THE CANARY CONNECTION

PHILLIP SPOLIN

The Canary Connection is a work of fiction. Apart from the well-known actual people, events, and locations that figure in the narrative, all names, places, characters, and incidents are the product of the author's imagination or are fictitious. Any resemblance to current events or locations, or to living persons, is coincidental.

First Printing December 7, 2018

ISBN 9781642555523
(ISBN Ebook 9781641365352)

Front Cover design by Per Lilistrom

Back Cover design by Mae Spolin

Map by Carolyn Joy Strauss, The Artists' Career Coach

phillipspolin.com
thecanaryconnection.com

Acknowledgments

Like the explorers in this book, mine was a journey, to understand theirs. In addition to those listed in the text and source reading material I'd like to express gratitude to my family and friends who encouraged me, and especially my deep affection and appreciation to friends and associates living in the Canary Islands. Without the inspiration and collaboration of my sister, Karen Spolin-Shivley, these pages would be empty. Through the years of writing The Canary Connection help came from many people and in many forms, including from Marilyn Atlas, Dr Susan Kushner-Scott, Jenny Laper, John Perry, Roberta Floden, Carolyn Joy Strauss, Wolfgang and Bridget Keisling, Scott Spolin, Per Lilistrom, David Valcarsal, Avi Schefres, Elizabeth Lopez, Christina Fanti, staff of the The Los Angeles County Library—Agoura Hills Branch and Marina del Rey Branch, and staff of the The Santa Monica Public Library.

Table of Contents

PART I

PART II

PART III

"O sea! O myth! O sun! O wide resting place!
I know why I love you.
I know that we are both very old,
And that we have known each other for centuries.
O Protean, I have been born of you — both of us
Chained and wandering,
Both of us hungering for stars,
Both of us with hopes and disappointments!

JL Borges"

PART I

Chapter 1
Trouble in Palos

D ante was running, trailing his dog Lusi. The dog was partner to
the boy's day-dream stories of danger and violence. Together,
their adventures were imagined with courage and daring speed. The
brown and white spaniel, camouflaged in the rolling pastures of south-
western Spain, charged across a stream and over a hill into a golden
meadow of millet.

High above the laurel trees a red tailed hawk soared on the summer
air-currents. Lusi exploded through the tall fescue grass, her tongue and
ears flapping. The hawk dived, struck a rabbit, and rose into the sky,
its talons clutching the meal. Defeated, and conceding the prize, Lusi
slowed to a loping gait toward a distant Dante. The boy heard a sound
like an insect buzzing, then a muffled crack. Despite shading his eyes,
momentarily blinded from the sun's glare, Dante did not see Lusi falter
and disappear into a soft patch of purple heather.

This is a time when the world itself is sentient, experiencing its own
feelings. Purple mountains breathe a haunting purr, the sky smiles in
contentment, and the endless ocean celebrates its regal, blue wetness.
Man lives in nature's indifference, evolving through ancestral extinc-
tions, migrations, and plagues. Now, in the 15th century, man is living
his deepest fears and hatreds.

Just before dawn, Dante is last to wake in the room he shares with two
of his three brothers. Also shared on the Osorio family farm are the
fields, each season defining their duties — the sod broken in March,

seeded in May, harvested in August, threshed and winnowed in December.

On this summer day, Dante dresses his skinny body and eats a breakfast gruel prepared by his older sister, Revela. Early, on his way to the barn, a dark sea mist mixes with the acrid odor of goat scat. The boy snorts, muttering his discontent. Passing the solitary elm behind the house, he glances at his name carved several years ago with the farmer's shank tied to his side.

From the window Revela calls, "Mind that you take care of that feed bin." Although Dante loves animals, he resents the menial chores— feeding, milking, the shit detail – and does them half-heartedly. Then at day's end, the work ritual finished, his spirits brighten in anticipation of going to the village port. There, at La Taberna Sirena, he will play his concertina. In the moldy air, sailors will favor him with a few coins that will provide family amnesty for his perpetual slacking. The boy looks forward to these eccentric, seafaring characters with tar-stained hands, coming from exotic lands, singing sea shanties with their bawdy mouths.

> *Anna Tee's a hansom dame,*
> *She's not a day past twenty.*
> *And when she's had 'er fill o' ale,*
> *The focsil's where you'll find 'er.*

La Taberna Sirena serves as both a tavern and inn, and is as old as the port. Because of the sagging low beams that canopy the dirt floor, it stands at an angle, like a ship hard-heeled. Strong wine from the island of Madeira, *malmsey*, fuels hard-shell men who revel in drinking, swearing and the company of prostitutes. For these men, slapping backs, trading lies, strength is the only quality that really matters to a life at sea, an honest life free of hypocrisy and deception, where the fear of death is their constant shipmate.

The alcohol produces song and laughter, but also a constant tension of meanness and violence. It seems at times the devil itself lurks in the shadows, waiting to cajole a man to cruelty and brutality. The year is 1492 and evil is pervasive, like a hellish virus, as the Spanish Crown and the Catholic Church cleanse God's earth in Spain of witchcraft, satanic worship, and all non-Catholic belief.

Palos is a port city on the western most jut of Spain into the Atlantic Ocean. Smaller then Mérida, its neighbor to the north, it has a crusty reputation in the nautical community. Palos born sailors are sought after by ship owners to be captains and navigators on vessels that ply the nearby North African coast, the Maghreb, for gold, slaves, and, spices. Often youth awake after a night of drinking to find themselves crew aboard outbound ships.

On this sweltering August day, Revela, tall and with a friendly face, accompanies her younger brother, Dante, to La Sirena. She occasionally works at the tavern, serving drinks and washing what there is to wash, her hands bearing the roughness of heavy work. To her, Dante is a free spirit, defending all things noble in a clumsy, teenage huff of kindheartedness. With a motherly instinct she is quick to shield him against the cruelties of their older brothers. "Stop that!" Demanding, "Get off him now! Leave him alone!"

They walk together toward the busy port and Revela's brown eyes drop as she tries to console her brother over Lusi, killed that afternoon by a musket ball. Buffing her brother's stringy hair and smiling, she says, "She certainly was lovely. Best hunter of the three. But don't worry. You'll find another just as fine."

Dante snarls, "There will never be another dog like my dog." He had found Lusi hours earlier with flies buzzing thick around the wound at the base of the dog's neck. Despite his sister's soothing words, it is unbearable for Dante to believe his dog is gone, as if the lead shot that killed Lusi had pierced his own young heart. A stark vision of the laughing group of musket-bearing men stays with him. Their uniforms said they were the civil guard's elite, the *Cronistas de Armas*, and Dante swore a child's complicated revenge. He carried the dog home, sobbing, holding her against his chest, the slack body spilling over his arms, and buried her at the edge of the alfalfa field.

Approaching the port, they see the tavern's familiar wooden sign swinging in the wind, a rough carved mermaid with a curled fishtail and flowing hair. The sea-nymph's tempting eyes and inviting smile echo the lure of the sea. Here, seamen exchange tales of voyages and ship gossip. Little that occurs on the western coast of Spain is unknown to the inn's patrons.

"I'll meet you by the well-tree," Revela calls out to Dante. "Let's leave early," she adds, mindful of her brother's afternoon tragedy.

La Sirena's rugged, barn-like door opens to a large room lit by oil lamps. The yeasty air is a mixture of sweating men and stagnant harbor water. Planked benches and tables are lined with ragged, dimwitted sailors, their brains liquor pickled. Most are whiskered, lethargic men, wrecked by every mortal calamity and often crushed by disaster. Many are without fingers and with poorly knit bones, the price of being a worn skinned old salt. Mixed with the sailors are a group of shop keeps enjoying the day's reward before the trek home, and fishermen about to head out for the nightly haul under cod attracting lanterns. All devote themselves to the pursuit of a pleasurable inebriation.

Conversations are muffled. Muted voices tell of a recent voyage to the Maghreb, the Mediterranean coast of Africa, for a cargo of slaves. Others speak of men lost overboard in fierce gales, their eyes dropping to hide thoughts of the sea's fury. Some complain of the harsh discipline from ship marshals and their lash. Low voices echo familiar names like Ole Cap Nesnidal, 'The Priest', mate on the trader Vestland, Almut on the Yeoward.

Dante enters the tavern playing his concertina, knowing that to appear without a purpose is to invite dangerous scrutiny. He squeezes the bellows, air sucks in and then launches out as he fingers the shiny black buttons and sings:

Oh, I'm a simple fisherman,
I haven't any money,
My hands they stink, my arse is hard,
my nose is dreadful runny.

His lanky, farm-worked body meanders among the tables and he sings in a voice not yet settled in its range. He avoids the truly besotted, for alcohol is a god of vengeance, and these wrecks are more likely to gift him not coins but anger and enmity. Dante's mind is clouded by the events of the morning meadow as he circles the room with a smile, unaware that this evening a devil has a corner seat.

Ensconced in an alcove at the rear of the tavern is a group of five uni-formed soldiers, members of the revered *Cronistas de Armas*. They drink deliberately, whispering to each other, observing the scene as if keeping score. These are the kind of men careful not to make enemies, or at least, to choose their enemies from among the defenseless. Well armed, they are dressed in black and red, the colors of Ferdinand, the King of Aragon and of Spain.

The tallest of the group has dark, shark's eyes, and lips that curl unnat-urally on a jawbone set in prejudice and hypocrisy. He sits in a corner with his back to the wall, listening to each snippet of conversation. When voices pause, the men lean in, and looking down his long nose with a slight nod and raised eyebrow, he grants permission to continue. When he speaks, the others hesitate, then lift their mugs to drink in uni-son, as if in a ballet of fear. Something dark oozes and crackles within this man, something built up in a thick black gob, barely held in check, as if any moment he might explode.

Singing shanties helps to take Dante's mind off the day's tragedy, but his performance lacks heart. He is knotted in anger, anger at his arms and fingers for the sour notes the concertina whistles, anger at his feet that trip over chairs, anger at every sideways look, every smile, every watery eye he encounters.

Warily, Dante slides closer to the soldiers, singing, unaware this was this same group who had taken musket practice that morning using Lusi as target.

> *Old Stormy he is dead and gone,*
> *Oh, poor old Stormy's dead and gone.*
> *We'll dig his grave with a silver spade*
> *And lower him down with a golden chain.*
> *O Stormy's dead and gone to rest;*
> *Of all the sailors he was the best.*
>
> Folksong

One of the soldiers, a man with a wolfish face and bloated eyes, turns slightly and without acknowledging Dante, tosses a few coins in his direction, deliberately throwing them to the floor rather than passing them into his hand as is customary.

Stooping, Dante overhears, "We'll be busy as flies on a dung heap tomorrow."

"And I'm for starting with that bastard tailor, Snyder"; from another, "He'll crisp up nice and tasty."

They are listing names, people soon to receive a visit from these messengers of the Crown. This is the day they have been thirsting for, the third of August, 1492, the day all Jews and Muslims of every age are charged to leave all the kingdoms and lands of Spain - on pain of death. The large ports along the Spanish coasts, Cadiz, Cartagena, Valencia, Barcelona and Tarragona are now inundated with escaping families. The human overflow has found its way to Palos, this small port down the Guadalquivir estuary, northwest of Cadiz, and the last deep water harbor in Spain before the Ocean Sea.

The group of soldiers has lingered past the hour of normal departure, as if they have a late appointment. The captain and another sweep into their capes, leave the corner table, and slip out a side door.

Dante leaves La Sirena early to meet Revela near the well-tree. He stomps through the deserted street, alone in his thoughts, the afternoon burial repeating in his mind's eye, his jaw with its caterpillar fuzz clenched in bitter anger. He is unwilling to accept his loss, yet ashamed of his behavior, the little boy who grieved for his dog. How could he let it happen? How could he cry about a dog, and in front of everyone?

The terrain at the port is not the sea, yet not completely land, so despite the dry season, Dante's leather boots collect mud. In the distance he spots Juan Abreu, the local gravedigger and sometime ship's ferryman, sitting alone, his arms and legs too long for his body drooped over an edge of the pier. A scraggly beard frames his broken front teeth that produce a whistle when he speaks. When not burying bodies he sails his skiff, the Spray, hauling cargo to and from ships in the harbor. A character among characters, he is famous in the port for the goods and gossip he trades, and that uncommon whistle when he speaks.

Dante hails the gravedigger and pauses to stomp off a clump of red earth. He thinks he hears a dog bark. He looks away from the pier, toward a sound coming from close to the well where he will meet Revela. In the distance he sees what appears to be a drunken group dancing and singing. Did a dog bark again? He listens and straining to see, considers that perhaps the sounds are not singing, but rather muffled cries, and the dance not a private tryst, but a struggle.

Alert to danger and loss, his mind sparks. He thinks he recognizes a voice. Those cries are his sister's. Revela is in trouble! His mouth drops open and his eyes goggle. He hears screams, muffled words, and a blind foreboding possesses him. The boy, frightened and enraged, charges the swirling group.

Yes, it is Revela! Struggling with two soldiers. The shorter man chortles as he grabs and tears at her skirts from the rear, while the taller man faces her, holding her wrists secure, her raised arms violently jerking side to side.

Revela whimpers, her endurance ebbing.

Dante throws his body into the taller soldier, forcing the release of his sister, crashing the man face first onto the hard ground. Semi-drunk, tangled in his cape, and with the wind knocked out of him, the soldier treats the unexpected attack as if it were sport. Moaning, rolling on the ground, he is disoriented, unable to get his feet underneath himself.

Dante turns to the other man still wrestling with a cursing, pleading Revela. The boy seizes the oafish man from behind and the trio whirls in dance until the soldier releases his hold on the girl. Dante and the soldier spin off, staggering in mirrored steps toward the massive tree where they bounce off the burled trunk. Dante's hand smashes against the rough bark, and the soldier brakes free.

Revela glimpses her brother in the moonlight, his eyes cold, metallic. Blood trickles over his brows. He is expressionless in the midst of frenzy. She calls out, "No! Dante. Stop!" Then the shorter soldier and Dante find each other and when the boy sees the man reach for his knife, he does likewise. Dante has practiced with his shank, playing swordsman, but this is not a game.

The soldier's blade is a true weapon, a coal black handle secured to a long stiletto. Dante's pitted knife is a worn farmer's tool. They tumble on the ground wrapped together, each trying to free their knife hand. Dante's quickness overcomes the inebriated soldier's experience. Revela watches her brother grab the soldier's hair, hold his head against the ground, then jab his pitted blade into the man's throat; one, two, three times. An arrow of blood shoots from the man's neck with a low stuttering sound, the gruesome gurgling of an old faucet. The soldier's body shakes, and his final blank gaze announces the cruelty of life's end. The boy stares into that face, still grasping the limp man's hair in one hand, his bloody knife in the other.

Then, cautiously, without letting go of his victim, Dante looks up. The other soldier, the taller one with the lupine face, blood dripping down the side of his head, lips curled to one side, slowly rises. Dante stares, fixed on the man's awful, black eyes. He drops the head of his victim but remains in a crouch. The tall soldier, now on his knees, grips the long, bone handle of a double-edged dagger. For a moment they both are perfectly still. Then the soldier's eyes flash and he leaps to his feet. They grapple, holding their breath to muster strength, grunting in exasperation. The soldier drives his forearm at Dante's chin, raking his signet ring and leaving a red gash across the boy's face. He struggles to pin Dante's arm to his side and wrap his legs at the same time. But Dante, slight, with quick, teenage reflexes, manages to spin free and get behind the soldier. The boy knows this advantage will be momentary. He wants nothing more then to escape this conflict, but as the man spins, Dante strikes out, swinging his arms wildly, stabbing, kicking, and pushing, until somehow the soldier's weapon is knocked to the ground behind Dante. In his frantic gambit the boy stumbles and, almost comically, throws himself to the ground on his backside. Reaching back to push himself up, his left hand takes hold of the soldier's fallen weapon.

In this moment, time stops for Dante. His subconscious screams to his conscious mind that the power is his, a knife in each hand and a disarmed adversary. He can get up and run or simply stand and avoid any further conflict. He knows that by surviving, his heroic effort to save Revela is validated. But the soldier is again in a posture forewarning attack.

With one soldier already sprawled in a pool of blood, dispatched like a lamb at slaughter, a demonic smile twists Dante's lips and creases his eyes. The moment has come to step up and take his place as a man of courage, a man to be feared, a man of his time.

The unarmed soldier pounces, his eyes focused on the hand holding Dante's knife, the very hand moments before the soldier held harmless. Dante seems to surrender the advantage, holding his knife aloft, inviting the soldier to grab his wrist. Then, without stabbing, without force of any kind, Dante raises his left hand holding the soldier's double-edged dagger. The man pushes forward, his own weight forcing the weapon to pierce his doublet and slip between ribs into his abdomen, gathering the blade home. The soldier drops onto his knees, astonished to see his weapon returned to him in this unexpected manner. For a moment he remains as if in prayer, staring at the bone handle protruding out his belly, then topples over.

Still semi-crouched, animal like, his heart racing, Dante studies the scene with a savage attentiveness. His mind in turmoil, unable to control the content of his consciousness, he feels he is witnessing a future event, what might still occur, rather than what just happened. Seeing the pool of blood oozing from beneath the soldier's body shocks him back to reality.

Awake to the consequences of what he has done, Dante swoons with instant regret, sensing he has taken one step too many and is now falling headfirst over a cliff.

Chapter 2
Escape!

They ran. The air is thick with dust and despair, the dirt road home filled with travelers their possessions in an array of sacks and bundles carried on their backs. Dante looks as if he emerged from a butcher shop, his clothes, face, and hands smeared in blood. Yet no one takes notice. The minds of these poor souls are occupied with a more urgent matter, their fear of annihilation. Going in the opposite direction, Dante and Revela seem to be standing still as a tormented world passes like a boat straining at anchor against a fast current.

Dante walks in the ruts made by farm carts, breathing hard, a fugitive's gait, each step its own revelation. Revela tries to settle her thoughts, to focus on the moment. Her heart thumps and fear pulses up her spine. Her face is blank with the look of a woman in controlled panic. She says, "It's important that we move quickly. They'll be after us like dogs." She didn't wait for a comment, and despite the constriction in her gut and the desert in her throat, continues, "Oh Dante, you shouldn't have, I was..." then cuts herself off, wanting to console her brother, not scold him.

The three-quarter moon is high when they reach the farmhouse, the dogs barking absent Lusi's howl. Their father blanches when he sees his two youngest children. Dante's swollen face is smeared in blood and throbbing from the long crimson gash left by the captain's ring. There is a misty emptiness about his dark eyes. Revela sits him down and begins cleaning the wound.

Revela is frightened to look at her father. "He tried to save me, Papa. These, these soldiers had me, and Dante tried to save me." Gulping and sniffling. "There was a fight, and Dante slipped, and he got up, and the soldier fell. He just tried to save me. It wasn't his fault. Oh, Papa, it wasn't his fault."

Juan José turns, eyes widen in his ashen face, the sunken cheeks and withered skin of an old man. His brows pinch considering the predicament. The rest of the family filters into the room. Revela feels dizzy with anxiety. Pepe's wife, Josefina, takes over from her to apply a lead acetate on Dante's slit cheek, sterilizing the wound. Danger permeates the silent household like a noxious odor. Segundo breaks the tension. Fearing what would be coming, he asks the question on everyone's mind, "What do we do now?"

Pedro, the eldest, knowing the truth, hard and dark as a bitter seed, exchanges a resigned look with Revela and announces what the others are afraid to say, "You both need to leave at once. That's for certain." Taking command, he asks, "Who were the soldiers? Are they dead? Did anyone see you?" Revela shakes her head, not knowing or not telling, as he continues, "Whoever it was, they'll be after blood. You've both got to get out now. Josefina, put some food together."

The degree of peril could not be overestimated. If caught, Dante and Revela will suffer a very unpleasant death, and perhaps others in the family as well. They must escape and remain far away for a long time.

A plan is quickly formed. With the Jews in exodus, all the roads are in chaos. The nascent fugitives will join the confusion and head back to the port in Palos and attempt to gain passage on a ship. As a diversion, Pepe and Josefina will take the mule in the opposite direction, north, to visit Josefina's cousins near Moguer. Pedro and the twins will care for the farm. Juan José, knowing it wise, will go see Father Baragio, the unyielding, dour prelate at the Church of St. George, and ask him for guidance.

The provisions are divided into two carry sacks. Pedro takes Revela aside, speaking intently to her for several minutes. Revela listens, nodding in agreement. Brief farewells are made, ill matched to the magnitude of change overtaking them. Juan José sits at the table his head in his hands; Pedro and Josefina stare at each other, bewildered; the twins stand behind their father, Segundo's hand on Juan's trembling shoulder. The Osorio household is not a happy one as Dante and Revela leave home.

All roads and weedy ditches near the port are choked with activity. Despite the flood of travelers everything is doubly and triply quiet, accentuating the outrageous direction life can take in an instant. Men and women do not call to their horses and mules, children do not cry, the wagon wheels move noiselessly in the ruts.

It has been four months since the royal edict of King Ferdinand and Queen Ysabela commanding the expulsion of all Jews and Muslims. Devout Christians assume that Jews should suffer as foretold in their own writings, the fulfillment of their own prophesies. Also in danger are those who secretly practice Jewish customs, Christians in name only who publicly observe the least of their new faith while maintaining in private a maximum of the old customs. They are said to subvert the faithful Christians from the holy to the Jews' wicked beliefs.

The last of the escaping Jews make their way to ports up and down the coast of Spain, their property forfeited to the crown. Their goal is survival with a lifetime to appreciate what a supreme achievement that would be. The vast majority have already fled. In three months, a quarter million souls left behind their cherished land, the home of their ancestors for centuries before the birth of Christ. They left behind their family graves, the synagogues where they prayed, their friends, their schools, their homes, their gardens and orchards, their businesses, their lives and future lives. They took with them their mothers and fathers, their children and grandchildren, their brothers and sisters. And they took with them their Torah, their laws, and their covenants with God.

The port of Palos appears as a river of humanity rushing to the sea, as if the world was migrating. Despite this disorder and the deep night sky, Dante and Revela feel conspicuous. Shivering in a chill of loneliness, they have no real plan. In a stroke of luck they encounter Juan Abreu, the gravedigger, who tonight is busy ferrying people from the crowded harbor out to anchored ships.

A peculiar looking man, the gravedigger's stick-out ears start midway up his long fleshy neck, and his wine stained front teeth are broken at various angles. His looks match his voice, a high-pitched, scratchy tone that comes from a breath that smells like crushed insects. "Oh, its syou, is its? Ya knows they're looking ups and downs for your bottoms. Ya did sat captain real bad."

Good at being furious, Revela, her spine carved from oak, takes control. "Never mind that you old flea carpet, how about getting us on board a ship out tonight?"

"Oooh, sat would take some doings, and risky for mes too" Abreu trills, rubbing his grizzly face. "I don't suppose syou ave any moneys, do yas?"

They have no money. Revela blurts, "Now look, we're no Basque mountain goats passing through. You've buried half our family." Then she catches her breath, considers her tone, and pleads, "All we need is a little boat ride. Can't you help us Juan? Please!"

Juan Abreu weighs the situation. Many ships are set to leave with overflow cargoes of Jews escaping this last day of the edict. Knowing he might suffer severe consequences, he whistles, "Swell, I do knows your papa a pretty long time. An your mom swer always skind to me...c'mon then."

Joining the mountain of humanity moving to the water's edge, Dante and Revela slip into the gravedigger's five-meter skiff, the Spray, shunning the benches to huddle hidden in the bottom of the boat. Revela stubs her foot on the middle bench as they both curl beneath it and around the short mast. Juan Abreu's calloused hands haul the lateen rig, and the patched sail fills in a cat's-paw breeze to a course toward three ships anchored at the far end of the harbor.

Two of the three ships are 'caravels' owned by Paloans. These vessels are state of the art shipbuilding, designed by the Portuguese for exploring the North African coast. The third ship, a 'noa', called the Gallega by its crew, in reference to Galicia where it was built, is similar in shape but a bit larger, bulkier, and less agile in sailing coastal seas.

The Spray scuds like a ghost ship toward the mouth of the harbor. Juan Abreu, who knows that the sea is far from waste and empty, hums, feeling not entirely safe from the sea monsters lurking just below the surface, the ones he is certain will take him to a watery cradle someday.

> *Hey, hey, hey little sailor boy by the boat,*
> *Ho, ho, ho little sailor boy in the sea.*
> *My, my, my little sailor boy can you swim?*
> *My, my, my little sailor boy float like me.*

The gravedigger knows the captains of the two caravels, Martín and his brother Vicente Pinzón. They are Paloans and part owners of the ships. The vessels have been placed under control of the Spanish Crown as payment for 'undetermined crimes' – in fact, they had been caught trading in Portuguese controlled waters on the coast of Africa. The third vessel, the flagship of the enterprise, is captained by an Italian from Genoa.

The small skiff carrying the frightened youngsters slips silently through the calm harbor. From a distance, the three anchored ships with their elongated bows and high sterns appear like birds with wings arched to the sky. The gravedigger laughs to himself, amused by his own vision of the ships, wide hipped women on their backs, legs stretched in the air.

Revela and Dante feel almost safe, as if the ocean will protect them from the chaos on land.

"Can you see anything?" Dante asks from under the bench... "Shush," Revela admonishes. "We're almost there. Stay down."

Juan Abreu heads for the middle ship captained by his childhood friend, Martín. The Spray settles silently amidships near the boarding ladder against the ship's strake. The gravedigger does not call out to the watchman for permission to come aboard, his friend Mervino, thinking he can better handle the situation once on deck.

Abreu snakes up the wooden ladder followed by Revela and Dante. They find the watchman leaning against the mizzenmast, snoring, a half empty bottle of *malmsey* on the mast step, the first unexpected circumstance. The second is encountering a group of men, women, and children on the deck pressed against the forward bulkhead. Juan Abreu silently swings his skinny arm in wide circles, directing his cargo to join the exiled Jews.

The gravedigger waves a quick good-bye and scurries down the ladder to the skiff, giggling to himself. He knows it was a stroke of luck to get Dante and Revela on board so easily. He also knows these poor wretches are fugitives, and that on weighing anchor they will be stuffed below in the cargo hold along with provisions for the ocean sail. He knows they are headed to the Canary Islands, seven islands laying one-hundred-fifty kilometers off the northwest coast of Africa. And he knows that these three ships are headed beyond, on a journey never before tried. The gravedigger knows that if Revela and Dante remain on board past the islands, he most likely will never see them again. And finally, he knows that someone might be willing to pay for information about these two young farmers. What he doesn't know is that they are not on either vessel captained by his friends the Pinzóns. He has brought them on board the flagship of the expedition, captained by the Italian.

Chapter 3
Memories of Family

O n board the Gallega Dante and Revela fold into the rear of the group, next to children with smiles practiced for older brothers and sisters. Dante slicks right up under Revela's arm, the spot that's fit since childhood. Her arms wrap his shoulders, his heart beating against her hand. They share the feeling of loneliness that escape brings, a kind of desperate helplessness.

The decree of expulsion forbade Jews to leave Spain with any money or valuables, under pain of death. Still, despite persecution and despair, there is a sense of righteousness and deliverance. Refusing to renounce their religion and convert to Catholicism, they honor their heritage, and are steadfast in guard of their five-thousand year old religion and its Torah.

Dante and Revela merge with the small group of exiles, but the whispered conversations and murmurs hardly inspire their confidence. The ship rocks and the moon shifts from one side of the mast to the other. The thread of time is broken for these victims. Terror has dislocated both their past and future, and for them, the passage of time takes no time. They all look the same. They all smell the same. They all fear the same. It is as if they have been born from the same mother at the same moment, one dismayed, terrified, glob of humanity. Clustered on deck, praying, bodies and heads rocking and bobbing, a bizarre vision to Revela and Dante, if not pitiful, then comical, like a shrub of misery that bloomed on board.

Revela feels a tugging low on her dress. A small, round-eyed girl clings to her knees. As Revela strokes the blonde curly hair, the urchin looks up. Revela bends to hug the child, and lips to her ear, whispers, "What's your name?"

A delicate voice, "Chavery."

"Is that your mommy, Chavery?" motioning to the closest woman. Chavery's lips purse and she shakes her head, 'no'.

"Is she over there?" Again the lips and the 'no' face.

A woman leans in, "She's traveling with the Brezlo family," pointing. "They've been caring for her. Someone lost her. She was just wandering in the crowd."

Revela thinks, 'What does a child do when she has no family?' "Well, Chavery," her motherliness easily accessible. "we both need a friend. Will you be my friend?"

Chavery's curls bob 'yes'. But Revela's smile fades thinking of the anguish Chavery's parents must feel.

Revela thinks of her own family. Her mother, Concepcion, had died from consumption three years earlier. Revela, then sixteen, inherited the responsibilities of the household. She is built like her mother with broad shoulders and wide thighs, thick brown hair framing wide eyes, and a pouty mouth. Though a canny girl she was content with farm life, the daily routine of cooking, cleaning, caring for the livestock, and serving men.

After his wife's death, Revela's father, Juan José, became less mercurial and more tolerant of his six children. Like all sun-wrinkled farmers he was resilient to the labor that saps the energy of all peasants. A caved in side of his forehead notched his face so it seemed in secret disagreement with itself. Not a patient man, his pent up anger made him impatient with all. A schemer, when he felt the need he outright lied, becoming outraged if disbelieved, even to fight another man though he knew him to be right. His oldest child, Pedro, twenty-four, never married, but Pepe, did take a bride, Josefina, who shared the household burdens with

Revela. The twins, Primero and Segundo, were hard workers but fought constantly. Dante, the youngest, remained an afterthought to his father.

Revela, taught there was something noble in self-denial and suffering, unselfishly cared for her family. Of her brothers Dante was her favorite and he gladly collected her nurturing. Shielding him from their older brothers' constant teasing was simply another routine chore for Revela. She saw Dante as unique, a rebel, with the fortunate gift to be easily amused. Intelligent and quick to learn, he had not yet discovered his own inclination. With his boyish beam of innocence, Revela imagined him a missionary. She was certain that the abysmal emptiness of farmland would never satisfy Dante's curious mind, that blood had cast him into this family, as if into a doom.

Now, her life irrevocably changed, Revela is aware Dante feels responsible for their situation. Although he excuses himself, believing his actions heroic and their consequences unavoidable, there are two handles to that pot. He had acted courageously, but the attack on two soldiers was also foolhardy, and speaks to his reckless immaturity.

Intelligent and with a practical nature, Revela is accustomed to small but dependable successes. Now, circumstances have put life beyond her control and tied it to the fate of society's victims. She has lived in an innocent world of the poor, where poverty takes the place of ambition, where hunger changes everything you ever thought you knew. Familiar with death, she knows that all one can do is wait and accept it when it arrives, not to think about it, but to live with it's coming.

Still, there is a more immediate matter feeding her anxiety, specifically the very real question of her behavior at La Sirena. Self-condemnation and shame humble her. Can she put aside remorse and survive the certain adversity that lay ahead? She has only the comfort of memory and she lets her thoughts drift to the family life that is no longer.

Dante was always Revela's favorite and she watched over him like a mother bear. For her, the boy's gentle face, generous nature, and kind manner, mask his resolve. It leads people to underestimate him. Yes, he is impulsive, but he also has a man's practical, sharp, intelligence; and Revela also sees calmness, modesty, and sadness in him, traits genuinely female.

Their father, Juan José, a man who enjoyed no pleasure, thought Dante soft, lacking grit, and so turned from him. "Toughen him up a bit." her father would say, dismissing the boy.

At times Revela felt her father's eyes on Dante's neck, like a noose. 'That man is so cruel', she thought, resenting the injustice in him. She watched his old face harden, wavering between fear and spite, never acknowledging Dante's kindheartedness. Choosing to close his eyes to his son's merit, he shrugged off the boy's spirit, the way Revela shrugged off everyone's faults.

Worse still was Juan José's attitude toward her, "Use the tiny brain that ya got ya foolish woman. That's what it's there for." As Revela matured and became more recusant he would complain to his wife about her, "She's arrogant I tell ya. A little she-devil." He didn't hate women, but lived in a constant annoyance, an ornery man in perpetual animosity.

Revela's mother, Concepcion, barely aware of her own suffering, always tried to lighten everyone's mood with a playful aside. The daughter was grateful to her mother for the name she gave her brother, Dante. She had heard the lyrical name at a sailor's funeral, and after her husband named the twins Primero and Segundo, she felt entitled to the choice.

A hard woman, her narrowness of mind was a family tradition and her cagey eyes and cajoling voice undermined her. A conscientious mother, she sought to inoculate Revela from the perils a young girl was certain to encounter. At twelve, with Revela's first flow, came her mother's cautionary advice. She took her mother's worn, wood-like hand, and listened, "Love and passion are as different as the moon and the sun. A man will tell you that he can't live without you, that he can't eat or sleep for thinking about you. There will be no doubt about his eagerness to touch you. Then as soon as you say, 'yes', he'll turn his head as if you never existed. And he won't want to be with you. And he won't want to talk to you. And he won't love you."

Perhaps most difficult for the daughter to accept was Concepcion's advice; "sometimes being a bitch to a man is the only thing a woman has to hold on to." Revela took these admonitions to heart as she grew into womanhood and understood that for her mother marriage was a resignation to endless insults tolerated through endurance and forgiveness. Any love received, seldom satisfying, demanded a lifetime of payment.

Revela witnessed her mother battle against both her mulish husband and the lengthy ravages of her final sickness. Death, like a rolling force, took revenge for its sustained wait and humiliated her, stripping away her sense and memory. In perpetual misery, the woman cried herself to sleep every night until she let go the burden of life. At rest in her coffin she looked different, Revela thought like a bride, that perhaps death had given her back the grace of being a woman.

Setting up house in death's wake, never questioning the terms, Revela was resigned to life in her mother's shadow, as if it were a tether that tied her to the Earth. To guarantee her mother's soul rest peacefully, she danced seven times around the body and opened every window for her soul to escape. It could be said that Revela's hatred for her father was awful, as was her love for him; and that she loved her mother, but because she resented her appeasement of him, she also loved to hate her.

Growing up, the girl often became absorbed in whims the way any child might, but her enthusiasm was never childish. When she daydreamed a fantasy, something vital was always at risk: a treasure, a knight's honor, a Crusade battle. Sometimes she would imagine herself a princess in a far away land, the daughter of a mighty ruler. Or she might be a noble lady traveling the countryside on horseback, performing magic to rescue children from evil men, or saving families from burning barns. She was never the one rescued. At night her dreams were ghost like, with animals that spoke to her.

Once, around sunset in the late fall, Revela was washing clothes at a bend in the river. The slow current was half in the shade of tall alder trees. Their black, ropy branches etched eerily in the sky, reaching over to the water's sunny side for something to hold when the wind blew hard enough to sway them. There among the estuary weeds and the wind-blown puffs of silver grass seeds, she saw something that looked to her like a man draped in a dark shroud and cowl, very tall, almost too tall. She could not be sure but thought it might be the de Silva boy who was known to spy on people. A low mist hung above the water just beneath the bright sunlight flashing through the overhanging trees. The intermittent glare prevented her from being certain she was seeing a man. As a child she was taught about the presence of the spirit of the devil, *La Duquende*. She grabbed at her hair, feeling something in it, then was startled by a form swooshing over the water at a great speed, it's black cape flapping behind. The figure rushed past leaving an acrid odor.

When she heard an owl screech, a sure omen, Revela said softly to herself, as if ending a thought, 'Death'. The feeling would pass but leave scar tissue in her memory and she knew better than to ever mention it.

Despite her daydreams and the demands of religious superstitions, in her everyday life Revela wanted nothing to do with conceits. She lived resolutely in reality, relishing the household's turmoil, and accepting ordinary life and the destiny of family. However, she did want to escape the odd small things that offended her. She despised the belittling circumstances of farm life, poverty, the little meannesses she endured that pleasured her brothers, and the trivial matters loudly complained of by her father. She yearned for her life to hold something beyond ordinary. Yet despite all her confidence, she could not form her dream.

The struggles of daily life and the chronic illness of poverty, made it difficult to find a time and place for the Church. She believed religion confused matters. Yes, there is sin, supreme sin, but this is not a part of her every day. When her father abused her mother, or when Segundo teased Dante, or when her friend Elena stole from the baker, this was misbehavior, not sin. Sin is forever. Sin is entwined with spiritual life, like believing in false gods or torturing animals. Ordinary wickedness, perhaps artificial sins, are only imperfections, ephemeral acts, and her judgment of it was fleeting. The girl was satisfied with Father Baragio's clarification of Catholicism. The father was a good Christian, ordering a great deal of torture, and himself fasting for two days out of seven, although this would not prevent him from dying obese. She accepted that we must examine our consciences, as he said, "and understand that we are in this world only to do God's will and to save our immortal souls. All else is insignificant and worthless".

When she was younger her friends thought Revela distant, aloof. She refused to share in their frivolous schoolgirl confidences, and opposed their false mysteries, their backbiting spites, their half concealed whispers and giggles that denied girlfriend merit. Revela thought them mean, especially when they ridiculed Marta. Marta drew up close when she spoke to you, looking deep into your eyes, as if she could see something more interesting inside your head than what showed on your face. The others shunned and made fun of her, mimicking her by widening their eyes and pushing their heads forward, awkwardly, into her face, saying something stupid like, "My dog's name is Beany." Revela would put her arm around Marta's shoulder, leading her away and whispering in her ear to ignore the taunts.

It was agreed, Revela was not like the others. Some saw her as quiet, others as mature. Her cousin, Karina, was tortured with misery if someone didn't like her; Revela cared little for anyone's approval. Her neighbor, Francesca, collected dolls; Revela pressed flowers. Lily San Pedro was attracted to arrogant men; Revela saw men as mostly bluster, concealing their incomplete selves.

Now all the hard earned acknowledgment of her true values, the years of compromise and no compromise, the groundwork laid to gain respect from her father and siblings, her community reputation as honest, matters she had cultivated all her life, seemed of no consequence.

On the deck of the vessel that would provide their escape, Revela pondered choices made that night. The comfort of the farm and family was gone. In a lucid moment she thought, 'good riddance'. After all, what loss was there to suffer? Cleaning and cooking for brothers who had never given her so much as a 'thank you sister' for her efforts? A father, who was a sour man persistent in his stupidity, a man anxious to demean anyone, who believed his presence alone sufficient to satisfy family affection, who had kept her mother in a state of numb existence.

Tears washed Revela's cheeks. Jews were less than an afterthought to her. Although she longed for something greater than the farm, she had little insight to what she and Dante were now a part. She did understand that not only her life had changed, but also, it was now her own.

She cried openly, not for herself, but for Dante, the boy she had so dearly protected from the moronic onslaughts of his older brothers, and from the silent, disapproving menace of their father. The boy who always returned her devotion with abounding affection, and made her life feel purposeful, who conspired with her to love the meadow and the ocean, who in a moment of teenage impetuousness, had cast their lives together as salt in the ocean.

Death was stalking them and it was her fault.

A gust of wind rocks the ship and Revela's mind returns to the present, huddled next to Dante among the exiles. A shadowy form appears near the stern, a man facing the endless Ocean Sea. In the dim evening light, Revela can see an aura about him, a diffused purplish glow. His gaze seems to draw the ocean, as a child might wind in a kite. Revela stares until her eyes water, gratefully anticipating the suffocation of sleep. In that silent moment, the kind of moment that can last a second or a lifetime, she still believes there is something for everyone on this cruel earth. Drifting into sleep she thinks, 'Sometimes you just have to trust the world'.

Chapter 4
Dante on Board

In the silence of that first night of escape, faced with the reality of the Jewish exodus, Dante recalled how nonchalantly he had accepted the disappearance of his neighbors, the ben Tarnof family. Their absence meant but a few empty chairs at school, a smaller team to compete against at harvest, one less topic of ridicule for his brothers. He remembered the story; Sarah ben Tarnof had made what she thought was a pretty good joke. "Those two dogs won't eat pork. They must be Old Testament dogs."

Unfortunately for the ben Tarnofs, a neighbor who coveted their land overheard the comment and denounced her to Father Baragio at St. George's. Nestor Baragio, a large man with lazy folds of flesh around his eyes, a funereal, effeminate man as pale as a lily, a man with autumn in his heart, was anxious for recognition as defender of the faith. He excelled partnering in broken oaths, tortures, and false witnesses. With a calm face the prelate set aside his conscience to institute a charge of heresy against the Jewess, and Sarah ben Tarnof was found guilty of communicating with animals.

The image of Serwan ben Tarnof lashed to the killing table, his limbs chopped off with a dull hatchet, never entered Dante's mind. Nor had Dante heard the screams of Sarah ben Tarnof being raped, or her three children's skulls caving to the crush of the pendulum swing of a cross-engraved boulder. Sarah, a gentle woman of cheerful spirit, was tied to a stake on the holy ground of St. George's Church and roasted like mutton.

Yes, though he was not cognizant of it, the flow of blood and the killing of humans was a part of Dante's life. That night's earlier drama now revisited his mind's eye, the ease with which the dagger had entered the soldier, the small red lake that filled beneath the body.

Dante's throat closed and his mouth went dry. He envisioned the instant when the accursed blade plunged into the second soldier, the moment of his decision to kill, the moment when he need not have raised his arm and struck down the body of Captain Ygnacio de Silva. The moment time stopped. Closing his eyes, he sees the blood soak the ground. His hand cramps. The thought of Hell flickers in his brain. Was he merely defending himself and Revela? Never religious, he could not decide if he was in mortal sin and he asked himself over and over, 'Why did I do it?'

Then he considers Ygnacio and the stories he knew about that ruthless man. How many bodies had that knife entered, the men, women and children, their blood drained by its thrust and twist? How many would now escape that ruin?

Revela, his sister, in attempting to save her, he has condemned her. He could not envision his future of farm life, but Revela was the lynchpin of the family. What would now become of her? He pushed these worries from his consciousness.

The young fugitives slept fitfully, clinging to each other, as the night passed in fertile silence. The Gallega was now two days beyond the expected departure. The small group of outcasts asleep on deck breathed in communal rhythm.

They would soon to be below, packed beside the provisions stored for the ocean passage; barrels of salted beef and pork, anchovies and sardines, kegs of wine and olive oil. Stacked near the cargo hatch secured in wooden casks is enough fresh water to last two weeks before it stales. The water, along with bread, fresh vegetables and fruits, will be replenished in the Canary Islands.

Expulsion from Spain places the Jews one step lower in humanity's pecking order. They serve no purpose on board other than as paid freight. The deck is their sleeping quarters, and the Jews shift positions as best they can in the small area allotted them. Dante and Revela become shadows disguised as cargo, and the air crackles in anticipation of setting sail.

A long bearded Jew with querulous eyes, wearing a heavy coat, speaks to Dante believing him to be crew. "I am Moav ben Meywud. Do you know our destination?"

"No, sorry I don't."

The Jew shakes his head and turns away. Another man, tall with a stately bearing, introduces himself. He had seen Revela and Dante board the ship.

"Good morning. I am Rabbi Moises. I have heard we are on a long journey, my son."

Dante mumbles, "Good morning".

"Most of us have already fled. They were wise to leave for more hospitable lands. To Turkey and Morocco. Some went to Portugal, but I suspect they will find no respite there.

"Yes" from the boy.

"It seems we are the last to leave and are in God's guidance, merciful may he be. How is it you leave so late?"

The Rabbi's kind but piercing eyes fluster Dante, who fingers the wound on his cheek. The young fugitives had conspired to present themselves as married, believing the status would protect them. In a low voice, as if to mirror the Rabbi, he reveals, "I am Dante ben Osorio and this is my wife Revela. We were slowed on the road from Valencia. We've never been on a boat before."

Revela's eyes narrow and she considers her brother's inventiveness. She thinks it would have been wise to select different names but realizes that neither their youth nor their marital status matters among these weary, dispossessed victims. She wonders if Dante is at all aware that their lives are on the brink of becoming a continuous subterfuge and falsehood.

The Genoan captain orders all three ships to be ready for sail by eleven that evening. He is not pleased with the extra cargo, the Jews, though they brought a substantial price paid to the ships' owners. When Juan Abreu, the spidery gravedigger, unloads the last barrel of water, his eyes meet Dante and Revela's, but no words are exchanged.

Yesterday's events are dream like for the brother and sister. Intent on remaining obscure, they communicate only with the Jews, who share with them their food and their terror. Playing his concertina at La Sirena had been a bridge from the farm to the sea for Dante, a bridge never crossed. Hearing stories of danger and exotic places, he often wondered if a man should seek great adventures. He wanted adventures, but adventures do not happen for boys who stay at home. What was out there, beyond what he knew? Now, having crossed the bridge, he knows that his old life is over.

Dante recognizes many sailors he knows from La Sirena, their skin cracked like dried mud, their faces freckled from a life on deck. He thought these men to be drunkards, degenerate buffoons. He smiles remembering the sport of spotting a sailor with a full complement of fingers, hands, and legs. Wondering about their skills at sea, he pairs their sober faces with the slobbering, wasted, sometimes weeping men he remembers from La Sirena. But here he sees them working together, belaying heavy ropes, securing unwieldy cargo, doggedly dragging their bodies aloft against the forces of the earth and sea.

There are many friendly faces. Arching his neck to see thirty feet up, longhaired Lorenzo works the mainsail, a man often comfortable on the tavern floor babbling nonsense, a simple fool. Nearby is Marko, an obstinate man, a chronic drunk, guiding on board a load of barreled wine. Tontas the Greek, Juan de Nevtan, Kiril, Unai, Orkon the Turk, so many familiar faces, as if La Sirena had shaken out its patrons from above onto the Gallega's deck. Among them is Juan de Moguer, a man all in Palos feared. Dante had heard he came from prison scheduled to be hanged for murder, the town's weekend entertainment denied.

Men strain with the cargo using crude block and tackle. As they work, the sailors sing shanties to synchronize their strength, and their collective strength will be needed to move a host of men through a raging wind and sea. Dante wonders, 'are these men sad drunks or skilled mariners?' He grips Revela, his lips purse and eyes narrow mistrustful of his judgmental nature.

Revela also recognizes sailors from the La Sirena, but it is the men she does not recognize that draw her attention. Standing close by is a short, bald man wearing a red cap. He has rat like, dark eyes, and is lipless with tiny sharp teeth. Diego de Harana, the *alguanal*, the ship's marshal, in a raspy growl, directs the men working aloft. Revela watches the marshal, he coughs and fingers a bone handled scourge in his belt. Harana, perhaps not suited for deep thinking, is justly feared and regarded by many as a tyrant. His command, often an extreme and dangerous physical task, is obeyed.

High on the poop deck at the stern, to port and above the large tiller that will guide the ship's course, Revela notices a man dressed more for a royal court audience then for going to sea. He is examining scrolls while leaning over the cover of a hatch serving as a table. His shoulder length brown hair is tied fashionably in the back, and his furrowed brow evokes a serious demeanor. Luís de Torres is a newly converted Jew, a Catholic of two weeks, who speaks, besides his native Spanish, Hebrew, Arabic, Portuguese and French. The Genoan Captain has brought him to the enterprise, not so much as a crewmember, but as an intellect whose court and language skills will be needed at their destination.

Revela surveys the crew spotting more familiar faces, then in the distance sees another she does not recognize. Near the aft bulkhead is a thin, almost transparent man of indeterminate age, who would be tall in a land of tall men. He appears as part of the background, even while standing in the forefront. Wearing a loose fitting tunic, his deep, milky blue eyes, capture images rather than see them.

At the man's feet is an equally diaphanous ash grey dog with a white blaze on its forehead. Before Revela sees the dog, it sees her, and moves toward her. After a cocked head and mutual scrutiny, the dog drops its head to be pat, then returns to the side of the man. The crew's activity on deck slows to a seaman's routine. Alone with her thoughts, Revela stands amid-ship looking out over the flat harbor water toward the farm. She imagines her mother saying, "Life is never what we expect."

Chapter 5
Ygnacio & Lily ; Baragio & Debrun

E arlier that summer of 1492 at the monthly market in Palos, Captain Ygnacio de Silva first sees Lily San Pedro. He watches from a corner of the square near a church fountain. A small girl with a pleasant face and round, honey colored eyes, she wears a peasant dress tied with a yellow ribbon around her narrow waist, accentuating her developing hips and breasts. Always gentle with animals, she speaks softly to her mule and chickens, and treats her vegetables likewise, harvesting the carrots and beans by tenderly shaking the dirt away, picking apples and peaches with a slow twist being careful to leave those still hanging undisturbed. Lily's faith is kindness, and she smiles with her chin uplift as if singing.

Activity in the market increases as buyers begin to outnumber sellers. Lily tosses her auburn hair from her face and goes unnoticed in the busy throng, except for de Silva. He watches her small hands spreading carrots on the blanket, arranging them for examination. When de Silva saunters up to Lily she smiles, an innocent, trusting smile, a smile suggesting her playfulness and vulnerability, a smile that announces she finds something fun about life and good about people. Tilting her head to one side, she asks the uniformed soldier, "Would you like some fresh vegetables?"

De Silva hears her voice as the warble of a wren. He smiles as if they have met before, a cunning, wolfish smile, like an animal that might devour Lily on the spot, slurp her blood and squeeze her young organs in his mouth. "That's all right, I'm looking for something else. What's your name?" he coos.

She tells him her name, where she lives, whom she lives with, and what makes her laugh. De Silva, captivated by her naivety, notes the information. As he turns to leave, a bead of saliva appears at the corner of his mouth.

Three days later monks from St. George Church under the order of Father Baragio escort Lily from her home to the House of God. No reason for the command attendance is given to her or to her family. Her audience with the friar is misleadingly congenial. "You have nothing to fear. This is a matter of concern for your well-being", he assures her. His puffy face hacks a phlegmy cough as he wags a finger to pardon the nuisance.

Lily is led to a small dark room where a candle on a rough hewn table barely illuminates the gray walls and the wooden image of Christ hung over a low pallet bed. She sits at the table on the one rickety chair, folds her hands into her lap, hums a nursery rhyme, and waits.

She is seventeen, a lifelong friend of Revela. The oldest of three sisters and four brothers, she knows what it is to live in the perpetual cyclone of babies. However, the mature talent to accomplish something worthwhile is a riddle to her, and she accepts being powerless. Her sisters took on the responsibility of the boys while Lily stayed the shy child, ever playing make believe, clinging to a naïve sense of magic. Unsure of her worth and afraid to grow up, she left matters of significance to others, trusting them completely. Unworried about what her life might become, but tormented of inheriting the burden of living, Lily cannot help but exude victimhood.

The friends were like night and day. Where Revela believes one is accountable to the world for her actions, Lily opts to avoid commitment. While Revela tends animals, Lily plays in the shallow brooks, happy to be running and singing. Revela might put up preserves, Lily watches the birds and indulges in thoughts of ghosts and fairies.

When asked a question, Lily would feign mistrust shaking her head in doubt, making time to ponder if she is being fooled or if she might get in trouble. She lives in the world of hair pulling, teasing, snitching, lying, and petty meanness. Still the friends did both agree of their affection for Dante and that each enjoyed tatting lace.

In St. George's Church sitting on the bumpy chair in the dank cloister, Lily waits, imagining her life as a forest princess having the keys to a magic world. But in the back of her mind she wonders what the church could possibly want with her.

Seven days later, Lily wakes on the dirt floor of the now familiar subterranean chamber. Each day Debrun, a small, thick man with kneeling, hooded eyes under a stringy mop of colorless hair, brings her a meager pot of gruel and exchanges the refuse bucket.

The demonic man is dressed in blood splattered rags, panting noisy, short breaths as he moves his top-heavy body. His voice, high pitched like a schoolgirl, sputters words of obedience.

Talks with Father Baragio serve to steadily weaken Lily's spirits. A toady in de Silva's command had advised a monk of seeing Lily dance naked in the woods in singsong conversation with an invisible devil. Baragio asked, "Tell me Lily, when did you first speak with demons?" The cleric was not far from wrong.

Disheartened, Lily memorized prayers. Reciting the litanies and long sections of the liturgy provided a peaceful detachment from the monotony and fear. She did not beseech God to be spared pain or death. Her requests were modest, and she prayed for the safety of children and animals.

Debrun opens the wobbly wooden door. He motions and grunts to Lily to come with him, and leads her to another small chamber where a menacing figure stands near a pallet bed. Ygnacio de Silva turns, takes Lily's trembling hand, and to assure her, strokes her hair. Lily has no recollection of the man from the market and surrenders to his cunning manner.

"How are you faring, my dear?" he asks. She looks at him and weakly nods. De Silva continues, "I have spoken with Father Baragio and we are certain that we can release you from this demonic affliction that has contaminated your spirit." He offers her a small crystal cup and says, "Here, drink this." And she does.

De Silva cajoling, certain of being irresistible, croons, "It is a mark of your innocence that the devil has sought you out, my dear. We must drive the fiend from your body. Take my hand."

"Yes sir."

"It is important that you do as I instruct, my little birdie. I must reach deep inside you to ensnare the curse placed there."

The potion quickly disorients the young, half-starved girl. In a moment, she is disrobed. Seeing her nude de Silva trembles, his hands shaking in anticipation of bursting into her slight body. He ravages her, and in his maniacal excitement, ejaculates prematurely. Chagrined at the physical release, his lips curl, and he leaves.

Ygnacio de Silva visits Lily often that summer. The girl is barely kept alive, even with the extra food she would find waiting in her cell after each visit. De Silva no longer requires her to take the opium laced drink, but she requests it every time.

Each time Debrun leads her to meet Ygnacio, Lily keeps her eyes on her feet, unwilling to look at the stone labyrinth. The winding passageways of the dungeon promote silence; still, she can hear awful screams of pain, unworldly shrieks, shrill and rattling, as if exploding from a doorway quickly opened to hell.

Often after a chilling concert, Debrun, dumb as a fish, would appear at Lily's side, smelling of death sweat, trembling in fresh blood splatters, his mouth contorted. His presence has no purpose. He simply stands there in her cell panting, bulging eyes staring at the ground, like a dog.

Cruelty often employs spontaneity, a certain creativeness, but Debrun has settled for the tried and true, and is an expert in his craft the same way others are experts in husbandry or masonry. The Inquisition's machines of torture are constructed to expose the sinner's lack of power, to inflict agonizing pain, the path to atonement and purification. At the sight of Debrun, heretics are quick to confess, even before they arrive at his isolated chamber deep in the bowels of the abbey. Suspended by their wrists, perhaps with weights tied to their ankles, a sample torture, like an hor d'oeuvre, to moisten their lips and dispense a hint of death's foretaste.

There was talk of innovative devices labored over by holy men, designed to keep the victim alive while being roasted. Proud torture machines were constructed with counterweighted beams that could dip a heretic to burn in the fires, then lift him out for the crowd to watch his agony.

Debrun was not aware that his profession was informed and guided by no less than the seminal work, 'Summa Theologica', authored by the revered theologian and philosopher, Thomas Aquinas. It canonized any confession into a death sentence.

"In God's tribunal, those who return are always received, because God is a searcher of hearts, and knows those who return in sincerity. But the Church cannot imitate God in this, for she presumes that those who relapse after being once received, are not sincere in their return; hence she does not debar them from the way of salvation, but neither does she protect them from the sentence of death."

The Catholic religion uses its authority like a whip, making people kneel, forcing their surrender, lashing them into obedience and meekness. The superstitious nature of the average man is never overestimated. Threats of an eternity in hell are meant to keep simple people in fear and submission; tales of ghosts and curses take advantage of their stupidity and cruelty; doubt, the enemy of faith, is never tolerated.

As Debrun knelt before the prelate, Baragio, working his lizard tongue told him, "The heretic has no right to silence, so it does not matter if one lies to dupe them into confession. If they will not speak then hang them by their wrists, break their fingers, then a bit of kindness, and then rack them, burn them. It is a blessed act. Torture is therefore charity. It only follows that the greater the heretic's collapse, the more valid the torture and the greater the charity."

He cautioned Debrun that Satan would attempt to prevail by means of superstition and ignorance. "Any pain suffered by the heretic is also suffered by the devils within him. The best cure is to make the heretic suffer so much that the devils will decide to abandon him. The evil within will be exorcised by his screams, this will become the confession."

And Debrun asked, "What is the confession I am to listen for?"

"Why, that they are a Jew."

"But they confess that right away."

"Yes, but are they telling the truth?"

With this logic, as if its senselessness was key, Father Baragio made himself as stupid as his congregation who believed they were as clever as he. What could they know? There were few matters to think about, but there was always the Jews, and they burned so well. After all, the divine mandate he preached was in Latin, a language the parishioners did not understand. Surely he was one of the select few who possessed the secret of the holy code.

Baragio was a genius in divining irrationality from a rational argument. He reasoned that where evidence is lacking, it is only logical that a conspiracy exists, one so successful that it leaves none. He never consciously wondered if he was disbelieved. He had been honest and well liked as a boy, for even monks have a past, but his life became filled with sacred oaths broken, exotic tortures, false witness, and countless burnings. He was often late for supper because of an execution. His oldest son, Ernesto, then sixteen, witnessing his father direct the torture of a young girl, left home without a word, and was never seen again. The churchman had made himself unfit to pray to God. A sinner so mighty as to be beyond mercy, the meagerness of his soul was not punishment enough. Deservedly, his near future would provide him no mercy from the agony of the plague.

"Yes, I did Judasize," the heretic would cry. "Yes, I did deny the purity of the Virgin Mary." They would even deny that Jesus was the Lord Savior, and when entering Debrun's exclusive alcove, they confessed they had spoken with the Devil and conspired to destroy the Church. Placed on one of Debrun's extraordinary apparata, his *trampa*, his special table, they revealed that their mother and father had joined with them, that their spouse and brothers and sisters had conspired with them. Even their children, especially their children, were guilty, for they had introduced them to the devil.

But Debrun could not be fooled. He knew that the rants were only to avoid the application of his talents, that these were not true admissions. And so feet and hands were tied to the frame of his cherished table, the rack, and the handle turned, pulling legs and arms. Muscles stretched, ligaments ripped, tendons popped. It was only then that squawks and squeals would transform into a genuine, unfaked, heartfelt confession.

Debrun's *trampa* was lovingly efficient. The deformed cretin watched the death agony, that slow expiration that gives off a sparse smell of rot. Yet, Debrun had more toys to favor his guests. Those who survived the rack visited his *potro*, a trestle table that inclined the head lower than the feet, the throat and forehead held fast by a metal strap, arms and legs secured by ropes. Now, bound and secured like a gaffed fish, their mouths were forced open and a strip of linen, the *toca*, inserted into their gullet. Debrun poured water down their throat, chortling as they swelled, exhorting them to tell the truth, all the while knowing they couldn't even sputter, "Help!"

Before any torture began, Debrun would be mesmerized by the rituals. He gripped the sinner as they walked on dirt floors through the murky halls, condensation dripping from high stone ceilings. Tapestries of holy bible scenes covered the walls to smother the ghastly cries of pain. A dozen inquisitors gathered in a circle around the accused, their nostrils burning from the musty smell of deep earth mingled with the stink of old blood and human excrement. Draped in hooded monk garb, faces hidden in cowls pulled tight, the twelve held candles, the flames flickering light onto the crosses hung from walls and posts, as they administered their didactic cruelty. The high prelate intoned the benediction:

"We stand here in the name of our savior Jesus Christ, the Lord our God, and we confront the devil in this poor soul who must, as we all must, embrace the end of life."

Then, as instructed by the Suprema of the Church, they recited the prayer of absolvement:

Christi Nomine Invocato: Having paid attention to the evidence and merits of this case, we have grounds to suspect the prisoner, and so have found that we must condemn them to be put to the interrogation of torture, in which we order that the prisoner should spend as much time as we see fit, so that they should tell us the truth about the accusations made against them. And in addition we declare that if the prisoner should die or be injured or suffer heavy bleeding or have a limb mutilated during the torture, this will be their fault and responsibility and not ours, because they have refused to tell the truth. Amen

'Embrace the end of life', an edict to be honored ad infinitum to a cacophony of pain and pleas for mercy. Then the strange habit of human death, as if it was the miracle they waited for. Lily waited her turn.

Chapter 6
Welcome to the Inquisition

Twenty-three years earlier, before Revela and Dante were born, in October of 1469, Queen Ysabela I of Castile and King Ferdinand II of Aragon were married, uniting the crowns of Spain. Jews and Muslims were tolerated at the time, generally allowed to follow their precepts and customs for domestic matters, though subject to discriminatory economic and political laws. Called *The Convencia*, this period of tolerance ended in 1478 when the royal dominion, in order to maintain orthodoxy in its kingdom, inaugurated the Spanish Inquisition. This new era of intolerance was accepted as casually as the coming of the next season, as familiar as air.

The 'New Inquisition' produced 'New Christians', *conversos*, devout Jews who did not believe in the myths and magic of the Catholics. They prayed in the cathedral as a public show, but met in secret to honor their true faith, their daily reality being oppressive fear and danger.

Tomas de Torquemada, the Queen's confessor, advised her, "The Jews serve Mammon in Spain. Let not Your Highness' gracious mind be disturbed on account of these descendants of our enemies, the crucifiers of Christ. If they suffer at all, do but suffer justly, for the unutterable sin of their forefathers so many centuries ago."

Between 1480 and 1492, thousands of Jews and conversos were arrested, imprisoned, tortured, and burned at the stake. The ceremony intoned by a high prelate included, of course, the benediction:

"We stand here in the name of our savior Jesus Christ, the Lord our God, and we confront the devil in this poor soul who must, as we all must, embrace the end of life."

Diego de Suson who washed his hands before praying, and Juan Abola-
fia and Manual Sauli, who would not eat rabbit, were tortured, burned,
and called to embrace the end of life.

The Crown felt it necessary to remove a genuinely mortal danger from
Spanish society, reasoning that Jews, masquerading as Catholic Christians, were like wasps depositing eggs in a caterpillar. Jewish falsehoods,
inseminated in Christian minds, incubated, and would breed thoughts
destined to destroy the host.

When the Church found pages from the Torah buried on Samuel de
Eli's land, he was burned at the stake. Juan de Esperandeu and Vidal
Durango, seen washing their hands before praying, were tortured, quar-
tered, burned, and called to embrace the end of life.

Many ordinary citizens, singled out by the circumstances of common
human prejudice, were subjected to the worst of terrors. A simple jealousy, a social snub, a perceived insult, a spurned suitor, a minor financial question, any matter of humdrum daily life could result in being
denounced. Mateo Ram, who did no work on Saturday, Pedro Muñoz,
Jaime Monfort and his wife, seen blessing and passing a cup of wine—
all charred at the stake and called to embrace the end of life.

The consequences of not confessing were as brutal as those of confession. Imprisonment, whipping, limbs chopped off, bodies drawn and
quartered, hanging, decapitation. Andreas and his wife Blancha Colom,
who gave Old Testament names to their children, were tortured, staked,
burned, and called to embrace the end of life.

Even those Jews and conversos who had faithfully served the crown
with honor and skill in high positions, found themselves and their families persecuted. Juan Pedro Sanchez, Garcia Lopez and wife Brianda
Sanchez, who on the Day of Atonement neither ate nor drank, went
barefoot, and asked forgiveness of another, were set afire and called to
embrace the end of life.

The extended Santangel family living throughout the realm, a bastion of wealth and respectability, prominent in all matters that advanced the culture and reputation of their country, and whose wealth was often advanced to the crown, these men, women and children, were persecuted, tortured, and systematically murdered. Martín de Santangel, because he recited the Psalms without adding: "Glory be to the Father, the Son, and the Holy Ghost" burned at the stake in July, 1486, in Saragossa. Mosen Luís de Santangel, father in law of the King's treasurer, Gabriel Sanchez, met the same fate, called to embrace the end of life.

Believing in the magic power of signs and exorcisms, Spanish society lived in the darkness of ignorance and savagery, the victims of pestilence, accident, hunger, and wars. Despite the numberless fates they were ever inventing new ways to die.

When the pyres to burn Jews were lit, the choir sang, Te Deum Laudamus, the Hymn of Thanks. It was as if civilization had collapsed and beasts reigned.

Dominican friars, the Domini Canes, the Hounds of the God, promoted a Catholic creed of fear, greed, cruelty, and murder. Because the church was not permitted to shed blood, they preferred burning at the stake. Dazzling and memorable, it was considered a purification. Driven by blind fanaticism, the New Inquisition used only those words of the church that served their purposes. They found justification in the Gospel of St John:

> If a man does not abide in me, he is cast forth as a branch and withers; and the branches are gathered, thrown into the fire and burned... John 15:6

and of St. Matthew:

> Depart from me, ye cursed, into everlasting fire which was prepared for the devil and his angels... Matthew 25;41

Consequently, the *auto de fe* ceremony, the heretic's punishment, the burning, was administered by civil authorities.

There was no monopoly on stupidity, as judges became murderers by following the religious philosophy of honored thinkers. Thomas Aquinas, the immensely influential 13th century Dominican philosopher, decreed it was not enough to excommunicate heretics, they must be "excluded from the world by death".

Many of the 'purified' had served the crown as physicians, counselors, lawyers, mathematicians, navigators, scientists, and even high bishops of the church.

The mother of Gabriel Concalo de Santangel went to the funeral pyre, called to embrace the end of life. Jaime Martín and Donosa de Santangel, burned in 1488, and Simon de Santangel in 1490.

Men and women who had escaped to another country were condemned and burned in effigy in order to legally confiscate their property. Even long buried bodies were exhumed and the bones burned. The Crown usurped generations of family property. People who wished nothing more than to live their lives following the traditions and customs of their ancestors were tortured by fire, the foulest treatment conceivable, regarded as the instrument of divine vengeance.

Blood boiled in veins, brains boiled in skulls, and bowels formed a mash of burning paste. Hearts swelled and burst. Soulful eyes flamed out, revealing the dark, empty sockets of skulls. Burning, the vilest torment to which a tyrant has ever subjected his wards left its awful stench.

An accusation of heresy found ample reward for accusers, as the Crown shared in the confiscated property of the condemned. The Spanish treasury, depleted to nothing during the ten-year Granada War against the Muslims, was replenished.

Ferdinand and Ysabela were strong leaders, monarchs of a newly united Spain at the dawn of the modern era, who also had other interests. It had been an act of religious promise to complete the 'Christian Reconquest', and retake Granada, the last Muslim outpost on the Iberian Peninsula where the Muslims had lived for 800 years. In April 1492, after ten years and many battles, the war came to an end when the Emir Bobadil surrendered the keys of the Alhambra Palace to Castilian soldiers. Six weeks later the proclamation to expel all Jews was issued.

Chapter 7
David & Revela

Early August, 1492, is a sweltering day under high, thin clouds as sailors load cargo on the Gallega. Dante and Revela cluster with the Jews near the aft hatch, taking pleasure in just being alive. In this new restrictive space they devise a routine to accommodate their daily human needs; to eat, drink, eliminate and sleep, with deference given to women and children. The foremost need, to get ready for death, each tends to in silence, the thought lingering in no motion in the back of their minds.

The hour of departure has been anticipated for days, and each new dawn brings its own anxiety. But today the Jews seem unusually active, even disturbed. Their speech is more animated, their prayer louder and more intense, their tender of comfort to each other more heartfelt. Many of the ship's crew, *conversos* themselves, lament the exiles and their fate, abandoning that peculiar air of tolerance that seamen affect toward unwelcome passengers.

An intermediary emerges, David de Violina. He is the son of Rabbi Moises, a textile merchant from a *judería* in a hill village near Sevilla. Orders from the marshal, Harana, are given to him to inform the others. A young man with an engaging smile and natural charm, David is a fountain of encouragement. He is escaping with his father, his mother, Merosa, and two cousins. David's beloved Uncle Aaron, his father's brother, recently had the dubious honor of meeting Tomas de Torquemada, the Inquisitor General, and was called to embrace the end of life.

David is tall with broad shoulders and a confident walk. The look of a hero, Revela thinks, but she also sees the boy in his honest face and gentle manner. When he pushes back a curl of dark hair that conceals a small scar above his eyebrow, she imagines herself doing this for him. She asks, "What is everyone so excited about?"

David's attention was on Dante and Revela from the moment they boarded, but he remains uncertain of their status. He says, "Today is the Ninth of Av. It's the anniversary of the destruction of the Temple of Jerusalem, first by the Assyrians then the Romans. May darkness devour the memory of that dread day." Then, seeing Revela's questioning look, "It is our greatest day of mourning."

For the briefest moment, the circumstances of exile escape David. Only an instant, but an instant that gives him time to consider who Revela might be and what they might do if this was an ordinary meeting of a young man and young woman. In that timeless moment, David becomes his own representative, imagining how he would impress her with a childhood lesson about the Ninth of Av. He would describe how both holy temples in Jerusalem had their walls breached and tabernacles destroyed. How they were razed to the ground on that date, 'Tisha B'Av'— so long ago, in the first century after Christ's birth and again seven centuries ago. He wants to sing to her the song of deep lamenta-tion for that day, Al Naharot Bavel.

> *By the rivers of Babylon,*
> *Where the waters flowed down,*
> *And yea we wept,*
> *When we remembered Zion.*

But before he can speak, Revela breaks into his thoughts, "Oh, is that why all the commotion?"

"Well, yes. But there's more. We seem to be making ready to leave. But it is said that nothing good can come of undertakings begun on this holy day. The prospect of leaving today has everyone nervous."

Revela nods her head as if she should have known that. She also wants to continue the conversation, but is tongue-tied, flustered as any young woman might be talking with a handsome stranger. Suddenly feeling dizzy, as though her blood pressure had dipped then soared, she asks, but too late realizes it will result in herself being questioned.

"Are you all from the same place?"

"No, my family is from Sevilla and the Bartlets are from Aracena. Near the Sierras. The others are from further north. Aroche, I think. Or perhaps Carmona. Where are you from? Your name is Revela, right? And your husband is Dante?"

Revela's lips tighten and her eyes drop. She had counseled Dante to be vague and she gropes for an answer.

"We're from a small village to the east." Her eyes widened and she seizes the opportunity to avoid another question and cries out, "Here, don't do that!" In an exaggerated manner she bolts past David to prevent one of the youngsters from climbing a railing. Herding the child away, she looks back over her shoulder to smile.

At dusk, as the last of the provisions are brought on board, Diego de Harana spits out to David, "Have those Jews ready to get below. And quickly!"

David nods and turns to the group, "Be prepared now. Quick, Get ready. It's time."

Dante and Revela maneuver their way to the group's center with the children. She asks why they are crying, a small voice says, "Because we're lost", and they gather close to her. That is the way with Revela, never having time to become desperate, an island of integrity in the midst of despair. The two escapees follow the group of seventeen Jews below. They shuffle through the hatch, pass a bulkhead, and into the foc'sile, the very prow of the ship. At sea this area, ill-suited for cargo of crates or barrels, is normally used as storage space for the anchor line. Humans, irregularly shaped and flexible, are a better fit, but the space will soon take on the feel of a communal coffin.

The surface area allotted the Jews is a meager triangle connecting port and starboard at its apex, and aft about five meters to a bulkhead. The ship's deck is directly above, barely a half-meter over their heads. David sorts the exiles like carrots, fitting bodies between the ribs of the ship, splitting families, the shorter children placed forward. Mothers whimper at the separation, a cruel turn at the start of a tortuous journey. Their backs to the hull, as close as raindrops, they stare across the narrow space, Revela and Dante at the Rabbi and his wife, Merosa. They wait, listening to the watery slap against the hull.

Harana comes below, inspecting with his rat-like eyes. His teeth and whip threaten as he confirms that all cargo is secure. He knows well the ride on the sail southwest down the coast of Africa. If the seas are rough, a loose crate could be a costly disaster. His scrutiny includes the Jews, although not with concern for what the fury of the seas would inflict on organs and bones of human freight.

In a voice like a fist, he booms, "Now you Jews keep your place. No wandering past this 'er bulkhead, 'cept for you two." He coughs harshly, pointing with his lash to ten-year old Joshua and his younger brother, Jacob. "You devils 'il pitch the buckets an get yer meals and water topside once a day. Ya understand?" And he thinks how little that will serve.

The Jews shed layers of clothing, using them to cushion their wasting, bony bodies against the ship's inner hull. There is no wiggle room. A small movement by one inescapably provokes the next person, creating a Jewish wave rolling to the end of the pitiful line.

Stifling heat compounds their confinement. With no hatch above them, the only source of air enters from the passage to the cargo hold then forward past the bulkhead. As dusk descends these cargo hatches are battened down, eliminating any airflow to the dank foc'sle.

Unable to stand upright, the Jews lean against the hull, crammed together in the dark, sucking the inescapable heavy heat. Solitary spirits embrace and their suffering together relieves their suffering alone. As their bodies adapt, their thoughts drift to memories of better times.

Merosa thinks of her cousin, Edit. In 1468 Edit and her family escaped death from a pogrom in Sevilla by fleeing to Sicily. She wonders, "Could I have helped?" If she had, "Would I have put my family at risk?" Merosa wants to forget but she cannot forget, she will never forget. She often tried to put herself in Edit's place, to fathom the deep tragedy and hardships her cousin underwent. What was it like for Edit to be separated from the land of her youth, lost to the impossibility, the absolute futility, of finding a new homeland. Exile, what she understood now only too well, Merosa could not imagine then.

Deep whispering voices break the silence. "This is it, motek."

And a mocking, "You think so?"

"You see we've stopped running away."

"You're right, I feel that too."

"We're sailing to freedom."

"Anywhere, please. It stinks in here."

There would be homes again for many surviving exiles of Spain, all that any human on earth truly wants. But here, in this strangest of places, no one escapes the unbearable heat and putrid aromas of the journey. Soon, as the ship surrenders to the pitiless sea, they will feel as if they'd been turned inside out. Sleep will not be sleep. Awake will not be awake. As they vomit on each other they will curse life. The pain and taste of their own raw organs will prove a test of their grip on reality.

The day after the bloody evening at La Sirena Taberna. Dante is not a thoughtful youngster and he seldom considered much of anything other than avoiding farm-work; not friends or school, not the Church, not the crusades, not the King and Queen, not the decade long war against the Moors, not the persecution of the Jews, not Jesus Christ. And he never considered, much less questioned, the tenants of his religion. Perhaps he knows marginally, like he knows about sex, that his church nourishes racism and sadism, and sponsors their champions. But he believes this is

God's work. He wants God to exist. Not for reassurance of the promise to survive death, his youth bestows immortality, rather, like most, Dante seeks an answer to the question, why? Something has to make sense in this life. The irony that religion makes no sense never occurred to him. Now, confronted with monumental injustice and senseless immorality, true to his nature, he joins the side of the oppressed.

Late that Palos night pressed against the hull like cloaks on hooks, a deafening explosion shocks the Jews from the monotony of the foc'sle. Coming through the thickness of a deck plank above them is a piercing discordant crack, like a splitting glacier. Heavy chains, links thick as an arm, rake aboard over the ship's rail. Jewish arms thrust up to grab ears and block the roar that seems to originate inside their heads.

Harana gives the order to weigh anchor. Twelve men strain to lift the huge kedge, Esmeralda, from her snug rest in the mud of the Palos harbor. The marshal sets the rhythm to pull in the thick hawser by slapping his bone handled whip against his palm. The men understand what will happen once the ship is set loose. It will not rear like a stallion, but rather draw on the power of the sea to gain its freedom. The haul starts, the men grunt with each pull. Then Kiril, the shanty man, begins his song. It is heard below and it is heard across the water, from the harbor mouth out to the world.

"O dio", Kiril sings as the men haul in line.

At the end of the short pull, the men reach forward to secure a fresh hold, singing the response, "ayuta noy."

Kiril sings, "O que somo"

and the men pulling, "servi soy".

"O veleamo – ben servi"

"O la feda – mantenir"

Muscles strain. Sweat breaks on the men's' brows as the chant continues. Esmeralda holds the earth as the ship is hauled through the water forward.

"O fillioi – dabrahin"

"O non credono – que ben sia"

Reaching a point above the anchor, the Gallega glides past, the force of the ship's momentum breaking the fluke free of the muddy harbor ground, dragging the great hook over the seabed.

"O non credono – la fe santa"

"O di Roma – esta el perdon"

"O que ruegue – a Dio por nos"

The Gallega is unchained. Esmeralda hangs in the sea six meters directly below the ship. The haul-up is now the anchor's dead weight plus the clump of muddy Spain attached to its flukes. The men lean to it, the sheen of sweat on their bodies. The other two ships haul their anchors and sing in the false-dawn light. From across the water a concertina, soft, barely heard. The sailors of the caravels wonder if this is an omen, perhaps a saintly-spirit come to guide and protect them.

Esmeralda's line is secured to the cathead and the men begin rowing the sweeps, propelling the ship out the harbor and down the Rio Odiel. The cool terral, the night wind that blows from the mountains to the sea, joins force with the ebb tide. The ships gather way, moving slowly downstream toward the broad estuary where the Odiel joins the Rio Tinto. The Genoan captain, standing tall against the Spanish coast, smiles as they pass the cliff that houses the priory of La Rabida. His son, Diego, lives there.

In the new daylight, the evening star, Venus, becomes its own twin, the morning star. The fleet approaches the Tinto's mouth at the Saltes Bar. The eastern land breeze, the Levanter, falls as the sun rises. Out beyond the bar the wind blows from the Ocean Sea, fresh and strong. The ships slide down the protected passage, the Canal of the Holy Father, and plunge into the ocean rollers.

The crew stands ready, every man intent on doing his best. As soon as the Gallega's bow crosses the wind, Harana, atop the foc'sle, gives the order, "Let go the canvas". All hands bolt into the rigging, the heavy cloth falling and the two heralds emblazoned on the mainsails fill the morning sky. An 'F & Y' for the king and queen mark one mainsail, and on the other the Green Cross of Castile. The canvass fills to the steady wind and the three bows point to clear the Spanish coast, pushing the square-rigged ships south by southwest toward Africa. Warm waves slap against the hull as the voyage begins, the course set direct for the distant Canary Islands.

In the foc'sle, the exiles line against the hull, muscles tense, jaws set, trying to find a rhythm in which to breathe. With nothing to grip for support, they slam against each other. From the deck above where Harana stands, comes a maritime symphony; wooden planks creak with the boat's pitch and roll, taut ropes hum and groan, winds hiss into the sails, waves slap the broadsides, and men shout across the deck.

That first wave gives the sailors the ride they want, the ride they are there for. The Santa Maria, the Nina and the Pinta are at sea. The three captains, including the Captain General of the Fleet, stand their posts—Cristóbal Colón, Martín Alonso Pinzón, and Vincente Pinzón.

It is August 3, 1492, dawn of the first day of exile for an ancient people, and the dawn of the first day of a new world.

> *Look they move! No comrades near but curses; Tears gleam in beards of men*
> *sore with reverses; Flowers from fields abandoned, loving nurses,*
> *Fondly deck the women's raven hair.*
> *Faded, scentless flowers that shall remind them Of their precious homes*
> *and graves behind them; Old men, clasping Torah-scrolls, unbind them,*
> *Lift the parchment flags, and silent lead.*
> *'Mock not with thy light, O sun, our morrow, Cease not, cease not,*
> *O ye songs of sorrow! From what land a refuge can we borrow, Weary,*

thrust out, God-forsaken we?
Where, oh! Where is rest for thy long-hated, Hunted folk, whose fate
in death unsated? Oh! Where is God? So swelled the wail unbated,
From the mountains down unto the sea.
Cold ye, suff'ring souls, peer through the Future, From despair you
would awake to rapture:
Lo! The Genoese boldly steers to capture Freedom's
realm beyond an unsailed sea!

Christ Columbo By: Ludwig Agust von Frankl Translated by: Minnie D. Louis

Chapter 8
The Castle Meeting

It is 1486, six years before the sail of the Voyage of Discovery's three ships with their cargo of exiles. The town of Medinaceli, Spain, situated on a small hill overlooking the Jalón valley mid-distance between Madrid and Saragossa, separates the Muslim and Christian territories. Nearby, the Jalón River serves to transport the region's salt as it flows from the foot of the Sierra Ministra to join the Rio Ebro, the largest river in Spain. Entry to the dukedom is through an arc built by the Romans in the second century. After a season of above normal rainfall in perpetually arid Spain, generous fields of alfalfa and meadows of blue sorghum, veronica, and flax fill the rolling hills. Near the center of town, not far from the castle, is a *beatério*. Now inhabited by the sisters of San Roman, it was once a synagogue serving the *judería* of the town. The Jewish and *converso* population are gone, having suffered cruel persecutions from their Christian neighbors before fleeing.

Count Luís de la Cerda y de la Vega fought at the side of King Ferdinand against the Moors and was rewarded with the title of First Duke of Medinaceli. His castle, walled on three sides, a refuge for ambitious men, encloses an area large enough to encompass a small village. It sits strategically on a bluff with a view of the Jalón River Valley to its embrace with the Erbo. The Duke's private quarters are high in the castle's center. Below, various courtyards connect six distinct areas like spokes of a wheel.

Muffled voices come from behind an archway concealed by a heavy, dark curtain caked with mildew as if it stored the past. Three men are in conversation in the high walled room well lit by ornate oil sconces.

"Someone's going to do this, Santangel, I'm certain of it."

Cristóbal Colón, a tall man with piercing, blue eyes, speaks as he leafs through a thick book. His crossed legs propped on the corner of a long wooden table show the worn heels of his leather boots. Plates of congealed bits of bread, fruit, and fried fish scraps are scattered among nautical charts and drafting tools.

Luís de Santangel nods to his friend, "Well, with King John turning it down twice." And he shakes his head. "It's clear he's banking on Dias rounding Africa. Who else now besides Ferdinand?"

Santangel, a 'New Christian', is King Ferdinand's Chancellor of the Royal Household and Comptroller-General of the Royal Treasury. Like Cristóbal Colón he is in his mid thirties, but his face is worn with worry lines.

Being reminded of his visits to Lisbon and the off-hand dismissal he received there from King John, Cristóbal Colón mutters, "Ah, the Portuguese".

Santangel says, "The war is the principal obstacle for Ferdinand, my friend. The money is there, but it's the war. Right, Deza?"

Hieronymus Deza, seated at the other end of the table, signals his agreement. Deza is a short man with a hooked nose. Summoned by King John, he has travelled from Germany en route to Portugal, bringing with him the newest chart that shows the world as a sphere.

Deza purses his lips as he examines a small African statue and asks, "You know why primitive art is so magical, Santangel?" Then without waiting, "Because it is shaped by terror."

Colón ignores Deza and responds to Santangel. "Yes, of course it's the war. I know it isn't the money. Were you in Sevilla last March? At that wedding? The Infanta Ysabela. A ten-year-old! There were twenty voyages spent on that carnival."

Deza, through a mouthful of pear, laughs, "Yes, I was there. They spent a chest-full. You'd have thought the Pope was getting married."

His face relaxes and Santangel wonders if he should speak in the presence of Deza, then inquires "Tell me Cristóbal, do you think it would help to reveal where you learned Spanish?"

Cristóbal Colón closes his book. He understands the intent of the question. He has scrupulously adhered to the commands of Rome, devout in both his public and private conduct. To reveal that he learned Spanish at home in Genoa would raise eyebrows in the court. His adversaries would gleefully claim his ancestors to be part of the diaspora from the 1391 Jew killings in Sevilla. He would risk exposing his support from the Jews, both a boon and a curse to his efforts.

Colón opens his mouth to speak but hesitates, as if considering his words or listening to a voice only he can hear, and then says, "As you well know, Santangel, I am a reverent Catholic. The day of my first holy communion was the happiest day of my life. It is for good reasons that I have avoided explaining my family history. As Christ is my savior and witness, it would serve no useful purpose. You know I have a *limpieza de sangre*, and am in compliance with the five generation precept" he lies. "Any controversy would endanger my divine mission to spread the word of Jesus. Remember, Santangel, it was only ten years ago that Peter Albano and Cecco 'd Ascoli were burned for declaring that the world was a globe."

Santangel slightly bows his head. "Yes, of course. I'm sorry. I spoke without thinking. Your service gives great hope to our dream."

But the Royal Treasurer cannot contain the urgency he feels. With Torquemada now supreme, the vehemence of the Inquisition has seen the most prominent Spanish families annihilated. "Did you know of the burning of the Bisques in Latona and the entire Apriles family in Qunice? I was told they even desecrated the family mausoleum. They burned the bones of four hundred years! The morons!"

Luís Santangel paces the floor, wringing his hands, agitated by the recanting of these atrocities. "If ever there was a time for asylum it is now. Oh, the times we live in. Terror is rampant and total disaster only a matter of time. We cannot keep the beast away forever, my friend."

Just then, the heavy magenta curtain that divides the room from the foyer, parts. Cristóbal Colón sighs, welcoming the close of his conversation with Santangel. The Duke of the castle and a woman enter.

The Duke of Medina-Celi, like King Ferdinand, like Deza, like Torqemada, is the grandson of a Jewish woman. A stout forty-seven-year old, with a short-cropped reddish beard and melancholy eyes, he walks a bit crooked, the result of a fall from his horse while in armed service at the King's side. As any man would be who has enjoyed the lifelong privileges of title and wealth, he is direct and outspoken. His relaxed sociable presence is an attribute of never having had an unpleasant moment in his life, and never expecting one.

With his cousin, the Duke of Sidonia, Meli owns substantial holdings in the sugar plantations of the Canary Islands. The commodity has recently surpassed honey as the sweetener of choice in Europe. On the Duke's arm is a striking female, a raven-haired Spanish beauty. She is Elenora Bobadilla, the governess of Gomera a small island in the Canaries, and the sister of Beatriz Bobadilla, the Marchioness of Moya, the Queen's confidante and best friend. Elenora has a mutual interest with Meli in the export of sugar, and she clutches the Duke's arm, elated by his early knowledge of a large contract offered by the Genoans of Majorca to buy first sugar crops.

Meli works his tongue as if searching for water to moisten his parched mouth, and says, "Aha, here's our friend, Cristóbal."

Elenora glides forward, her hand extends, her head slightly tilts.

"Hello Captain," she says, the provocative lilt in her voice aggrandizing the title. "So good to see you again."

"Contessa, always my pleasure. You know Luís Santangel, our regent's Treasurer."

"Of course", extending her hand to receive his bow.

"What a surprise to see you, Lady Elanora. I am most fortunate."

Turning to the older man she says to Deza, "And Hieronymus, you are here also? How are you, my dear friend?"

"Lady Elanora, wonderful to see you again. How long has it been?

The last time was Toledo, was it not? Where you served the Queen of Castile. So long ago." He continues to hold her hand.

Withdrawing her hand, "Yes, it has been much too long. You promised to visit us in Gomera", and in a pout, "but you haven't come, Hieronymus."

Deza, is a portly forty-two-year old man who has learned well the value of appeasement in service to the royals. Around his gelatinous neck he carries a magnifying glass on a lanyard that he fiddles and points with when speaking. "I know, I know, Contessa. It's this gout that vexes me. I simply cannot travel by sea. I'm afraid I shall never see your marvelous island."

Cristóbal Colón says, "I've offered to take him, my lady, but he's a difficult man to convince. I'm afraid we must enjoy his friendship here on the Peninsula."

Meli agrees, "Yes, let's do that."

They settle on sofas in an alcove alongside tables set with bowls of fruits and bread. The conversation proceeds in a semi-courtly manner, a well-practiced social repartee, recounting current and past intrigues of the palace - who has distinguished himself, who is in disfavor. Cristóbal sits to one side of Elenora, which makes her somewhat uneasy, but gives himself the advantage of watching the other three men posture before the dark haired beauty.

This is an unusual woman, a calculating strategist, adept in the politics of persuasion and money. Educated, sophisticated, she deals with life as if every decision is critical, all the while harboring a streak of cruelty and contempt for the masses. Strong willed and confident, an expert in the game, her presence charges the atmosphere. Life has taught her to favor each man with attention, her lingering eye contact complimented by a seductive smile. Her eyes then flutter to another, only to slowly return to her target with a nod of her Venus head as if to say, "I could be yours". The man's chest puffs. That's the way of it.

Cristóbal Colón considers how easily one surrenders attention to her musings. She might simply ask, 'How are you?' and one believes she truly wants to know. Sometimes her fingers impatiently pull at her crucifix, or she tucks her arm up her sleeve, a woman reluctant to show her hand. Most of all, Colón admires the way her slight emphasis on a word, a subtle lowering of her tone, a gentle touch, hints that she will share a secret with you.

Cristóbal and Elenora exchange private glances. At the right moment she turns to him and asks, "So Captain," again that flavored intonation, "tell me how your venture advances." They all understand how his success would greatly favor her interests. Future voyages would repeat his nautical course and her small island could become the entry point to the riches of the East, benefiting her with great power and wealth.

"Not that well, I'm sorry to say. Still, thanks to Meli, I'm about to present the matter to the Queen again. But I am afraid her confessor, Talavera, advises against it. The court's focus is the war."

Luís Santangel sums up the situation. "Yes, unfortunately, our efforts to send the Captain on his voyage lack the force necessary to convince the Crown. They feign interest but it is like sailing for the promise of the horizon that one never reaches. So long as the war continues, the commissions of inquiry will remain skeptical, and approval unlikely."

Meli blusters. In the attitude of a man with little to fear, a man enjoying his age and influence, he says, "These 'King's advisors are basically dimwits. They scurry about like mice to find out what the King wants to hear before they say anything. And then they say only that which they believe he wants to hear. He might as well have dog-fleas as advisors."

Being closest to the King, Santangel has the only opinion that matters. Words of encouragement are all that's left to be said, words too familiar to Cristóbal Colón.

Meli says, "Come my lady, let me show you to your quarters." and they leave the room.

As the Duke and Elenora leave, Santangel gives Colón a knowing look. "Still a beautiful woman, wouldn't you say?"

Deza adds, "Simply exquisite. But like all her sex she is fickle and easily led into intrigues. No wonder the Queen despises her very presence in Spain. Probably all women do."

Colón holds his thoughts to himself. He first met Elenora in the Canary Islands years before, while on a sugar trade mission for Meli. Colón's wife, Beatriz, had just died. Although Elenora's allure was renown, no man is ever prepared for such exceptional beauty. A realist, Cristóbal Colón had accepted his fate as yet another man haunted by the image of a radiant female.

Cristóbal next encountered her years later in Barcelona, and he savored the memory of that month's euphoria. Elenora Bobadilla, then a recent widow, was unsure of her future. Her husband, Hernan Peraza, had been assassinated, making her the Governess of Gomera. The Queen's jealousy of Elenora's beauty was well known, and although Elenora avoided any contact with the King, her name became a constant topic of court intrigue. Bearing the curse of glaring sexuality, she suffered slander from many, including accusations of debauchery, licentiousness, even nymphomania. Cristóbal Colón, mature, intelligent, and unallied with factions in the court, became a welcome friend to her. She was attracted to his rugged countenance cultivated by long days at sea. He relished hearing her sultry purr, "You know, I love to call a man 'Captain'."

The accepted social order in the 15th century predestined their liaison to be short. She was noble; he was not. His status a constant wound, Cristóbal Colón intended that his plan would cure that lack of nobility. He demanded, as reward for a successful mission, to be granted the inheritable title of 'Don' as well as other appellations. Until then, there could be no future with Elenora Bobadilla.

The very place of Elenora Bobadilla's castle, San Sebastian de Gomera in the Canary Islands, was the last deep water port on the Ocean Sea, and the exact position from which Cristóbal Colón intended to launch his enterprise. Colón considered this implausible fact to be divinely inspired. Their month together in Barcelona began an intense period of dreaming, dreams he considered to be God's manner of messaging him. How could time and circumstance be more serendipitous?

That night in the garden of the Count of Meli, purple jasmine perfumed the air and crimson bougainvillea climbed the walls to lattice balconies. There, on a stone bench in the courtyard alongside a fountain adorned with winged cherubs, pretense and formality dissolved.

"It is wonderful to see you again, Elanora. I have thought of you often."

Conscious of his physical presence, his assertive body, she remains distant and non-committal, but feels herself succumbing to the latent power of his will. He is again the dominant male.

"Yes, and I you, Christopher. You're looking well. And the leg pain? Is it gone?

"Oh, mostly yes. It comes and goes, but not like what it was then. I try to stay off horses. I think that helps."

"Yes, of course."

The Governess dips her hand into the water and then shakes it off. "We are both widowed now, aren't we?" He nods. "Oh, I see you still carry that book. What is it again?" Cristóbal fingers what has become his companion, Imagio Mundi, by Pierre d'Ailly. The book is bound in dark green with a tooled border of gold, its pages edged in gilt. A compilation of science and philosophy from the ancient Greeks and Romans, it is Cristóbal's primary source of calculations, the reasoning behind his enterprise.

"Oh this? It's my best friend."

Not waiting for anything further, Elenora continues with a smile. "How fares your son, Diego, and your brother, Bartolomeo?"

He is touched by her expressions of concern, its intimacy.

"They're fine. Bartolomeo is in Lisbon and has become a talented cartographer. And Diego is at La Rabida with Fray Marchena. He studies history. And you, what of your situation? Why are you here in Iberia?"

The woman makes light of her motivation. "Oh, I am very busy, trying to keep order among the primitives. I've only come to the Peninsula on a small matter concerning my son, Hernando. Changing the subject she asks, "Do you remember when we were in Cordova?"

The question is a tease. "Yes, of course I do." His mind's eye travels to the thrill of that wild ride through the forest in Catalonia.

She smiles and takes his arm as they stroll in the garden. "Yes, I do also." She has reconnected with a unique comfort she feels with Cristóbal, so unlike her associations with other men. Something about him rings true. She senses a mantle of respect in his presence that encourages candor, and says, "I have always been desired by men, you understand that Cristóbal. But now I am valued. Which I find quite a different thing."

"And well you should be. I am hopeful that soon someone will sponsor my voyage. And if they do, I will need your help, Elanora. Gomera has always been my point of departure."

"Of course, Captain. Whatever I can do."

Chapter 9
At Sea

Ship's Log

Friday, 3 August 1492

Most Christian, exalted, excellent, and powerful princes, King and Queen of the Spains and of the islands of the sea, our Sovereigns: It was in this year of 1492 that your Highnesses concluded the war with the Moors who reigned in Europe. On the second day of January, in the great city of Granada, ...based on the information that I had given Your Highnesses about the land of India and about a Prince who is called the Great Kahn, which in our language means "King of Kings," Your Highnesses decided to send me, Cristóbal Colón, to the regions of India, to see the Princes there and the peoples and the lands, and to learn of their disposition, and of everything, and the measures which could be taken for their conversion to our Holy Faith.

I informed Your Highnesses how this Great Kahn and his predecessors had sent to Rome many times to beg for men learned in our Holy Faith so that his people might be instructed therein, and that the Holy Father had never furnished them, and therefore, many peoples believing in idolatries and receiving among themselves sects of perdition were lost.

Your Highnesses, as Catholic Christians and Princes devoted to the Holy Christian faith and to the spreading of it, and as enemies of the Muslim sect and of all idolatries and heresies, ordered that I shall go to the east, but not by land as is customary. I was to go by way of the west, whence until today we do not know with certainty that anyone has gone.

Therefore, having banished all the Jews from your Kingdoms and realms, during this same month of January Your Highnesses ordered me to go with

*a sufficient fleet to the said regions of India. For that purpose I was grant-
ed great favors and ennobled; from thence forward I might entitle myself
Don and be High Admiral of the Ocean Sea and Viceroy and perpetual
Governor of all the islands and continental land that I might discover and
acquire, as well as any other future discoveries in the Ocean Sea. Further,
my eldest son shall succeed to the same position, and so on from generation
to generation for ever after.*

*I left Granada on Saturday, the 12th day of the month of May in the
same year of 1492 and went to the town of Palos, which is a seaport. There
I fitted out three vessels, very suited to such an undertaking. I left the said
port well supplied with a large quantity of provisions and with many seamen on the third day of the month of August in the said year, on a Friday,
half an hour before sunrise. I set my course for the Canary Islands of Your
highnesses, which are in the Ocean Sea, from there to embark on a voyage
that will last until in the Indies and deliver the letter of Your Highnesses to
those Princes, and do all that Your Highnesses have commanded me to do.*

*To this end I decided to write down everything I might do and see and ex-
perience on this voyage, from day to day, and very carefully. Also, Sovereign
Princes, besides describing each night what takes place during the day, and
during the day the sailings of the night, I propose to make a new chart for
navigation, on which I will set down all the sea and lands of the Ocean Sea,
in their correct locations and in their correct bearings. Further, I shall com-
pile a book and shall map everything by latitude and longitude. And above
all, it is fitting that I forget about sleeping and devote much attention to
navigation in order to accomplish this. And these things will be a great task.*

*We set sail on this third day of August, 1492, at 8 o'clock in the morning,
from the bar of Saltes, The wind is strong and variable, and we had gone
45 miles to the south by sunset. After dark I altered course for the Canary
islands, to the south by west.*

Diario de a Bordo, Bishop Bartolome de las Casas — *El Libro de la Primera Navegación*

It is a well-known adage that the first scent of the ocean air brings out the philosopher in a man. Cristóbal Colón, the Captain General, looks back toward land, where time was the past. As the three ships slip by the rock barrier and enter the open sea, he turns to de Torres and says: "To be true to yourself is not an easy thing, Luís. It requires being on the verge of disgrace. I was there, and now it doesn't matter."

Luís de Torres holds to the rail with both hands as the Santa Maria settles into the rhythm of the first rollers. A surreal silence announces that present time has fractured. Men are now moving through a singular opening.

The Captain General continues, "Look out there. Though the salt smells like memory, still the water has no trace of us, or of history. And without the past, there is only the future."

Luís de Torres steadies himself against the rail. "My father, rest his beloved soul, often said to me, that in order to reach truth, one must first live in a state of extreme humiliation. Everything must be endured – disgrace, poverty, oppression. The hope is that the next day something will change. A miracle, to make life tolerable."

"Oh I have done that, my friend," replies Colón, "as you well know. Yes, I have tasted the depth of humiliation. I have been annihilated." He pauses, turns his head to the left as if someone had spoken to him from behind. "But in some matters you need only answer to yourself. And now, God willing, the truth will be known."

The moon is sewn into the late night sky. The fleet is one hundred fifty kilometers west of Gibraltar, Spain's strategic outpost guarding the entrance into the Mediterranean Sea. Following winds fill the sails and push the square-rigged ships southwest toward Africa.

Life at sea has its own rules, its own delights and difficulties, and a veto, belittling all man's attempts to challenge its power. With the land behind, and with reference only to the water and the sky, a sailor has, at the same moment, a sense of leaving and arriving. This day's mild weather and following sea make for an easy run. Still, there is the ever-present threat of disaster. A slight wind shift from the offshore breeze catches the Captain General's attention, and his eyes trace to a loose halyard causing a shake in the mainsail. As if in mirror to Colón's thought, Harana's voice booms, "Orkon and Nevta, ya bastards, get over an put that sail right." He slaps the rail with his whip handle and glances astern to the Captain General and de Torres.

Cristóbal Colón buttons his patched leather doublet. He thinks about the land he cannot see lying far out to port and the land he is certain will be much farther to starboard. They are sailing ships specifically designed by the Portuguese for the exploration of this stretch of land, the coast of Africa. The Portuguese, preeminent sailors of the European world, hold dominion over these waters through an agreement with the Spanish, brokered by the Pope. The ships are small, about twenty-two meters in length and seven meters of beam. Their shallow, three-meters draft and lateen rigging, not only enables their sailing close to land, but also allows them to reverse course, and beat into the wind for the open ocean.

The Captain General thinks back to his audience in Lisbon with King John II. John was nephew to the legendary Prince Henry the Navigator. Ironically, Henry was a small man averse to going to sea, yet he reshaped the world from his easy chair. Colón holds King John in high regard, aware that by rewarding bold navigators, he has pushed the known world farther. John's goal, the same as Henry's, is to establish a southern sea route around the tip of Africa to the riches of India. King John had been royally dismissive when he declined the Captain General's solicitation to participate in a voyage west to the Indies, and it stuck in Colón's craw.

Colón slaps his hands behind his back. Knowing his route will be much faster, he relishes the thought of his success leaving a bitter taste for the Portuguese and halting their exploration of Africa. Perhaps more importantly, it will serve to flatter Ferdinand and Ysabela.

The Captain General has been disturbed these past days by several un-expected circumstances; the ship owner's decision to carry the escaping Jews, the unexplained one day delay, that familiar looking boy among the exiles, and the dog with the Canarian, Gotzun. What steadies him is the participation of the Pinzón family, especially Martín Alonzo who captains the Niña.

With the ship making good headway and faring well, the marshal, Diego de Harana, is in good spirits, testing the humor of men he did not know with a wink to those he did.

"Hey there, Gotzun. You'll be losing that pesky dog afore this here sail's done. Ya know the Turk fancies 'em,'" he says, patting his stomach. Oth-ers laugh, as Gotzun, the tall, inscrutable sailor, smiles.

The dog, Yoggi, looks from one sailor to another, as if noting those who might be in agreement. Gotzun replies, "Oh, he wouldn't want this old piece of meat. It'd be nothing more than gristle. Full of worms and feathers. Not a meal for a sane man."

"An who says the Turk 's sane, 'eh?" the marshal coughed back. "Why I've seen 'em try an suck water outta beach-rocks."

The men bend to the work at hand, making certain all is secure. The sky is clear, a sweet taste floats in the brisk air. Birds appear from time to time anticipating a scrap of food as the Santa Maria pitches forward then rolls to its side in an easy rhythm.

The untitled Spanish nobility on board, the hidalgos, all non-sailors, line up at the prow of the ship, divided to port and starboard. Each possess a specialty that the Captain General or Queen Ysabela believe import-ant to the voyage's success. They have discovered that the stability of their stomachs is directly related to their perception of the horizon.

Closest to the bowsprit on the port is Colón's friend, Luís de Torres, a skilled interpreter, aboard to communicate with those potentates and rulers they might encounter. Alongside him stands Rodrigo Sanchez de Segovia, cousin to Santangel, the Crown's treasurer, signed on as comptroller at the specific desire of the Queen. Next in line is Rodrigo de Escobedo, recruited as secretary to record possessions the expedition might secure in the name of the Crown.

The starboard pair is Pedro Gutierrez, employed as the royal butler, and Maestre Bernal, the ship physician, who though he had sailed before, has never been able to convince his digestive system to enjoy the journey.

They stand a small distance from one another, arms outstretched and grasping the rail as if letting go meant they would fly off the ship. Each wave lifts the ship high as it sweeps past from behind. At its peak the men lunge out, their chests pressed to the rail, heads thrown forward and overboard. Then down into the trough of the wave, a simultaneous scream of surrender, and the sea receives their gifts. As the vessel is lifted by the next swell, knees buckle and the dance repeats until utter exhaustion drives each man to his knees in capitulation.

The exiles huddle directly below the deck and the puking hidalgos. For these passengers the ship's movement feels very different. As the Santa Maria rides the waves, each blow of the ocean batters the hull. The seven children in the prow bounce like falling acorns. Absorbing each wallop, the adults' necks snap, their heads bang against the hard, pine hull, and their teeth slam inside their jaws. With no visual reference to establish equilibrium, the hyperbolic motion, the up and down, the high and the low, the roll right then left, each moment of unceasing blows demands attention from their exhausted senses.

The exiles hold each other and the ribs of the ship. A protocol evolves for use of the vomit bucket. The children fare no better than the adults. The women, in particular, are distressed by the putrid smell. The children beg to alleviate their suffering. David's father, Rabbi Moises, beseeches his son to do something. Despite a fear of being severely reprimanded, David crawls through the bulkhead and goes topside.

Revitalized by the fresh ocean air, he seeks out the marshal to plead for some measure of relief. Harana sees David stagger out of the hatch. He grips his scourge and coughs a smirk.

"Please Don Diego, permit our children and women to come topside and escape the punishment of that pit. There are several very sick older people. Please show mercy and spare them."

The marshal answers sharply, his teeth flying out at the young man, his whip pointing threateningly at David's chest, "Get back below there, Jew. Who am I to be kind? You're on board as cargo, this ain't no passenger ship. Here!" and he throws another bucket at David.

From the prow, sprawled on the deck in exhaustion, de Torres watches Harana chastise David. 'What irony,' he thinks. While he curses the moment he had agreed to go on this voyage, he realizes those below believe the ride topside to be a sailing picnic. He considers that without the smell, the heat, the jammed space, and the pounding sustained below, perhaps it is.

The Spanish hidalgos live a duty of *noblesse oblige*, the concept that privilege includes a responsibility to help those less fortunate. Their aristocratic manners, an attempt to hide the foibles of human nature, are not expected to be perfect. Little by little, commonness leaks out. Hidalgos do no manual work, regarded as contrary to their honor. Farming a crop, building a ladder, sweeping the floor, or even peeling an onion is taboo, the trade-off for acceptance of their status. And so, despite his nausea, with an air of beneficent authority, and painful identification, de Torres hails the marshal to plead the case of the banished Jews.

Approaching the small tyrant, he says, "Marshal Diego, wouldn't it be merciful, as a Christian act of charity, to permit those poor souls below, which the Lord Jesus has put into our care, a brief respite from their wretched ordeal?"

As his chest puffs, the marshal thinks, 'You pigheaded peacock. I'll pluck a few 'o yer feathers 'afore this sail 's over.' But aware of the confidence the Captain General has in de Torres, he says, "Perhaps it would serve St Francis and the saints of the sea, in the name of Jesus Christ, to permit some minor breach of the rules."

As the marshal spoke, creeping from the cargo hold, led by Gotzun, his dog Yoggi strutting alongside, are the seven children. Emerging onto the deck they looked drained of all their blood, like mushrooms after a rainfall.

Harana, not missing a beat, shouts to the tall man, "Here you, Gotzun, get t'em minnows amidships and see they've some fresh water." And then, "And see to it that the women get a turn topside. They're all in your charge, Gotzun, an' if any of 'em dies, ya'll be answering ta me. An yer little dog too, ya scurvy ridden devil." The tirade provokes his consumption, and he coughs violently.

De Torres, pleased with himself, certain that his intervention has appealed to the benevolent nature of the marshal, bows graciously and turns as if exiting a tribunal.

Gotzun and Yoggi lead the children to the very center of the ship, where the sea's motion is least felt. The Canarian had heard the orders barked by Harana, but they merely duplicated his own intentions. On several voyages he had been punished for the disregard of orders, still, logic and kindness first filter his actions. He huddles low on the deck with Yoggi, surrounded by the children now buoyed by their reversal of fortune.

Diego de Harana is not pleased with the challenge to his authority by either de Torres or the ghost-like sailor. His face twists, he coughs and then spits, marking each man.

Late afternoon, the third day out of Palos, David asks Gotzun, "Can you tell me about our destination?"

Gotzun replies without hesitation, "Why we're going to Hell, of course. Where else would you expect adulterers, thieves and assassins to be going?"

David, taken aback, says again, "No, of course. No, no, what I'm referring to is the port. The next landfall."

Gotzun looks to Yoggi, strokes the dog's head, and smiles, "Well, you'll be leaving the ship in about four or five days, in the Canaries, just off this coast. And God protect your souls. I can tell you that you might as well be in Africa itself. The great desert flies across the Ocean Sea when it chooses, much worse than this, with burning hot air, thick with sand."

David recoils. He is aware of the islands, but the stories he's heard were always mixed with excursions into Africa. Tales of wild black men painted as devils, dressed in the skins of animals, enormous terrible animals lurking everywhere that relish feeding on Christians as a delicacy of white meat. He rushes below to tell the news.

For the outcasts the information is an elixir, initiating discussions of the dangers ahead and strategies to survive. Dante and Revela receive the news with a rising sense of freedom and renewal. Although they've overheard talk of these islands as one of many possible destinations, they know nothing about them. Dante imagines the Canaries to be an exotic start for adventure. Revela understands that life seldom gives us what we want, and that it will be as good a place as any to begin anew. Both are eager to put an ocean between themselves and what they want to forget.

Dante says, "The Canary Islands! I heard about them at La Sirena. Palm trees and coconuts and golden beaches and beautiful happy natives!"

Revela notes how young and naïve her brother is, how she loves his lighthearted optimism. And she thinks about home, the predictable life and simple pleasures it offered.

"Yes, it sounds good. But you know we'll be foreigners with no friends. We're going to have to be on our guard and find some way to live, Dante."

David has been advised of the predicament their arrival in the Canary Islands will present for the Jews. They are not concerned with the stories of savages and hideous animals, for they know those tales belong to the interior of Africa. The Canary Islands hold no such frightening mystery. No, the news is ominous for the Jews because of the 1479 Treaty of Alcáçovas brokered by the Pope. The agreement ceded dominance on the African coast to the Portuguese, and to Spain, control of the Canary Islands and all lands and islands west.

So what have the exiles gained? The Edict of Expulsion clearly states that they are to leave all the kingdoms and lands of Spain. The Canary Islands are considered belonging to Spain. Yet all the islands in the Canarian Archipelago have not been conquered. Are these unconquered islands part of the 'kingdoms and lands of Spain'? Will they arrive only to be confronted with the Inquisition? Although David de Violina is still a young man, uninformed of the complexities of life, he carries an innate understanding that risk leads to more risk, and fear to more fear.

As David explains the conundrum, Dante considers that he and Revela are not in the same circumstance as the exiles. After all they are not Jews, they have nothing to fear from the Inquisition. No one will yet be aware they are fugitives from justice. Then, he has a most logical second thought. Haven't he and Revela pretended to be Jews? Doesn't the crew consider them to be Jews? Aren't they traveling with Jews to escape as Jews? Why should anyone believe they are anything but Jewish?

Dante was far from understanding what it meant to be Jewish in 1492. He considered it simply 'to be a problem'. Since the onset of the New Inquisition seven years earlier, the plight of persons of Jewish descent had become increasingly desperate. A virus of hatred had spread in this malignant atmosphere. The horns of the Santa Humanidad bloodied many unsuspecting new Christians. To avoid skepticism, *conversos* often exaggerated their passion for Jesus and the Church of Rome. Who could blame them? The fog of fear was thick, the penalties cruel and merciless. This was a time of unrelenting terror, and then, 'The Edict'.

Cristóbal Colón's behavior was similar to that of the fearful conversos. Like them, he deliberately obscured his past, seeking to confuse questioners. Like them, his devout piety and ritual praying overshadowed his evasiveness. Like them, he was obsequious to church prelates. Colón was considered a fanatic, a 'rabid Catholic'. He had a ready phrase from the bible rather than scientific facts to defend his actions and goals, any deviant action a message from God. Consequently, his suspicious behavior raised eyebrows of both the oppressed and the oppressors.

Much of the intelligentsia of Spain were of Jewish descent, and Cristóbal Colón's supporters in and around the court were overwhelmingly Jews, baptized Jews, or ancestors of *conversos*. They encouraged Colón despite the jeopardy of being considered a member of a cabal. If denounced, extreme punishment would result for them and their families. Despite the danger many of the foremost names in Spain were considered to be Colón's supporters. They had declared themselves to this improbable venture – and for good reason.

These were the last Jews standing, devout, principled, and proud. They flaunted the very character traits that the unloved and uneducated loved to hate. The Jews' hope was rooted deep in their soul, as deep in their spirit as the hatred and cruelty of their oppressors was in theirs. Annihilation was at hand. Fearing persecution of themselves and their families, Cristóbal Colón's plan stirred a vision of redemption. They brushed aside rational considerations.

What was it like to walk the streets marked for death? To see your neighbor delivered up to humiliation and torture? To be surrounded by faces contorted in hate; to have a sweaty arm tight on your throat; to have your head pulled back with a force that stretches your neck; to be persecuted and murdered? How do you explain this to your children? What kind of answer is 'because you're Jewish'? Because you're alive.

It was no wonder that the Jews were desperate for a plan that might provide a refuge, or bring closer the wish-dream of generations of Jews. Evil, as real as the mountains, had enslaved their country to the devil. They sought a plan that might fulfill the promise they had studied for centuries — a reunion of the ten lost tribes of the bible. Their hope was that Colon's 'Exposition of Discovery' might reach the Jewish lands in Asia recounted by both Marco Polo in the thirteenth century, and in the 12th century's travels of Eldad ha-Dani in his 14-year trek across Asia. For the Jews, realization of this quixotic goal paralleled the dream of Cristóbal Colón. It was worth any amount of aid and risk.

PART II

Chapter 10
Ygnacio de Silva

For the young Ygnacio de Silva, future captain of the Guard of Aragon and the *Cronistas de Armas*, life was horrible thanks to his father, but wonderful, thanks to his mother. He lived communally on a farm in Ciudad de Austina, on the Atlantic coast of Spain with five adults and an array of brothers, sisters, and cousins.

As a child, Ygnacio was shunned. Something about his face repelled people. Perhaps it was the nervous facial tick, maybe his perpetual sniffing the air, or perhaps the way his lips curled up to the left, as if pulled by a string. Slight of build, he developed a furtive demeanor, always the first in line throughout his youth to receive the abuse of bullies. As childhood requires, he learned to embrace this cruelty, for, after all, who isn't a survivor from the havoc and catastrophe of childhood? Punished, then punished again for protesting, he learned not to complain, arming himself with an attitude of homicidal resentment. Having endured the taunts and beatings from older children, the boy administered the same with a severe reverence, churchlike, to those smaller than himself.

Less raised and more pounded into growing up, Ygnacio learned to flinch and tremble. No one took his side. Simply seen talking to him might occasion a beating, so just knowing him was a disaster. Attempts to get what he needed, or simply wanted, invariably went pathetically wrong. Struggling to survive this ostracizing, Ygnacio spent many hours alone in the forest playing knight, throwing stones at animals, and trapping insects.

Reliving painful confrontations, he found solace in telling himself, 'Ha, I'm smarter than you, and everyone else too.' He was in fact smart enough to realize his anger could quickly spiral out of control, as it had when he nearly drowned the little Alisha girl. Each day brought another bout of suffering, more thoughts of doom. Aloneness became his dominant experience, and he dreamed of being invisible.

Ozwaldo, Ygnacio's father, a man who could not bend, only brake, was never, ever, kind to his son, providing him a particular physical education. The boy learned to avoid the knuckled fists and nails scalloped like sea shells of his father's ferocious temper by remaining silent and small in his presence. A man wanting the advantage in everything, Ozwaldo had a well-known reputation for cheating. Perpetually drunk, bellowing threats to get his way, he'd start a fight or joyously join one in progress.

One January when Ygnacio was eight, in the iron silence of a winter night, his father and Uncle Kolmus, both drunk on *malmsey*, began hitting each other with fists and firewood. On that icy evening, the same year his cousin Leo had died, the snarling Ozwaldo chased Ygnacio into the woods screaming curses and threats.

Terrified of the beating he might suffer, Ygnacio ran deep into the forest until the canopy of trees blotted out the stars in the moonless sky. Exhausted, he lay panting beside a downed tree trunk in a mix of leaves and frozen mud. His heart pounded in the icy silence. A panicky sweat dripped down his long nose, his hands squeezed into tight fists, and he closed his eyes to the world.

Shivering awake in the frigid morning, he wrapped his arms around his knees for warmth, then saw a nest of back ants, millions of them gushing out of tunnels in the gelid ground. A single ebony ribbon moved across the felled tree he lay against. He could smell their musty odor and was hypnotized by the in-line parade rounding a small burl. Placing his tongue on the bark, the ants marched up the pink muscle into his mouth, and he ate them.

Eight-year old Ygnacio stayed six days in the old growth forest, listening to the wind whistling danger. He carried a charm in the shape of a goat's head. It fit in his palm and was crowned with unusually sharp horns. He had stolen it from a dead body he once passed on the road.

Ygnacio used the prize to educate himself, eviscerating the internal organs of the frogs and rats he caught. At dawn, birds came to feed on the entrails, and he would coo to them, his friends.

Many lessons were offered a young boy in 15th century Spain, and the intelligent Ygnacio applied himself. The world was a callous mother to the boy. He excelled in learning true cruelty by inflicting the greatest pain. He learned the art of being a tyrant, remaining aloof to any pleas for mercy, how to take command when the mob rules, how to abuse women, how to betray at the right moment, how to convert any object into a weapon of torture, how to be religiously devout and self-righteously holy, how never to offend someone of higher rank, and how to sleep while covered in blood. But the lesson Ygnacio learned best and applied most often in his life, first came to him as a vengeful thought on that cold January night— how to call his victim to embrace the end of life.

For some reason, as unknowable as the answer to, Why does a man dream?, Ygnacio's mother, Amalia Maria, adored him. There was nothing smart about that for her. She found nothing to admire in him and never believed he accomplished anything of merit. He never did anything tender toward her. She even admitted he had an ugly, cur-like face. But in his presence, she simply had an overwhelming sense of wellbeing, perhaps not love, but a loyalty of heart. Unless his father was administering a physical lesson, she doted on her son to assuage his wounded psyche. No one could make sense of it, least of all Ygnacio.

One Sunday when Ygnacio was nine, he accompanied his mother to town. After the morning market they walked in a drizzle to behind the church where a group of people were gathered around a wooden platform. As was her wont, Amalia Maria cajoled and muscled her way to the front, pushing Ygnacio ahead, "Here, let the boy have a good look". So Ygnacio won a prime spot to witness the blessings of his religion.

In the center of the large platform was a stake anchored in a pile of stones, wood and straw heaped beneath. Tall, carved figures of the prophets stood watch from each corner of the platform as several men dragged a girl up the stairs onto the stage, to the stake.

The remainder of the day would forever be sealed in Ygnacio's memory. He returned to the farm and reported to his younger cousin, Leo, what he saw. Speaking, his eyes hazed:

"...onto the platform this girl, well I guess it was a girl, maybe it was a lady. They tied her up to the post with chains. The man next to me said it was because they didn't want to waste good rope burning it. Mother pointed stuff out, turning my face to see. Everybody was bumping and shoving and whistling and jumping up and down. It was really scary.

"Then the monks come up to her and said something about Jesus and power things. They waved wands and magic stuff and then got off. The big pole she was chained to had wood and straw all around. Piled really high. Bigger than this," Ygnacio stood tall, his arms stretched overhead. "And some old lady brings her own stupid little stick and puts it on the pile and everybody cheered. Mother laughed and said, 'Let's hope it's wet'.

"We had a good view. Then it stopped raining, and everyone cheered again. All of a sudden, a line of at least a hundred monks closed in from all sides.

"They're all chanting. Real low, magic Latin words." Ygnacio lowers his chin and voice, "'And you will die. And you will die.' And they're holding candles and crosses and swinging the smoke pot."

Leo silently mouths the word, "censer'.

"Then the monk with the big hat goes up to the girl and shouts something at her. Telling her she's a witch. Behind him is a big man with his hood up. You could only see his eyes. And he's got a torch really burning. Then all the monks sang together a special song."

Ygnacio closes his eyes to hear the monks chanting:

We stand here in the name of our Savior Jesus Christ, the Lord our God, we declare that if the prisoner should die, this will be their fault and responsibility and not ours, because they have refused to tell the truth and accept the Lord our God, and we confront the devil in this poor soul who must, as we all must, embrace the end of life. Amen

And then the monk with the hat turns and tells the crowd, 'It's her own fault' and walks off. The torch-man goes up to the girl, and I could see her. She was pretty, and she was crying a lot, and the torch-man raises his arms real high, turns in a circle, and laughs."

Ygnacio holds his arms high, turns in a circle and in his squeaky voice, "'Ha ha ha ha ha." He laughs loud and long. "Then he starts walking around the straw and puts it on fire. Pretty soon he's done and he gets off too."

Little Leo, sitting cross-legged on a large rock, rubs his hands on his thighs and adjusts his pudgy body. His lips are tight, his jaw stiff and hurting. He has heard about burnings from the older children but never like this. His excitement is in believing these are secrets.

Ygnacio continues; "Then the smoke makes everybody crazy cause they know it's lit. And then there's crackling as the hay burns, and the fire kicks up, and they're screaming and pushing up on us to get closer. Then they can't see through the smoke. They start coughing and choking. And everybody is still screaming."

Ygnacio whispers, "Calling her a whore. Saying they could smell her. I could smell her too, so I held my breath so I didn't get her inside me." Leo's eyes goggle and he wonders what 'whore' means.

Ygnacio whisper-like, "That's when mother tells me to watch close cause her blood is going to explode. She saw that happen before. And it did. Pwoosh! Ignacio swings his arms high and wide. "Blood all over the place! And then there was this popping. Pop, pop, pop, poppop! I thought it was just the fire. But it was her bones. They told me. Pop, pop, pop. The girl screamed a long time. People pretended they were her, twisting and swooping, and dance-dying. The fire was really big and really hot. We were too close. Then the girl was just gone. And we came home."

Leo thinks, 'I'm glad I wasn't there.'

Then one day when Ygnacio was eleven, while at play with his only play-mate, eight-year old Leo, Ygnacio de Silva succumbed. Raised on ridicule and rejection, always the outcast, he completely surrendered to the dark side of his nature. They often played a game of pretend in the fields near the forest, being soldiers and wheeling stick-swords. Ygnacio, a Crusader, carried the banner of the cross, and Leo was the pretend Muslim. But however well he fought, Leo never won a battle, all the contests ending with Ygancio's war dance of victory.

This autumn day attacking each other, circling a large ficus tree, Ygnacio cries out, "Submit to Jesus Christ you Saracen pig", and Leo responds, "Allah is great. Death to the infidel." Ygnacio, atop a small outcropping of rocks, suddenly slips, falling into a field of flowering wild onions. Leo is hysterical, laughing at the sight of his proud cousin, the perpetual victor, sprawled on his backside, legs sticking out of the purple flowers kicking in the air.

Bewildered by this absurd circumstance, humiliated to be laughed at by Leo, with a deep-throated bawl of disbelief, Ygnacio bounces up to confront his adversary crying, "Take that you dog". He swings his wooden weapon at his laughing cousin, and in one potent stroke, chops down where Leo's neck meets his shoulder. The younger boy folds strangely onto the ground. Ygnacio cocks his head, much like a dog might, unsure at first of what has happened. But quite soon, seeing the bulging, distorted, reddening on the side of his poor cousin's neck, and the funny way his head hangs too far to the left, Ygnacio freezes. His eyes goggle and the curl disappears from his tightly pressed lips. Going for help never crosses his mind. He realizes the finality of what he's done and tactfully removes Leo's wooden sword from his small hand. 'You won't need this, cousin', he thinks. His first thought is to bury the stick, but instead, he throws it into a mulberry thicket. Ygnacio takes a last look at his small, crumpled cousin, and thinking that although 'he had it coming', he would need to find someone else to play the Muslim. Then he turned and fled. When Leo is found the following day, it is clear he has fallen from the ficus tree and broken his neck.

Chapter 11
Romería

By the end of the fourth day at sea Dante and Revela acclimate to the ship's dance in the rolling waters. They are less worried but still cling to each other as if to their past. Dante says to his sister, "Do you remember that *romería* a few years ago?" She says, as if they were safe at home in the barn, "A few years ago? A hundred years ago, five years from now. What does it matter? *Romerías* are all the same."

"No, I mean the one with Lily? Uh, the last one when Mom was alive."

The thought of their mother brought the memory to her hard. "Okay. What about it?"

"Well, remember that story Lily and I told you about the burning cat?" Revela nods, her eyes asking for more.

"And remember we couldn't make out who did it?"

"Yeah."

"Well, I think I know who it was."

"Me too."

It was the summer of 1488 when Revela turned seventeen, and the Osorio family travelled once again to the *romería*, the yearly harvest celebration held in Moguer, fifty kilometers away. Originating in Spain in the 12th century as a pilgrimage to Rome, it quickly lost its religious purport evolving into a carnival of music, food, and drinking. Although the Church sought to regulate and rule everyone's conduct in all aspects of life, the feudal peasants of Spain appropriated the festival as their own and dedicated themselves to its observance the way a dog guards a bone. This was a true bacchanal. Families from all over the region came to the banks of the Rio Tinto, welcoming a respite from their hardscrabble existence brought on by the year's poor rainfall and meager harvest. They came not only to relive childhood adventures, and to reunite with friends and relatives, but also to proclaim their humanity. Despite the adversities they endured every day, they were here to enjoy life. During these singular days, the past year's squabbles and threats, including bad blood, were set aside, to be replaced soon enough by fresh quarrels and rivalries.

The Osorio family prepared for the journey as every previous year. Two short-legged oxen, stocky and stubborn, were festooned with colored ribbons, white oleander and garlands of purple lilacs. The thick horned animals moved steadily, their black, massive heads swinging from side to side, occasionally flinching off a swarm off insects. They hauled the cart through wheel ruts, putting the road behind them as they lumbered along. The cart's straw bed was loaded with several pigs, a goose, and the family. Dante's dog, Lusi, a yellow scarf tied around her neck, yipped along side. The children were dressed identically in the folkloric outfits of Castile with red and yellow striped blouses, red sailor caps, and white scarves. The adults were more refined, wearing crush hats, tooled leather vests, and woven tasseled sashes. From a distance they might be taken for a traveling troupe of thespians playing their parts in The Peasants of Spain.

Approaching Moguer, they joined other festival travelers converging in a parade of decorated oxen and horses pulling wagons crowded with rose-cheeked farmers, singing, drinking, and bellowing their presence. The procession meandered through the town's narrow cobbled streets.

The *romería* was the single event each year where behavior was exempt from the dour judgment of the Church. Everyone's door was open, food and drink freely shared. Young and old danced in the street to gypsy music, *botas* were held high to squeeze an arch of new wine into grinning mouths.

For the children this was a joyful escape from the harsh discipline of the farm. They were free to make fun of each other's family members, free to tease and belittle each other, free to run and wrestle, free to be bullies and free to be victims. The boys indulged in mischief, stealing sweet-cakes and *pinchos*, playing make believe games of crusader and hide-seek. The girls skipped through the compound dancing and singing, telling secrets, and tattling about what the boys had done to deserve punishment. The boys chased the girls, and the girls chased the boys through the campsites, or trailed older brothers and sisters, taunting the awkwardness of their adolescent pairing. A few severely inbred cousins stood watching, gapped-toothed and expressionless.

The summer evening sky, holding only a sliver of moon, was lavish with stars and ablaze with the embers from a hundred crackling fires. The smoky, acrid air mingled with the smells of spit-roasting animals, hares and chickens, pigs and goats, all crisping over hard *manzanilla* wood. Music surged and faded as guitars, fiddles, flutes, gemshorns, drums and tambourines were plucked, tooted, bowed, and beaten. The peasants lamented their anguish in a celebration of song and dance. Despite their wretchedness, their dashed hopes for a bountiful harvest, and another season of near starvation, they sang of heroes and victory, love and adventure, triumphs that never were nor would be their own.

The *romería* was venerated as a coming of age experience and in the Osorio family this was to be Revela's year. She was expected to make her choice of suitors from the eligible farm-boys. A pragmatic girl, Revela understood and did not exclude herself from local customs, at least not the sensible ones.

The family settled near a small brook, the same site as in the previous two years, in a clearing of laurels south of the main encampment. Their friends would look for them here, especially the boys who had sought to court Revela the year before.

"I thought I saw Ernesto talking to Chari at the Mikelo camp her older brother, Pedro, reported to Revela in a conspiratorial voice.

"And what would I care about Ernesto talking to Chari?" Revela snapped. Primero and Segundo raised eyebrows and stopped chopping firewood, but held back any snickering. They knew better than to antagonize their sister. Revela, immune to the teasing of her brothers, would not reveal her hand about any boy.

Romería festivities always included Saint Francis Day, designated for the blessing of the animals. The children brought their favorite pets to be sanctified, amidst a swarm of flies, tics, mosquitoes, and the pungent odor of fresh manure. Every animal known to a farm was represented; horses, pigs, snakes, roosters, rats, goats, cats and lizards. From morning mass through late afternoon, pets and livestock were led by the very old and the very young to the church steps. Their Father Nuri intoned a blessing on each animal in the name of Saint Francis of Asissi, sprinkling the startled pet with holy water:

> *All praise to you, Oh Lord, for Blessed are you, Lord God, maker of all living creatures. You called forth fish in the sea, birds in the air and animals on the land. We ask you to bless all these brother and sister creatures. By the power of your love, enable them to live according to your plan. May we always praise you for all your beauty in creation. Blessed are you, Jesus Christ, Lord our God, in all your creatures! Amen.*

It had become the custom for all eligible young men and women to accompany the animals to be blessed and in that way announce themselves available. It was then that commitments were made to meet later. Revela brought a new-born calf, and Dante his dog, Lusi, for the blessing. There was no particular focus on Revela, but Dante, now almost fourteen, was open fare for the courting game teasing.

"Dante. Dante." The voice was familiar as his neighbor Lily San Pablo waved for his attention. "I need to talk to you. I know someone who likes you." He blushed and looked to Revela.

Later that evening they played '*romería*-find-and-kiss'. Dante hid downstream near the mill where the old Arab, Menasha, ground grain to make bread in the community oven. On one side of the mill a mule kept in a corral turned the wheel when the water was low. After a while, Dante realized it wasn't necessary to hide uncomfortably crouched behind the gear wheel.

Daydreaming, he was walking aimlessly when he heard a soft voice say, "I see you, Dante." Lily sauntered up next to him. He'd not spoken with her since the church, but what he heard her say about someone liking him had been very much on his mind. Seeing her, he grinned in nervous anticipation.

Lily had played the game before, so she refused his demand to reveal her information, insisting, "Oh no, you've got to kiss me first. That's the rule." So he leaned forward, aiming his lips just above her charming teaspoon of a chin.

Lily raised her arms, draping them over his shoulders and around his neck, one hand grasping her opposite elbow as the other dug into is thick hair. She surprised Dante by pressing her soft body into his and her full lips found his mouth. His boyish, shy inclination to break off the kiss was forgotten as he felt the luxury of her breasts. She rose slightly onto her toes moving her body tight against his, touching him, and he staggered.

Suddenly, they both were startled by a high-pitched cry, a howling, coming from around the side of the mill, a forest-creature noise, uncommon to the human ear. They broke their embrace looking at each other wide-eyed. Keeping hands held, they ducked, sneaking to the corner of the mill.

The piercing wail startled them again, now sounding almost human, almost like a frightened plea. They moved closer, Dante's palm whispering along the wall. In the corral they could make out a shadowed enclosure. The waning moon barely shown when suddenly a torch illuminated the dark area with a flash so intense that an after image hung in their eyes.

They saw in the penned area a makeshift *quemadero*, a raised platform for burning with a pole in the middle, and in the maze of shadows, two skeletal apparitions, the silhouettes of a man and a small animal.

Lily huddled closer. "Who is it Dante?" He shook his head. They watched the shadow of the man awkwardly prance around the enclosure, quickening his pace, lifting his legs high in the air, stutter stepping, and singing, not a song, but more a chant. The faster he moved the louder his dirge, until his head fell backwards as he shrieked at the moon in a frenzy.

As he circled, the man torched the straw piled around the stake into a crackling fire. Tethered to the stake by its neck was a large cat, gyrating violently. It jerked and whipped its head, emitting a low growling screech of terror, its bray and the man's howl creating a grotesque duet. As the smoke and flames rose, the feline leaped up the pole. Twisting its body high in a frenzy trying to stay above the licking flames, it dug its claws into the wood so ferociously they pulled out of its bloody paws. Then, in a surrendering stillness, the animal ceased to strain against the noose. It mewed like a kitten until a final fierce ululation when the cat's fur, skin and blood exploded in a soft puff of black vapor and horrible stench.

Lily cried out and the laughing man turned.

Unable to see these uninvited witnesses, the man reasoned that neither could they see him. He cursed the interruption with an unpleasant snarl and with mouth and fists tightly closed, ran into the darkness, galloping down the riverbank toward the church.

"Jesus Christ, how awful. Who would do such a dreadful thing? Could you make him out?"

"No, not at all. Just a black shadow", Dante responded.

The ghastly odor stopped them from moving closer to the smoldering fire. They turned back toward the encampment at a quickening pace.

Dante struggled to shake the gruesome scene and recapture the memory of their embrace.

Eyebrows rose when the young pair entered the campsite together. Going directly to Revela, they told her what they had witnessed. Taken aback by the images, Revela impressed upon them the danger in telling anyone else. The culprit had committed heresy, a sacrifice to the devil, and must never know their identity.

Chapter 12
At Sea

It is deep summer and the sand from the great African Sahara Desert swims in the air, coloring the sea with a reddish-brown dust. The seasoned crew aboard the Santa Maria has settled into the routine of voyage. Because it does not skirt the coast as other European passages might, but rather is in the open ocean, the sail to the Canaries, never lacking wind, is the most arduous.

Sailors cherish these first days out, a time for forgetting, for clearing one's mind of the complications and demands of the last port. Those new to sail experience the endless expanse of open sea, like the moment between overlapping dreams. A smothering wetness replaces the fragrance of the land, and any natural resistance to the unfamiliar, dissolves. These daring sailors live in the mystery beyond the taunting boundary of sea and sky.

Curiously, for a voyage intended to spread the word of Jesus Christ, there are no clergy on board. The Voyage itself challenges the purity of the doctrine that the entire world had been visited by the apostles. The Church declined to participate in a mission that presupposed there were undisclosed parts of the world. That is not to say that the religion of Christ was not on board. Sailors are conservative, superstitious, and curiously devout. As dawn breaks each day, the ship's boy turns the sand-filled half-hour glass, the ampoletta, and sings:

Blessed be the light of day And the Holy Cross, we say; And the Lord of Verity And the Holy Trinity. Blessed be the immortal soul And the Lord who keeps it whole, Blessed be the light of day And He who sends the night away.

The Santa Maria, a small cradle rocking in uncertainty, the threat of death a constant companion, harbors countless visions of riches, adventure, and glory, as it pounds through the Ocean Sea. Although they find the Jews presence disconcerting, the crew are sympathetic, and refer to the outcasts affectionately as 'sojourners', as if they are on holiday. The Santa Maria flies the flags of Castile and Aragon, and all on board are bound as leaves on a tree.

Harana paces the deck, asserting his domain while checking to see that all lines and tackle are properly secure. He stops and says to Luís de Torres, "That's the Maghreb. 'Bout a hun'red kilos in. Nice 'an close for the kings of Europe to get their fill o' slaves and gold. An there ain't no one there to stop em, 'cept fer a few packs of Moors too busy fight'n each other to take much notice. There's a white king in there they call Prester John. His land is deep inside. With dark rivers, an full o' monsters."

De Torres answers, "Yes, I've heard of him, but some say he doesn't exist, that no one has ever seen him."

"Oh, he's there all right. An' there's a river o' gold he guards that splits off the great River Nile in the country Mali. It spills out that dark jungle, just 'cross from the Canaries." He looks in Luís' eyes to measure his belief.

'A river of gold', de Torres thinks. 'Perhaps in dreams.' The Jews continue thumping in the foc'sle, but so long as the seas remain friendly, and with frequent trips topside now permitted, the ordeal is almost bearable. The confinement challenges the children and, like children everywhere, they invent games. Rabbi Moises smiles under his heavy beard, relieved that the young ones no longer cry each day. But how can he alleviate the bitterness and anger of their parents? What can you say to a man and woman who have had to erase everything in their lives except each other?

Despite condemnation as heretics by the Catholics, worthy of torture and death, they live in dignity and honor. Exile is a test, a biblical journey, and their challenge is not one of physical survival, but of faith.

The Rabbi relies on the Jew's code of conduct and law, the Talmud. As the Torah is God speaking to the Hebrews, the Talmud is the Hebrews answering, often with a subtle humor. The Book presents life's trials and tribulations, typically in preposterous situations that deflate the pomposity of authority figures, especially the wealthy. Rabbis are made fun of, people ridiculed for their failings, the absurdity of life highlighted in silliness. Confronted with an aggressive, hostile society, a laugh is the best answer to sustain a spirit of courage and levity. So they mock themselves, even in the most desperate of situations.

Rabbi Moises thinks of the current anecdote: 'As the Santa Humanidad chains the old Jewish couple to the stake, and the monk raises the torch to set them ablaze, the bearded Jew raises his hand to ask a question. His wife grabs his arm and scolds, 'Shhh Mordachi, don't make things worse'.

Ravela and Dante, discovering the meaning of 'sea legs', roam the ship on the port side, from poop deck to stern, and back on the starboard. Their arms wrap each other as they stumble with the roll of the ship and laugh at their awkwardness.

"I wonder what Pepe and Josephina are doing?" she muses, thinking back to their escape from home, and the diversion provided by their brother and his wife traveling north.

Immersed in the excitement of this new life, Dante has left thoughts of Palos behind, and succumbed to the newness of sail. "Oh, they're probably chasing that roan horse at Moguer. Did you see those dolphins earlier? That was something."

What had been Revela's everyday on the farm, the work, the isolation, the boredom, has also dissolved from her mind into something new, a thoughtful design of courage to pattern her days. The immense ocean has paused time, suspended her old life, and she understands that to know its promise she must embrace this 'something new'.

Several crewmen linger at the prow and stop the siblings. Franco de Coastaba hands Dante a short piece of rope. "Here ya go lad, tie me a knot that'l save your life."

Dante confidently takes the hemp, reverses two overlapping loops, drops them over a marlinspike and pulls the ends. "There. That will hold a gate tight against any animal," he says proudly.

Franco examines the hitch. "For sure it will, lad. But there ain't no gates at sea, nor no animals. You best larn a few turns to collar a man gone overboard, or to bend lines together when one ain't long enough. Here watch this now."

Franco passes the line deliberately, looping it, then passing the lead up through the loop, around the lead, then back down through the loop. Pulling tight he hands it to Dante and says, "Here. This'll hold till the rope splits. You try it."

Dante fumbles with the rope but the line pulls straight, spilling without the knot. Franco shows him again, and on his second try Dante's knot holds tight. Proud for her brother, Revela smiles, but declines an offer to learn. She has watched her brother gain in confidence, and has purposefully separated as the crew accepts him. Revela prefers to join the group of exiles, and drifts away from the lesson.

"Here's another for ya, Dante. It's called a 'headhunter's knot'. Now watch close" and Franco starts an elaborate tie.

Pablo de Bimera nudges Aljanus and says, "It wasn't that far from where we sail. Just a bit further south on the coast beyond the Canaries." The men pick up on the story, lean in a bit. Dante's attention shifts and the rope goes limp in his hands.

"They're as real as spit. I've seen 'em. It was a slaver and we wer left beached on a low tide just afore Cabo Verde." Pablo's voice drops and he speaks directly to Dante. "Real tall, black as night and nakid. Covr'd from head to foot in blood and muck with thar legs and arms painted blue. Lips hangen low with silver discs an ears stretched down ta thar shoulders. Yellow feathers hangen off thar arses. They diden care for the slaves we took cause they were from a differn tribe then 'em. The chief, he invited Ricardo Besk ta marry his daughtr or else step inta the cookn pot. Well, we backed off pretty quick but they caught 'the goose', Testo de Galicia, and did 'im bad. They ate 'im on the shore right in front a'us watchn from the ship. They didn care. Ole Testo was screamn, 'Oooooh Nooo. Jesus save me. Ooooh no.' They roasted pieces of 'im and made 'im eat 'em. His fingers. And then his hand. Even his balls. They made 'im watch it char up in the fire. And then he et 'imself. Then they strung 'im on a stick and turned 'im over the fire real slow. His hair flamn off and his skin apoppn. And then they et 'im."

The men know the story to be true. On the west coast of Africa cannibals are not just bad dreams but, for a beached sailor, a horror-inducing fact of life. They watch Dante's reaction. Wide-eyed, the boy holds his breath, swallowing hard several times. When Pablo Is finished and 'the goose' eaten, Dante's stomach and throat feel as tight as the hangman's knot.

Revela, herded by Yoggi, drifts to the prow where Gotzun and de Torres are speaking. De Torres, gazing astern, smiles and sighs. "He's a man who has gathered his whole soul together. No alternatives for him. He thinks, 'I must'. No more than that."

Gotzun, looking even taller next to the shorter man, says, "Oh, I suppose so." "It's his time now, you see. I don't know."

Luís' dark wavy hair frames eyes that once lit up in conversation, but no longer. Now they are milky, ready to tear. Still, ever the scholar, he advises the curious man, "Our captain is the embodiment of the Bible passage:

Thy way is in the sea, and thy path in the great waters, and thy footsteps are not known...

Psalm 77:19

Gotzun, ever wary of Catholic references, remains silent as de Torres continues. "Many speak of him, but always with a taste of vinegar, as if it is too much to believe him right. That his thought is too bold, his dream too wild. Of course his constant muttering, those conversations with himself, raises eyebrows."

"Yes," says Gotzun, "That is curious. As if he listens to someone before speaking. Still, the Captain General has only himself to rely on. He has cut his heart on the high seas only to taste disappointment and suffering on land. It has made him wary of betrayal."

De Torres flashes a warning smile and points his finger, "You cannot fully know a person, my friend. There is always a piece missing, something you will never know."

Gotzun says, "With you Christians the more you know someone the more they disappoint you."

The men linger but no longer in conversation. Silence being the natural state of sailors, there are no uncomfortable moments of quiet aboard a ship. As night descends and stars fire the sky, the whine of a concertina is carried on the wind and Dante sings:

You know I'll never leave you, my heart is in your hands,

Your sweet breath of heather and angel strands.

Stay beside me as I brush away the mean and hoary,

surrender yourself to the days to come.

"That's a sweet song, Dante," says Orkon the Turk. "Did your mother larn you it?"

"She said I heard it first at her breast. But here's one you'd be more familiar to:"

Lovely Maribela has a basket full o'turnips,

she picks 'em when she can.

And if you care to look close,

She'll show ya where ya can.

"I know the breast you learned that one from," cries Smelly.

"He's never seen that tit," laughs Franco.

Dante is happy to be the target of good humor. Trailed by Yoggi, he plays his concertina, drifting on the deck as he did at La Sirena, giving men their space, careful not to step on their shadows. No longer feeling like a frightened escapee, he feels to be something other than 'Dante the farm boy'.

Chapter 13
Cristóbal Colón

Although some men are born out of their time, no man escapes being a product of his time. 15th century European culture endures in squalor and filth, but hungers for a perfect world. It prefers a code of chivalry, courtly love, religious rituals, and oaths of fealty. Life is dominated by extremes with no relief from nature's harsh oppressive summer heat or brutal winter cold. Political boundaries are approximate and change with the death of a local ruler or a lost battle. Authority is a blend of local custom and church law. Famine is commonplace. With a life expectancy under forty, and a third of the population under fourteen, society lacks the invaluable perspectives of old age — wisdom and caution.

Violence and early death are inherent in day-to-day existence. The roads of Spain are unsafe, the inns shoddy, and tradesmen are frequently robbed and travelers murdered. In every village local authorities mete out savage punishment on the scaffolds of public squares. The poor are shown no mercy, even paying money to 'fee the hangman' for a broken neck and a quick end.

Towns purchase doomed men and women from other towns to provide their citizens a spectacle of torture and death. The inventiveness of cruelty becomes a mark of celebrity, perhaps the primary form of entertainment in a shattered land, a world drained. Once the Iberian Peninsula had observed a complex ceremony of death. Now death is crude, vulgar, a matter of power and contempt, void of any spirit of mystery, simply a call "to embrace the end of life".

The 15th century provides a season for everything dark: a time to hate and a time to be hated, a time to bleed and a time to starve, a time to hang and a time to burn — with no shortage of terror.

The land is a caldron of carnage, a shadowy squalor threatening life. Assiduously feeding this macabre spirit is the 'New Inquisition'. The Church sustains an insatiable rage as thousands are tortured and burned. This pageant, a world of agony spawned by terror, is enjoyed by spectators as if a carnival. Body parts become gruesome souvenirs, collections for twisted minds. The country is a crucible of skulls. Religion, its red sandstone churches the color of dried blood, is a trade focused on power and revenue. It is as if evil requires maximum speed to maintain its balance, like a spinning top.

Death flourishes from the diseases that thrive in the crowded conditions and poor sanitation of the walled medieval towns — black plague, tuberculosis, leprosy, scurvy, smallpox, diphtheria, typhus. Bacteria dominate humanity. And when the primary grain crops of wheat and barley fail in the poor soil of Iberia, the scythe of famine, a devoted partner to disease, makes a wide sweep.

War, fought to wrest control of land from a neighbor, or to slay the heretic, manifests a cornucopia of violence, disease, and famine. Men march to their bloody demise obsessed with their menacing weapons and protective armament, displaying a unique talent for mayhem and destruction. Decency, honor, or restraint is imperceptible; absent is any adherence to the rules of individual combat or warfare, and consideration of mercy is non-existent. The killings follow no rules. Battles are short lived, but the vanquished suffer tenfold afterwards. Crops are burned, homes ransacked, women raped, ancient books and relics burned, clerics murdered and displayed naked in front of their defiled churches.

Each year, each season, each day, slaughter offers no explanation or resolution to the common man. No answer comes from the local authority, no justification from the church or the Crown. For an entire century tragedy permeates the mentality of medieval European culture, creating a crisis of its very soul. People are divided into the burners and the burned. Although morality existed before theology, in the 15th century compassion never supplants the wrath of religion.

What better diversion for a people imbued with life's misery and suffering, then a story of adventure, glory and fortune? How could Cristóbal Colón's tale not captivate at a time when the woes of life dominate all thinking?

Genoa, the city where Cristóbal Colón was born in 1451, is an important seaport in northwestern Italy, the capital of the Province of Genoa located at the peak of the Ligurian coastal arch. Colón's father is Domenico Colón, a middle-class wool weaver, his mother, Susanna Fontanarossa. Cristóbal is the older brother to Bartolomeo, Giovanni, and Giacomo. He remains purposefully vague about how his family has come to Genoa. Never formally educated, as an adolescent he works for his father in the wool trade.

At fourteen Cristóbal leaves Genoa and goes to sea, never to return to his birthplace. He begins an apprenticeship as business agent for the Centurione and Spinola families spending twenty years sailing between ports, trading various commodities, and educating himself in languages, navigation, geography, astronomy, and philosophy. He speaks fluent Italian, as well as Castilian Spanish, Greek, Latin, and Portuguese. He sails many years to Mediterranean Sea ports and further to the Aegean Sea and the Greek Isles; he sails the North Sea to Iceland and visits the ports between, Glasgow in Ireland and Bristol in England. He knows the coast of Portugal, including the great port of Lisbon, the center of world maritime exploration. He sails west to the Portuguese island of Madeira, where he marries Filipa Moniz Perestrelo, daughter of the governor of Porto Santo, and where his son, Diego, is born in 1481. He then sails further west to the Azores Archipelago. He explores the west coast of Africa, navigating to the Portuguese colony of El Mina in Guinea, and to the Canary Islands, the western-most deep water port in the known world at the island of Gomera.

Despite his common background, with extensive language skills and commercial knowledge he has become a shrewd, discerning man. He has the look of a man possessed with great energy and insight, the tenacity of the fanatic, every moment of his life dedicated to, and absorbed in his mission.

In 1440 the printing press was invented, a watershed event that revolutionized how the world is conceived and described. Books give Cristóbal access to the ancient philosophers of Greece and Rome such as Aristotle, Ptolemy and Pliny, and to world travelers like Marco Polo and Sir John Mandeville.

Cristóbal carries Cardinal Pierre d'Ailly's book, Imago Mundi, everywhere noting his own thoughts in the margins. He uses the tome to compare the cardinal's cosmography and estimates of world land- mass with known historical opinions and calculations. Also of immense importance to Cristóbal is the astronomical treatise of Abraham Zacuto, a Sephardic Jewish astronomer and mathematician who serves as Royal Astronomer to King John II of Portugal.

All this knowledge gleaned from ancient and contemporary scientists and philosophers is of little use in promoting Cristóbal's cause, however, without his identity as a devout Catholic. Aware of the power exercised by the Church through the Crowns of Europe, he conscientiously quotes the Bible. To bolster his vision, he finds a persuasive argument in the Bible's Second Book of Esdras, symbolic of his faith, posing as evidence of a short distance to cross the Ocean Sea.

And on the third day Ye united the waters and the earth's seventh part, and dried the six other parts.

The courts of Europe overflow with grandees of inherited titles, men of leisure and entitlement. In contrast, Cristóbal Colón is respected as a knowledgeable man of action, adventure, and ambition. And so, despite his commoner status, the nobility of Europe gives him audience.

Those who listen to Cristóbal's promised discovery of a new route to the Far East, do so at first because his enthusiastic presentation captivates them. He earns a meager existence, barely means to sustain himself, but incorporates drama and mystery into his stories of adventure and fortune, learning to say what people want to hear.

Like most sailors of his time, Cristobal is self-taught in the art of navigation and seamanship. The new nation-states of Europe have begun to expand their horizons, wanting more land, more wealth, more power, heralding the beginning of European worldwide exploration. All that is necessary is a little killing. The world is in flux and prosperity is fickle. Glory and wealth are the rewards of conquest.

Promoting trade by sea voyages across the Mediterranean Sea, the Genoans and Florentines establish contacts with the eastern shores of the Ottoman Empire in Turkey and India. The European connection to distant China and Japan is the land route across Asia, the Silk Road. Visions of vast wealth and exotic culture described by Marco Polo lure their mercantile ambition.

But there is a problem. On July 9, 1453, Constantinople fell to the Turks. Because most mercantile and royal dealings are in coastal cities, the thought to travel in safety means to go by sea, but the Red Sea and the Black Sea are now unsafe for Christian ships. The shore of the Eastern Mediterranean and beyond, the Silk Road through Mongol territory, comes under the control not only of Turkish sultans, but also of every warlord and thief in Asia.

Commercial travel with the uncertainty of profit is not acceptable, and the European merchants sorely miss the silk and spices. And so, due to the danger, there has been no measureable European trade with India for more than a hundred years.

Cristóbal Colón believes he has a solution. His goal is to avoid the disruptions of the land route and reach the Far East riches by a western sea passage. The leaders of this quest are the sailors of the Iberian Peninsula, now on the Voyage of Discovery.

This tenacious Genoese had searched all his adult life for financial support, a homeless trek between countries, a journey of poverty, often provoking ridicule and contempt, even odium. Like a man with a secret that is not a secret, he has promoted his cause to those he believes might provide financial support, those with contacts in the royal courts. He tailors his story to whoever will listen. With merchants and ship owners he speaks of an investment in glorious adventure with the virtual certainty of amassing vast riches in gold, silver and spices; to prelates of the church he portrays a holy mission to spread the word of Jesus Christ as commanded in the Bible; to hidalgos and courtesans of the European Courts he offers an opportunity for glory, wealth, and lucrative, uncontested titles.

As a well-travelled linguist, familiar with the protocol of European courts, Cristóbal Colón speaks with intelligence. He knows the names not only of the idle nobility but also of many learned men of the times. He quotes the ancients and the prophets, and understands the hierarchy of the church as well as the twisted reasoning justifying its actions. It is no wonder the nobility paid attention.

Chapter 14
The Dream

Cristóbal Colón held a secret. Ever since he could remember, perhaps beginning at five or six years old, he'd experienced a recurring
dream. Although not always the same in every respect, it was as real
to him as being awake. As a child he could not recall many details, but
sensed it meant something important. At first he spoke about it nonchalantly, with the childlike wonderment of describing an imaginary
playmate. But later, at the first quizzical look, he would become silent,
so he decided never to talk about it.

As he grew so did his enjoyment of the dream. Sleeping often meant
meeting an old friend. He could not summon the dream, and long periods of time elapsed, sometimes years, waiting for the dream to reap-
pear.

But even though he might forget about the dream, the dream did not
forget him. Without warning, it would recur. Invariably, Cristóbal would
experience a shift in his spirit the following day, a new energy, eagerness, and optimism. The dream might visit him several nights in a row,
pause, and then return frequently over the next few months. The older
he became, the more he dreamt the dream, and the more detail he remembered.

He kept his childhood vow to never mention the dream to anyone; not
his father or mother, not his brothers, not his wife, his lover, his son, a
friend, not a priest. As he grew older it became imperative that he keep
the dream secret, believing that if he spoke of it his enemies would call
it blasphemy bringing severe consequences.

In attempts to decipher the dream, his internal dialogue evolved into a conversation with not himself, but with someone that demanded his attention and obedience. Those silent conversations and their voice became a part of his everyday, extending even beyond the subject of the dream.

He was convinced there was a key, a hidden message. Experience warned him not to underestimate the significance of things he could not put into words. The dream remained a mystery and his most precious treasure.

The dream always included the ethereal sensation of soaring in air over water. Sometimes, gazing into the dream-water deep, he'd see a bottom that wasn't a bottom at all, rather the vision of an unrecognized land where everything felt foreign; trees, animals, flowers, insects, birds – even shadows of what might be men. Somehow it seemed natural for him to dream of these things. He was a sailor with deep-water sailing in his blood. Salt water and foreign lands were as natural to him as the wind.

Once, his father, brother, and a childhood friend, appeared together in the dream, asking like a Greek chorus, where he wanted to go. On waking he could not remember his answer, only that his answer was laughed at, and he woke ashamed. He agonized over the meaning of the dream, believing something was inside him, struggling to get out.

In the dream-flight, soaring high over trees, he had an endless vista of land and water. Coastlines of surf broke from turquoise waters onto golden sand. Asleep, he would hold his breath so as not to fall out of the sky, until the need to breathe overcame him, and he'd descend to scrape the leafy tree tops, scattering noisy red, blue and yellow birds. His flight path would sometimes be through a long, dark, narrow space, like tunneling through the earth and time. Anxious in the dark, uncertain of where he was, he'd seek an exit. When the narrow view was bright rather than dark, he encountered shapes he could not identify, and odors that burned, making him teary-eyed.

Dark or bright, the narrow vision seemed to have another side. He was certain if he could only dream long enough he would get there, that somehow, the way out was through the way in. To understand what was happening, it seemed the dream was demanding he hold on to himself and let go of himself, at the same moment.

Looking straight into a narrow field of vision he could see clearly, but the surrounding images became ghost-like. As with normal dreaming, daytime experiences might appear in the dream. Nor was it unusual for him to confuse events on a voyage with those he dreamt. This would trouble him for days, causing others to note his manner as peculiar.

The Captain General came to understand the dimension of time in his dream-state to be a trickster. The dream might surprise him with a new image, or bring people from his past together with people from the present. Events occurring years before might unwind backwards. Time refused to be linear. He'd awake wondering whether he'd dreamed about long ago, just yesterday, or perhaps, dare he think, tomorrow. He came to believe that his dream did have the power to see the future, but not a language to reveal it. Still, there was always the journey over water. And there was always one other thing — a boy.

The boy had no name and never spoke. He was perhaps twelve years old, but that would change from time to time. The Captain General did not recognize the boy, nor did he see the boy as himself, but he felt a serene confidence shining from the boy's deep blue eyes. In order to know the boy's secret, believing he had something important to tell him, Cristóbal concluded he could discover a clue by looking through the hole of the boy's cherry lips. In that lacuna he'd find a passageway to the other side.

A fierce sequence of his dream lasting years provoked the Captain General to attempt to dream the boy into existence. With fierce concentration he focused months of dream-nights on separate parts of the boy, his hair, an arm, his eyes, hoping to conjure him into the real world, to wake the dreamed boy from his dream into his world. But he did not succeed.

When he was twenty, a vivid image of the dream remained in Cristóbal's consciousness in extreme detail. This dream was only of that wonderful boy. The boy, about thirteen, sat serenely on a wooden fence at the edge of a cliff overlooking the Ocean Sea. He didn't shift or switch about impatiently as children often do, but gazed ahead, shoulders hunched, holding the top rail, legs dangling. The boy wore a string necklace that held a single stone resting in the soft cushion of his throat above his collarbone.

Staring into a golden bronze sunset, the boy's light brown hair was swept back by a sweet-smelling on-shore breeze. The Captain General felt an overwhelming comfort from that fragrant breeze. The boy glowed brighter than the sun itself, exuding a titanic aura of confidence, as if he was the center of life and the world could not exist without his presence.

Mesmerized, the Captain General stared at the boy for a long time. When the boy turned his head away from the horizon to stare at Cristóbal, the boy's cobalt eyes completely filled the Captain General's mind and he became frightened. Then, in a thunderous voice, unlike any boy's voice, he said, "I am here waiting for you. Will you come?"

The Captain General was never aware that his dream began only when he slept with his head resting to the west. He might go to bed hungry and dream of chasing chickens, but if he shifted to a westerly direction, he would settle into the reverie of effortless movement, marvelous sights, and the boy — that wonderful boy.

Thereafter the dream furiously occupied his mind for years, years that often marked his spirit with rejection and humiliation. But if Cristóbal knew anything, it was that his perception of the dream was no dream. Doggedly certain of his plan's veracity, to sail west to reach the Far East, he built his life on this vision.

Above all, the Captain General was certain the dream was a direct message from God to him, a divinely inspired command. Sometimes he'd awake trembling, asking himself, "Why does God speak to me like this? What does this dream want?" Perhaps to validate his appointment as the Lord's instrument, he maintained a reverent ritual of church doctrine, dividing his day into prayer on the canonical hours, matins through to vespers and compline, ending with evening recitations of Our Father and Hail Mary. And finally his chant of Salve Regina, the ancient Benedictine antiphon.

Salve, Regina, Mater misericordiae, vita, dulcedo, et spes nostra, salve. ad te clamamus exsules filii Evae, ad te suspiramus, gementes et flentes in hac lacrimarum valle. Eia, ergo, advocata nostra, illos tuos misericordes oculos ad nos converte; et Jesum, benedictum fructum ventris tui, nobis post hoc exsilium ostende. O clemens, O pia, O dulcis Virgo Maria.

Hail, holy Queen, Mother of Mercy, our life, our sweetnes and our hope. To thee do we cry, poor banished children of Eve; to thee do we send up our sighs, mourning and weeping in this valley of tears. Turn then, most gracious advocate, thine eyes of mercy toward us; and after this our exile, show unto us the blessed fruit of thy womb, Jesus. O clement, O loving, O sweet Virgin Mary.

Chapter 15
Luís de Torres & Cristóbal Colón

The Captain general stoops in his small cabin, astern, below the poop deck. Not exceptionally tall, still he must drop his head ever so slightly in the low, arched space. His light-blue eyes, somewhat hooded, appear at rest yet probing, as he scans the chart of the Ocean Sea. A soft-spoken contemplative man with an air of certainty, he has spent his life sailing on waters under a shadowless sun that has turned his fair skin ruddy and whitened the blond-red hair of his youth,

In thinking about his friend Luís de Torres, the Captain General sees much of himself; the seriousness, the intellect, the dedication to detail. He admires Luís' ready clear mind, his ability to immediately discern the essence of a subject, and is certain that de Torres' language skills make him the ideal ambassador to meet the Great Kahn of China. It is no coincidence they were introduced by their mutual friend, Santangel.

Luís was a Jew until his forced conversion to Catholicism two weeks before sailing. His conversion came after he witnessed the torture and hanging of his brother, Isaac, who was suspended 'mouth downwards' to protract his death and aggravate his agony, called to 'embrace the end of life'. Luís' psyche would never heal from that grotesque image.

Educated to be a scribe, de Torres grew up isolated in the Jewish community of Murcia in southeast Spain. He is as enlightened a man as could be found in the Middle Ages, immersed in the revered study of philosophy. He knows his Torah, and takes pride in the fact that his father, Rabbi Hyman, whose temperament he inherited, had been honored to script the sacred scroll. Modest, reserved and soft-spoken, though not withdrawn, he inherited attributes that pass through generations, the same as eye color and height. He is, however, uneasy about displaying his intellect, and often conceals his command of languages or disguises his perceptive nature. Confident because he thinks things through, people say he sounds full of himself. He censures his inclination to start a sentence in one language and finish it in another, and will be quick to explain in detail any metaphysical concept. When he speaks an uncommon word he immediately defines it.

But his soulful eyes have lost their warmth; his sagging lips forecast a permanent frown. His face suggests a kind of prescient awareness, as if he expects to be startled. His lean body moves at obtuse angles, making it difficult to tell where he has been or might be going. Cristóbal believes Luís to be like himself, a man who must keep moving.

In the Captain General's small cabin, sitting at his chart table, his back to Luís only a meter away, Colón works a vee shaped wooden tool, measuring distances on an open scroll. Noticing Luís' entrance, unsure if it is a disturbing or a welcome interruption, he is reminded of the hidalgos performance at the rail. He asks, "And how does the sail go for you? Have your found your legs?"

"Just one, Captain. It has not been entirely charming. But I am grateful to you for including me in your plans."

The Captain General shrugs and says, "I have no plans, Luís. I never had plans. Planning is fine. Five months, what to do in a year? But what does it all matter if there is no plan for tomorrow?

"But surely, captain, you've contemplated this voyage for a long time."

Cristóbal rolls the chart and replies, "Yes, that's true. It takes a long time for a man to call an idea his own. Oh, it's been a bit disheartening, even daunting, but now having begun, it brings comfort of another sort."

In his decade of soliciting invitations to courts and urging dukes to promote his petitions, Cristóbal Colón has adopted the romantic manner of the nobility, aping their speech and rituals of space. Perhaps as an influence of de Torres' presence, the Captain General continues his courtly manner, as if he was an aristocrat here on board.

"A man may have a notion of something for many years, but clearly understand it only at a particular moment. But that man is not me, Luís." He stands and turns to face the interpreter, his aquiline nose and high cheekbones pretend a noble bearing. "This voyage has not been a plan, but rather it's been a part of my soul forever. It seems some aspirations last a lifetime. God willing, perhaps I'll find 'peace of mind' before I die."

A gust of wind rocks the ship. The sudden movement is like an omen, and Luís de Torres casts his mind into the darkness of his past. 'Peace of mind before I die', he thinks. A dryness grips his throat, a burning agony, as if for him living is more terrible an issue than death.

Until last year Luís' life had settled into a long reverie. He had been an important part of his father's family, the eldest of three sons and two daughters. Training with his father and other rabbis, he pondered daily matters of faith, law, and family, reading not only the great Hebrew scholars, but also the works of world philosophers, the ancients and the myths they told. His life expanded when he married Judith, the woman his father chose, a bastion of tenderness for him. Their children, David, Aaron, and Edward, were his treasures.

But then, with no regard for justice or truth or the lowest measure of kindness or mercy, the beast reared its head and ravaged his soul. The insane Catholic purification, the Inquisition, rolled like a suffocating fog of poison gas into the life of Luís de Torres.

He and his family lived near a branch of the Rio Segura in the former home of his parents, dead for many years. A neighbor, the fat Ramundo, had long carried a grudge against his father over a misunderstood covenant in the sale of three goats. Ramundo was a farmer who seldom awoke with a sense of satisfaction or contentment. His mind lived in a jumbled past filled with remorse and insufficiency and he became senile. One morning he rolled out from his straw bed feeling not himself, yet someone he knew. By the end of the day Ramundo was convinced the goat transaction with his neighbor, Rabbi Hyman, had just happened.

He denounced Luís, believing him to be the long dead father. Of course neither the error of identification, nor the error of time, mattered to the abbot or to the sheriff who brought them all, the entire de Torres family, to the Cathedral of Murcia's dungeon.

Luís's mind could not get past that day, that hour, that exact minute when he was separated from his wife and children. The family was at table for dinner, the odors of cooked meat and vegetables mingling with the sweetness of his children. Then came the commanding knock at the door, the surge of the constables of the Santa Humanidad, the Domini Canes, into his home. Men at arms in black capes with dark faces and rheumy eyes. The cruel Hounds of God, bringing the stench of a rotting future, surrounded the table. Cries from his frightened children, "Papa. Papa. Help!" In the grip of a hooded monk, Judith's pale face froze as she watched her husband being lifted from the floor, a choking arm thick around his throat, his body twisting, legs kicking.

The loathsome memory startled him every day thereafter as his future ebbed like a retreating tide. Many nights he cried out in his sleep, "Mother! Father! Help me!" But this was a dream from which he would never awaken.

Luís was herded along a dank, meandering passageway lined with bleeding bodies chained to walls, a hellish prison with a lifelong lock. He passed the 'room of song', a confessional, where men, women and children were introduced to the holiness, then leaked out of existence. Luís was locked in a cube-like cell with seven other men. The smell of rot permeated the air, seared on the crusted chains and ropes hanging off the rock walls. Grainy screams erupted in waves and then, during moments of silence, he heard supplications for mercy until the call to 'embrace the end of life'. The thought his children and wife might be the source of those cries drove him insane and he prayed for death to escape the madness. He grit his teeth until his jaw throbbed in aching spasms, he dug at the walls with bloodied fingers, tore at his hair, and scored his face. His eyes screwed shut as he bit through his lips. Semi- conscious, his head snapping back to touch his spine, he wailed, howling for his wife and children, a deep, terrifying wrenching noise, severing now from forever.

Dead men left the cell every day, to be replaced with fresh victims. Luís de Torres was glad he did not know the fate of his family. 'Kill me.', he thought, 'At least it will be over.' But there was no death for him, just the stench and the screams.

There had been an error. Luís' wife, Judith, mistaken for someone else, went immediately to the stake for burning. She was given no opportunity to say good-bye to her children and husband or to make her peace with God. Simply in one door and out to a courtyard where three tall poles ringed with bone-dry hay and *manzanilla* wood, stood separated from each other on a large platform. Carved figures of the four prophets, Amos, Hosea, Isaiah and Micah stared down from the corners of the burning stage, the quemadera.

A cheering crowd surrounded the raised platform. Hooded monks chanting doom scurried from post to post. Two men stood holding green candles, one wearing a *corazaz*, the conical hat of shame. Guarded by monks, like herself, she wondered why she had no green candle. The three victims looked at one another, as if seeing into a mirror, a final, feeble, ghastly face of terror.

Judith had an awareness of real death, a death of hopelessness, and waited for it, the final horror. She shook in fear. She was ashamed to be on her own, ashamed of the true terror she waited to experience alone.

Judith suffered no broken bones, no tortured flesh. She was not numb from pain. In fact, her senses were heightened. The accelerating moment to her death changed her perception of time. In death's shadow, instead of feeling empty, nearly nonexistent, she felt overfilled with life. She could distinguish every stone on the ground, every crack in the wooden steps; she heard every hideous chortle, every wheezing breath from the crowd; she smelled the distinct odor of the executioner's sweat and the stench of excrement. In her heightened state, the world appeared outlined, alien, and ugly to her. She lacked the benefit of time or the deprivation of food and water to anesthetize her body in preparation for her annihilation. Nor was she aware of the chaos and desolation her death, soon to be in the past, would cause her husband, Luís, in the future. A robust, intelligent woman in the prime of her life, alone and fully cognizant of the injustice against her, she thought, 'Let it be quick'.

A priest came to whisper in her ear, "Do not be afraid. You've received the sacrament of penance and extreme unction. Give your pain to the Lord, who knows all human suffering." Then, with a tongue trained to spit torment, in a loud, practiced voice through whetted lips, the priest intoned the Church absolved:

...we declare that if the prisoner should die or be injured or suffer heavy bleeding or have a limb mutilated during the torture, this will be their fault and responsibility and not ours, because they have refused to tell the truth.
Amen

Her death a theft, Judith perished in the roaring inferno, called to embrace the end of life.

Luís de Torres remained in the Inquisition's hell for eight days until he was released through the efforts of Santangel and the Duke of Medina-Celi. Rather than ending their responsibility to Luís, his rescue and liberation actually began it.

Returning to the *judería* he learned what had happened to his family and he descended into a numbing silence, an undertow of utter hopelessness. Awash in grief, he lived on the edge of hysteria, profoundly paranoid.

Cheated of his wife and children, unhinged, ashamed, and riddled with guilt, he scarcely slept or ate. At first he thought praying would give God a chance to make retribution, that everything might turn out as he wanted, although he knew it couldn't. Then he prayed, not for himself, but to console God, in whose name such abominations were done. And finally, holding God responsible for punishing his children and for the stupidity of his tormentors, he concluded that only God's non-existence could excuse him. Luís, wanting no part of a Godless world, considered killing himself every day.

> The weeping child could not be heard,
> The weeping parents wept in vain;
> They strip'd him down to his little shirt,
> And bound him in an iron chain.
> And burn'd him in a holy place,
> Where many had been burn'd before:
> The weeping parents wept in vain

> William Blake

On board the Santa Maria, coming out of this loathsome memory, Luís de Torres trembles. Tears stream down his cheeks. He looks at Cristóbal Colón, unconsciously twisting a button on his sleeve, tightening the thread. He contemplates Colón's words, 'Peace of mind before dying'. What an idea, he thinks.

He says, "Death is hardly mysterious compared to living, Captain. It is life that is the mystery. One could die and be done, but living is never done, it can never be finished."

The Captain General rubs the back of his neck, stiff from his berth aboard the Santa Maria. He knows of the catastrophe of Luís's family. Watching Luís rake his fingers across his closed eyes as if trying to wipe away the crippling burden of memory, he says, "Yes, as they say, 'we live and we die, though we know not why'. Nothing can be solved, Luís, even by living. Life fades away and it leaves solving alone. You and I, we are alike in the same way all men are alike. We share the desire to extend our life, even for eternity, but death overwhelms everything."

"No, Captain. We are not alike. I want my life back. My family back. I want to begin now, at the end. To live my life in reverse, where time would flow backwards, undoing everything done. I curse the eternity of my life. And you think that death, the end, is the beginning. Could it be more ironic?"

The Captain General's eyes reflect his friend's anguish, but he says calmly, "A death does not revoke a life, it is one fact among many, never the end of the story." Cristóbal believes Luís will gather darkness and more darkness before he sees the light. "If life has taught us anything Luís, it's that for every end there is a beginning. Surely you believe that. Sometimes the past can vanish, Luís. They say that to forgive is the highest form of self-interest."

De Torres' jaw clenches. His fingers rub circles on his temples, testing the blood in his arteries. His intellect tells him that with the passage of time, memory is supposed to ease, that there is forgiveness with forgetting, but his sorrow keeps spinning out of control. A deep breath calms him enough to quip?' "You're not going to ask me to pray are you? Don't look to me for a happy ending."

"I am a devout Catholic. You know that, Luís. And I am a thoughtful man. For as long as I can remember, each day I have considered the width of this ocean. Do you think I believe that me praying one second of those years has narrowed these waters? Could change that fact? It isn't prayer that sustains me. I seek salvation for the glory of God."

Blood flushes Luís's face. "God again! And what of, 'in the name of God'? After all that's what we live and die by. Where was God when my wife was burned at the stake? I cannot bear this bloodthirsty cowardice, this bitter beyond bitterness. How can you? Who are these madmen killing anyone they choose?"

Here in the isolation at sea, Luís feels safe, released from the discipline of silence. His jaw squares, the muscles in his neck strain. At the edge of sanity, he balls his fists, his whole body seeming to leak tears. "This brutality! This cruelty and savageness!" Remaining in control, he wipes his face. He fixes onto his friend's eyes and in a hushed tone, as if sharing a secret, says, "Your religion is a cult of death." He blanches, astonished by his own words.

Taken aback, the Captain General disengages from Luís' glare. Wincing at the blasphemy, the unbridled vehemence, he sighs. There is no purpose in challenging this tormented man. Nothing must muddle his focus on the voyage. To comfort, he says: "I've often considered the words of a great poet, Aeschylus, who said, "In our sleep, pain that cannot forget, falls drop by drop upon the heart, and in our own despair, against our will, comes wisdom to us by the awful grace of God."

Luís is shaking, a tremor at the center of his body. He knows the Greek poet's words. Cristóbal wraps his arm around the trembling, hunched shoulders and leading him through the hatch says, "Perhaps we can delay further theological discussion to a later date, my friend. Right now I must calculate our distance for the day."

Topside, the sky nurtures the hour of both sunset and moonrise, dark in the east, a radiant, color-infused sky to the west. A vast new horizon. The ships scud for the channel between Africa and the eastern most of the Canary Islands, Fuertaventura. Infinite, huge waves fold under long, curling combers in a timeless rhythm.

On the poop deck, Harana has seen the dry land breeze off this coast of Africa before, churning sand and sea into a reddish brown air. He says to the helmsman, Lorenzo, "Thar'l be a 'harmattan' before long. That's a rain o blood I needn't see. Better ta lay on more canvas."

Amidships, de Torres yawns, a harbinger of seasickness. The blood-flush has left his face, but inside emptiness strangles him. He knows there will be no end to his memory. Where he was once in the middle of everything, now he feels in the middle of nothing. His consolation is that there are no new torments, just old ones. What more of him could be necessary? Mankind's activities mean nothing to him, he wants no part in them. What does he live for then? What did he want on this earth but a life with his children and Judith? Without the will to live, the idea of resuming life again is hollow. It would be so much easier to simply give up. He thinks of the Talmud, the rabbinic musings of Jewish law and ethics, compiled over thousands of years. It taught him that the only virtue left for the hopeless man is courage. He wonders what he might wish for.

Chapter 16
Gotzun

Ship's Log

Thursday, 9 August, 1492 P

The Pinta was able to reach Grand Canary this morning. I ordered Martín Pinzón, the captain, to remain until the Pinta could be properly repaired. I took the Santa Maria and the Nina, and set out for the island of Gomera. If I cannot find another vessel there, I will come back in a few days and help with repairs.

The distant sight is Teide, the volcano that dominates the island of Tenerife. After ten-days sail, its snow covered peak heralds the fleets arrival at the Canaries, the Fortunate Islands. The Pinta stops for repairs at Gran Canaria nearer the African coast. The Santa Maria and the Nina arrive the next morning further west at the port of San Sebastian, Gomera's deep water harbor.

One of the smaller islands, Gomera had been conquered and is securely under Spanish authority. The ships lie parallel, pointing into a warm summer night's breeze, swinging at anchor like slow smoke from a chimney. A silver moon rises over the sea, lighting the sky in the west through gathering thunderclouds, and a feeling of calm rises from the illuminated blue waters.

The ships are silhouetted on the flat harbor. Undersea, shoals of mullet darken the ocean like waving wheat. Just east on Tenerife, no longer a speck against the horizon but blocking half the sky, rises the massive volcano. The Santa Maria's herald-and-cross emblazoned sails are furrowed and tied fast to spars. It is late and the crew settles on deck, most asleep. At the bow, savvy tars discuss what concerns them, the weather, the sea, and the best entrance into the harbor.

Dante is amidships leaning against the rail, playing chords on his concertina, living thoughts he'd dare not dream. Arm's distance away, Revela, wrapped in her woolen farmer's shawl, stiff from the salt air, rests against a cradle of water casks lashed next to the mast. She stares at the constellations appearing in the black sky, thinking of others who had watched these same sky-lights and wondered these same farmer thoughts.

Across from her, Gotzun sits on the ship's winch-like pulley. Yoggi lies by his side, his tail tucked in, his pink tongue just visible. The dog eyes Dante who saunters closer to Gotzun.

A light breeze ruffles a cat's paw on the water's surface. In a boyish, cracked voice carried on the salt-air, Dante says to Gotzun, "That was pretty interesting, right?" Then pausing in the non-response, "You know, what Orkon said. About the gold."

Gotzun, twirling a bit of rope, aware of the boy's apprehension says off-handedly, "Gold always interests men." He drops the line, his eyes demanding, "Why are you coming on this voyage Dante?"

The boy answers quickly. "Well for that...the gold...and the excitement. And doing something spectacular. And, you know, to make my mark. Besides, I guess, they're probably after me."

Gotzun and Yoggi shift positions. With a nod toward Revela, the tall man says "And your sister? What will become of her?"

Dante blurts, "Yes, we've talked about it. And, well, you know she can't go with. It's no place for a girl. And this looks to be a pretty good spot." Dante slows his explanation as if to give it more credence. "She's with the Jews, and David says he'll watch out for her. And anyway, it's me they want."

His face flushes and his stomach tightens. To deflect the shame of abandoning Revela, he asks, "What do you know about these islands?"

Revela joins them and her smile serves to affirm Dante's explanation. She curls next to her brother, slipping her arm over his shoulder, leaning her head into him then turns abruptly and says: "Yes, Gotzun, tell us what you know about these islands."

"I know everything about these islands. This is the land of my forbearers. I am of the Vincheni, what you call Canarian."

Yoggi noses closer, nudging Dante to pet him, then lies down and puts his head on his paws. There is a small rise in the harbor waters and the ship rocks, creaking as it strains against the anchor rode. The moon floats between clouds. Dante and Revela's eyes widen. They lean forward, squeezing together as if listening to a bedtime tale. Lines of age on Gotzun's face relax, his eyes close, and in a soft, clear voice, he begins.

"I am the history of my people. I carry the true story. So listen to me. What I say is for you only. I am a reciter. A story-holder. The one who carries these words. Cross your arms like this and hold your shoulders. Do you hear me?"

They silently mouth, 'yes', and do as he directs.

"The creation of the Vincheni, the Canarian people, who you call Guanches, is from the beginning of the earth. Our story is much deeper than yours. You could not understand from where we came. You believe that Jesus God waits for you and that suffering is good. And then you turn your suffering into hatred of others. So my God, Eraoranzan, is not understandable to you. We are not a violent people. More like the Book People than like you Christers. But this I will tell you about the Vincheni."

The youngsters inch closer, eager to learn secrets. The orange moon breaks through the darkness, illuminating the phosphorescent microbes that saturate the summer waters of the archipelago.

"Before the deluge, the mountains were many and so were the Vincheni. The land was vast and from the tallest points you could not see the great water. There were green pastures and brown and yellow farmlands, deep forests, and cliffs to the sky. The world was generous. A bounty of grains, plants for healing, animals for food, skins to clothe us, and fish to honor our ceremonies. And it was thought that the mountains would sleep forever.

"Then in the 'years of night', the world changed as the mountains burned with fire up to the heavens. First the sisters, Tibiatin and Tamonante fought, filling the valley between them with their hot blood. Their fire laid waste to the forests. Then their uncles and brothers fought; Hyter the skull, Tifuya early riser, Chenauco the flowered one, and the twins, Teno and Taucho. The earth shook everywhere for a long time. Then the battle was joined by the White Mountain, Chineche, the great mountain you now see in the distance that you call Tiede, and Timanfya, the home of the beasts. There was terrible thunder, cracking roars and rumbles, and the sky exploded into a rain of red fear and green chaos. The air hurt to breath and smelled of burnt life. Smoke and fire covered the land. It was as if the world had been turned inside out."

Yoggi's hind paw scratches his neck, resettles to Dante's side and nuzzles his leg. The sister and brother remain still, transfixed by Gotzun's story.

"The Vincheni huddled together in mortal fear, sealing their ears with grass, their mouths open, their eyes rolled up into their brains, their bowels emptying. When the fire rained down on them they were frozen in the burning blood of the mountains and remained in pumice tombs. And when the earth shook and the waters came, those that hid in caves became fish. After many years the waters finally left. Out of the tumbling waters a new earth arose, but only small parts of the land and few people remained. The spirit of the Vincheni was close to leaving for the second sun. The great battle of the 'years of night' was won by the White Mountain and his brother Timanfya. All others perished into ocean graves.

"Thus began the next circle. Where once there was land there was now water. The Vincheni were broken off from each other to live on islands in the great sea. They forgot the lessons of their God, Eraoranzan, and fought each other. And it was decided that each would be a separate tribe and that the island they lived on would belong to them with its own King and counsel. For a very long time the Vinchenis' minds were dark.

"There have been many great kings and many years. I know all the years. I know all the kings. The first was Almalek, next Alalram, then his brother, Gilgatek. When I was born Ervalzan was king and then Urtoga and then Charval, a great king in the year of the dark wind when he found the great cave."

Revela glances at Dante, purses her lips and rolls her eyes as if to say, 'Fairy tales. Why should we believe Gotzun's fables?'

"I know all the stories. In the year of the red locust, one hundred years before your Jesus God, the fierce men with yellow hair came to the island of Titeroigatra. In the year of the drowning pig, black men were blown onto Tamaran and were killed; in the year of the suffocating storm of golden sand a man came called Lilistrum, who stayed and became King Per.

"There have been many years and many great deeds. In the 'year of the whales' twelve Vinchinee escaped from slaving on Majorca Island. Emmetak the rebel was one of them and they brought back the Portuguese tongue. In the year of the thieves, just before my life began, pinks captured four Vincheni and took them away to their land of Portugal. My sixth father, Moristak, chief of the Vincheni of Adeje, was one of those men. He, like his father, was a story holder. And that is why I am able to tell you this.

"In the year of the red worm when Unae was King, pink men again came to kill the Vincheni. That is when my first father, Davjo was captured. Five years later I hid on the sugar ship, Athelas, to find my father, who had been slaved.

"Discovered, I was taken to the court of the great King John of Portugal. He asked me many questions about the Vincheni and about the seas of Chineche, and he told me stories of the first circle, told to him by a man called Pliny. And, in Lisbon City, Prince Henry told me stories recorded by the invaders and showed me a parchment made by Dulcert with our islands in the Great Ocean Sea. The Prince Henry showed me the writings of Sr. Boccaccio and of Sr. Petrarch, who called us The Fortunate Islands.

"Prince Henry of Portugal commanded me to tell others the Vincheni story. Sr. Martín Behaim asked me in Lisbon City, 'When does the wind blow from the east?' And, 'when do the porpoise come?' And, 'when does the desert sand come from Africa?' Sr. Rosalv asked me in Madrid these same questions as did this very captain general, Cristóbal Colón, in Cordoba. And the Castillian King's man, Santangel, along with Luís de Torres, the man on this voyage, on the King's victory day when the Moors surrendered Granada, asked me these and many more questions of Vincheni life.

"And I told him how we have been lessened. About the Seviano, Fernando Peraza, and the slaughter he inflicted. The humiliation of having our King Guanareme and Queen Tinguafaya captured and enslaved. That the Spanish Henry III made an outsider, Juan de Betancour, King of the Canary Islands. That without our knowledge our land was given and sold many times by the Roman Pope, and by the Portuguese and by Spanish Kings. That in the name of your Christ, the Vincheni have been conquered and reconquered. Outlaws in our own land. Exiled to the mountains. Forced to renounce our Gods. Hunted, enslaved, tortured, and murdered. That we have fought for one hundred years with stick and stone against the steel sword, armor, canon, and horse of the Spanish. We will never surrender.

"Here is what you must know, Revela: Here on Gomera there is a woman, Elenora Bobadilla. She is the widow of Hernan Peraza a merciless man gifted our land by the Rome-Pope. He ruled here, enslaved and killed many Vincheni. And now she rules Gomera as its mistress. I myself met this woman long ago here in Gomera and again in Cordoba, the very month I first spoke with the Captain General. She is a woman who wouldn't tell the truth even by mistake.

"Then early this year I stayed at the castle of the Duke of Meli along with our Captain General, Luís de Santangel, and this woman, Elenora Bobadilla. From the castle I traveled alone with Santangel to meet with a man, Diego Deza, who served the Portuguese King John. Santangel told me that the Captain General had sailed the Canaries and had a bold plan to sail west from Gomera to the Indies. He said Deza was a supporter of the Captain General. We rode mules southwest of Cordova along the Guadalquivir River to a hamlet, Perivilla.

Chapter 17
Santangel & Deza

In Perivilla, at the modest home of the alcalde, Juan de Kwili, Santangel reunites with Hieronymus Deza. The ambassador is in the service of King John II of Portugal and is a man supremely confident in his privileges. They meet in a room used to store new wine, now brightly lit by the morning sun. Deza is a man of small stature with wild, white hair and a sour old-man smell. He holds a wooden crutch close to his round body. Hanging at eye level from his long billed hat is a palm-sized, square piece of glass.

The lanky Santangel leans over the smaller man in an awkward embrace. Gotzun, after being introduced by Santangel, goes outside. Deza drops into a chair, his knees cracking like twigs, signals Santangel to join him at the long worktable, removes his hat and pours pinkish wine from a *garafon*.

They eye each other, quiet for a long moment until a bird chirp enters the silence. Warming to the comfort of their fellowship, Deza says, "It's been, what, five years, since we last met in Sevilla? You were either taller or thinner."

Hearing King John's ambassador say the city's name provokes a crushing memory tinged with guilt for Santangel. A place of horrific atrocities and expulsions where Solomon Adret and his wife Rachel burned, 'relaxed' by the Inquisition. The synagogue's burial committee, the *khevra kaddisha*, had sought Santangel out, begging him to intervene, but he was helpless.

Deza's graying, shaggy brows pinch and he says, "A difficult time for many friends."

Santangel reaches across the table and grasps Deza's arm. His eyes rest closed for a moment as the memory passes. Then he asks, "And how is his Majesty?"

"Oh, King John is quite royal these days. What is it Ysabela calls him? 'The Man'? He approaches the age when one becomes indifferent to life. Still he is not a person to be happy for another's success, so of course he's totally jealous of your King. Is there something, some act, some conquest more noble, more Catholic, that Ferdinand might come up with?" Deza enjoys his tease, a puckered smile on his face. "By the Saints of Aquinas, there won't be a Muslim left in Iberia."

Santangel recalls King John, the way his compelling eyes blink as he fingers his chin, a man of long silences who speaks sparingly. How different a man is the King than Deza, a man who lifts your spirits, whose talent is putting strangers at ease, permitting others to go out of their way to do him favors.

Not to leave the mocking of his King unchallenged, Santangel says, "Well, as it will be said, 'Envy is lean; it bites but cannot swallow.'"

His jowls bouncing in laughter, gesturing flamboyant, Deza persists, "I hear that your perfect Christians travelled from battlefield to battlefield mounted on those magnificent Carthusians. Routing the Moors by their own soft hands. Tell me, Santangel, how does the victor fare?"

"As you might expect a man of his character to fare. The King expects his own way. He is good to those who think him good and snaps his fingers for God to make it rain." His King, a subject Santangel loves. He looks to Deza and continues, "His eyes close often in admiration of himself, and as anyone, he likes to be liked, and of course, everyone wants him to be happy. So he is always right and as impossible to trip up as a cat. He speaks as if he could learn everything he needed to know by listening to himself. He raises all topics and is brilliant in all topics raised." Again, the glance to the ambassador who encourages him with a raised eyebrow. "All matters brought are dispatched with decisiveness, any delay considered an affront, and each day is blessed by his presence." Deza is delighted, listening with full attention. "His dukes surround him, anxious in their pecking order, awaiting his gifts for their service. He prepares prizes for those who promote his wishes. He desires the impossible — both power and love at the same time." Then in a sober voice, Santangel leans across the planked table to whisper, "The elbows are sharpening my friend. Best to be cautious. There is some stink in Aragon."

The ambassador nods, "Ah yes. These are dangerous times." He adjusts in the wicker chair, rubbing his fingers together, and then reaching for his piece of glass says, "Well, 'tempus fugit'. Cristóvão Colombo is at the Count's also?"

Santangel notes that Deza uses Colon's Portuguese name. "Yes", and he pauses, knowing this will be compelling news to the ambassador, "as is Elenora Bobadilla." He lets the name float before Deza's widening eyes. "Of course you know the rumor of her husband's death by savages is common gossip. It's extraordinary the way the woman's mere presence starts tongues wagging." Motioning to Gotzun outside, "My friend there knows them both."

Deza, asks, "Does the King know she's here?"

"Of course he does. As they say: 'a fish does not swim in the Med without Ferdinand's permission.' A better question is the Queen. Does she know? I can tell you confidently that she has yet to take her heel off Ferdinand's neck about that dalliance."

Deza strokes a hand through his wild white hair. "I imagine the King would like to have the lady go home to her island."

Santangel tugs at his lapel, giving Deza time to think. Elenora Bobadilla is not only beautiful, but has the reputation in Gomera as that of a cruel woman, without tenderness. She exercises her power liberally, and men respect her only because she is dangerous. She is believed to be a colossal whore. Because of her liaison with the King, the Queen came close to having her 'relaxed', and she would have burned if her sister,

Beatrice, the Queen's best friend, had not pleaded to Ysabela to spare her life. Elanora's exit to Gomera with her new husband, Perez, virtually a banishment, was a relief to the court. Both men know her reputation but Santangel's knowledge of Elenora Bobadilla's relationship with Colon, is kept to himself.

Deza muses, and then first to speak, adds as if thinking aloud, "She could be of great use."

The treasurer, "I agree. I agree." Deza says, "Tell me, have you spoken with Colombo?"

Santangel winces and admits, "Not yet. Not completely anyway. I have probed here and there. Of course he knows what I want to know. It would do simply to say where he learned his Spanish. But there are times when the man seems absent. We only partly understand him."

"Yes, he has such a strange tongue, a deficient Spanish, almost as if from another century, everything so small, every 'casa' a 'casita'. And his hand, with all dots and virgules, he writes like a monk. Not to mention that constant muttering, like a child with an imaginary playmate."

Then in a serious tone, "His plans are of utmost significance to us all, Luís. His tale has taken hold. What the King has not confiscated from us could be dedicated to his voyage. There is fear of the worst, of doom itself. What is there left for us to do, Luís? We must exert all our efforts on the Genoan's behalf. Come now, tempus fugit. Much depends on us. Let us get down to it."

"Yes, of course. Your report. The bane of all emissaries, the dreaded scripting."

They move to the far end of the table where Deza sits behind a traveling writer's chest. The mahogany chest is about the size and weight of a carpenter's box, adorned with marquetry of kingwood and walnut veneers, with handles like parrot claws. Deza caresses the gilt ormolu trim. A brass escutcheon has a relief of his family coat of arms, a replica of the ring he wears, and he rubs it with his thumb. He slips a key into the lock and lifts open the sloped writing board.

Deza takes out the glass ink and sand wells, and opens the nook holding a variety of quills stored in skillfully dovetailed drawers. "See here. There are compartments for all the essential items," and he opens one containing a variety of threads and needles.

Santangel thinks, 'Ferdinand's secretary is twice as large and has its own mule.'

"Now watch this," and Deza presses on an ebony inlay, flush to his left, then slides a small knob. On the right side beneath the quill drawer, a small door opens. Deza lifts his snowy eyebrows to Santangel as if to say, 'Here my friend, I trust you with my secret.'

The treasurer feigns surprise, considers the other two hidden compartments he had secretly examined years before, and honestly says, "This is a fine piece, I've often admired it."

From the accoutrement space beneath the velvet-writing slope, the ambassador withdraws a sheet of yellow linen parchment and secures it with small silver paperweights. He has a natural inclination to espionage, the covert world of court. He removes the right-wing swan quill, crafted for his left hand use, lifts the ink seal, and brings his seeing glass close. His arms flourish in preparation. "How shall we phrase it for your regent? As if it were cheese or caviar?"

Santangel stands behind Deza and recites the beginning salutations of the ambassadorial letter. Deza writes:

"Your most Esteemed Majesty, King John II, King of Portugal and the Algarves, your most Perfect Prince and Protector of the Faith. Your humble servant Hieronymus Deza, has the honor to transmit to you, in complete confidence, a report on my journey in your service to the Realm of your Royal Friends and Allies, Ferdinand and Ysabela, King and Queen of Aragon and Castile and all Spains."

The two friends settle into composing the letter from Deza to King John, one often finishing the sentence of the other. Deza's meticulous scripting takes time, his left hand limping behind the right, as he pushes it through the words.

While Deza writes, memories of childhood cartwheel through Santangel's mind. Deza had been there in Catalyud with Santangel's father and uncles, all of them scholars in the community. After each Friday night service, the men would gather the boys together— himself, Daniel, Michel, Matiaju, Aidan, the Bolkar twins— too many to remember. The men would quiz the boys on the Torah, the five books, and the story to be read at the next morning's Sabbath prayer. His sisters and the other girls joined with the women to receive dietary instruction, and to be taught that women are an inferior gender.

At home they spoke 'Ladino', a blend of Spanish, Hebrew and Aramaic, a 'family language', meant to be confusing to an outsider. In centuries of wandering, Jews had discovered that having a secret language was beneficial for survival, their principal achievement. Outwitting the Inquisition was good reason to resort to deception. Ladino, incomprehensible to outsiders, more than a language, was a spoken attitude, guarded and rebellious, fortifying the cultural bonds that united the Jews.

Santangel's father would direct him; "Tell me from Maimonides. But briefly."

The boy would respond, "Yes father. In the 12th century there was a pogrom in Toledo. In the 13th century we were driven from England by the blood libel fakery, and in the 14th from France and Germany."

"And when was the great pogrom of Castile, Luís?"

"In 1391 father. In Sevilla, when thousands of our brethren fled or were slaughtered, and thousands were forced to choose between death and becoming Christians."

Santangel reeled in the scorched memory of the corpse-strewn *judería* in Sevilla in that *anni horribile*. Hiding in a crack in a wall, Luís saw men of the cross shepherding the mob to kill Jews. The demon Ferrand Martínez. The twin monster *conversos*, Paul de Burgos and Joshua Lorqui. They led wild eyed, stiff-jawed, rabble, screaming their thirst for blood, demanding a Jew's pain. Traces of Jews from the mass burnings swirled in the air, leaving a pall of ash over the plaza for a week.

"And what became of our brethren that fled?"

"They went to Portugal and Maghreb and Sicily and Italy, leaving their homes as they were forced to do in the bible times when the ten tribes were scattered to the world, father."

"And what do the rabbis say?"

"The rabbis say that it is no sin to say whatever necessary to stay alive. That once a man is chained to the stake, it concentrates his mind, but agreeing to be burned does not make him a hero."

"And what is our dearest hope Luís?"

"To have a homeland again, father. To join with the ten lost tribes and to live in freedom to worship God as we did in Jerusalem. To have a homeland again, father. To join with the ten lost tribes and to live in freedom to worship God as we did in Jerusalem."

Now, seeing Deza who like himself had escaped the carnage of Sevilla, Santangel asks himself, 'What did a boy know of a homeland or of the Diaspora of the lost tribes? He thinks of Yitzak the Jew, from the ninth century, sent by the Emperor Charlemagne to Harun-ar-Rashid the King of Persia; of Sir John Mandeville's account of the Ten Lost Tribes of Israel, imprisoned between the mountains of Goth and Magoth by the Caspian Sea; and he remembers Rabbi Benjamin of Tudea who travelled in the 12th century a hundred years before Marco Polo, to Greece and Persia and throughout Europe, Asia, and Africa.

There were Jews everywhere. It could happen.

Deza is saying something. Santangel looks to him, puzzled from indulging in his reverie.

"I said, should we mention 'the eight excursions'? Is it too much?"

Santangel is immediately back. "Not directly, but we might allude to them."

Deza smiles. "Yes, an obscure mention, for him to figure out. The plan must be Ferdinand's. He'll like that, being clever to himself."

Santangel ruminates, 'was this too much to hope? Am I but a conjurer explaining one trick by performing another? Hope is an advantage. After all isn't the solution to a mystery always less inspiring than the mystery itself? Ferdinand lies without batting an eyelash, his deceit a tool. Why not me? Hope is an advantage. There is always a choice to parse together unconnected events, one true and one perhaps not. Secrets live in silence, but when someone confesses, it sets a power free.'

Deza looks up, "How does this ring?" He clears his throat and reads;

'Why not have a larger stake in the game to India with your reach across the Ocean Sea as well as round Africa?'"

Santangel admires the shift from sincerity to mockery and says, "Yes, that's good. It will squeeze his balls. Use it."

From over the ambassador's shoulder, Santangel assesses the parchment. Deza's immaculate handwriting, the text without punctuation, written in the manner of the Church. He thinks 'skillful and smart.' His own talent, to deduce where a person had lived by seeing their script, was more than a game. It had served him well and trapped not a few spies. 'You are from a place in Italy?' 'You lived with the Franciscans?' He thinks of the dots, curlicues and virgules of Cristóbal Colón's hand.

Deza says, "Just one more now, perhaps about the coming edict? Shall we get ahead of the future, mark the history now? What do you think?"

Santangel says, "Why not?" And then musing, "My cousin, Leon, he was the one for history. When he was six he was a walking Jewish encyclopedia. His father, Hyman — you remember him — rest his sacred soul, was so proud of him. The boy would perform as entertainment, lecturing like a professor at *yeshiva*." In his mind's eye Santangel sees the diminutive Leon standing in front of a rough-hewn table. Dinner over, the families sit talking before clearing the dishes. Someone calls his name. 'Leon'. Others echo and clap, "Yes, Leon! Leon! Leon!" The boy looks to his parents who encourage him, and then he walks to the open area near the hearth. He stands, feet together, his oversized tunic gathered by rope around his tiny pot-belly, pudgy arm raised, his finger stabbing the air:

Santangel can still hear the child's high-pitched voice, "In the late 14th century the Jews of Spain entered a new era of persecution. It was a time of lawlessness and King Henry II decreed..." and the boy would launch into a litany of forbidden acts carefully pronouncing any word with two or more syllables:

"Jews cannot be near castles, hold public office, wear fine clothes," and he would sweep his arm across his body as if he did wear fine clothes. "Ride mules, use Christian names, carry or sell weapons, practice medicine or chemistry."

He pauses to draw his breath, his beany eyes searching. "Sell bread or wine or flour or meat. Work in any trade. Hire Christian servants or farmhands or gravediggers. Change money, cut hair, eat or drink with or visit or converse intimately with Christians"— always stumbling here, pronouncing it 'inmitantly' — "leave the country. And Jews must live separately from Christians in enclosed *juderías*, wear distinct badges" and he would point proudly to the *Magan David*, the shield of King David, on his chest, "And women will wear garments of coarse material reaching to their feet", and he reaches down to the floor.

Everyone cheers, pounds the table, and whistles as Leon bows three times, then marches into his mother's lap.

Now Santangel wonders, 'Why didn't they teach Leon the procedures that sealed their punishments and doom? How a learned anti-Semite such as Fray Alonso de Spina or Fray Alonso de Hojeda would begin the secret 'edict of faith'. How the *calificadore* would examine the charges, and the certainty of issuing a *calidad de oficio* to prompt the *promotor fiscal* to present the *clamosa*, the formal demand for the arrest of the accused; or the secret trial that excluded witnesses for the accused as untrustworthy because they knew him; the accusers who were never confronted but whose accusations of mere personal cleanliness could result in death.'

The Christians, repulsed by the Jewish humane ritual of butchering animals, were maniacally crazed to engage in the ritual butchering of Jews.

Would it have made a difference if they heard Leon recite that after dinner? Would they have prepared somehow? Was there any way to prepare?

Deza finishes writing, carefully replacing the swan quill, the inkwell, the blotter, and the six silver paperweights in their home drawers. From another compartment he removes pellets of dark magenta wax and a brass spoon. First melting the wax in the spoon he then pours it on the linen parchment, just overlapping a portion of his signature. A twist of his wrist and his signet ring marks the imprint of his office.

Santangel watches Deza's every movement. When the wax burns and the scent reaches him, he thinks, 'Consider a country where a boy smells his father's burning flesh. Does the monarch not hold his subjects' trust and owe them his guardianship? Aren't his people due his protection from those who would instruct them how to speak to God? What kind of a ruler unleashes that Hell?

Deza beams, "And now the final touch, my friend."

He slips the letter to King John into the dispatch case and folds the flap-cover through a loop. Using a thick purple, linen thread and heavy needle, he begins to sew shut the dispatch buckle, using a sailor's-palm that fits snug in his hand to push the needle-point through the leather.

Deza works the beginning anchor-point slowly, then proceeds quickly and deliberately, his body rocking in rhythm with each stitch of his spotted hand, humming like an old woman sitting by the fire repairing a granddaughter's blouse.

"This is my pic-poc stitch Luís. See how I double back to lock each knot? See, pic——poc. It won't be a problem will it?"

Santangel purses his lips, his eyebrows squinch and he shakes his head, "No, it won't be a problem". He grins, thinking, 'pic-poc, pic-poc'. There is no going back. The question is, what is the way forward? Can the fate of a people be determined like this, two men in a small room? In reality, didn't a shifting wind, a sudden storm, or a man's hangover often change history? Santangel admires his friend's skill, and knowing the talent it will require to duplicate his work says, "Don't make that too difficult."

Deza examines the case knowing it will be intercepted and brought to King Ferdinand. "That should do it. Play your cards well, my friend."

The Letter:

> *Your most Esteemed Majesty King John II King of Portugal And the Algarves Your most Perfect Prince and Protector of the Faith I Your humble servant Hieronymus Deza has the Honor to Transmit to You in Complete and Absolute Confidence a Report on my Journey in Your Service to the Realm of Your Royal Friends and Allies Ferdinand and Ysabela King and Queen of Aragon and Castile and all the Spains The King's health is robust Daily After early Mass His Highness rides His magnificent Carthusian in the morning hours and then has a small Meal His Highness then receives His Grandees' reports from Señor Santangel regarding the Depth of the Royal Treasury And the Debts Owed And from the Duke of Lotus regarding the Garrison at Santa Fe And then he hears Petitions from the Court After which He retires to his Bath and Pleasures The Queen attends early and mid- day Mass between which Her Highness carries out the Duties of the Court Her Highness joins with the King At the End of Day After late Mass for the evening Meal On certain days Her Highness is Accompanied by Her Ladies in Waiting in Visits to the Infirmary to Comfort the Sick She attends late Mass*

It is my most honored privilege to inform you that I have seen the Secret Dispatch between the Duke of Meli and the Genoan merchant from Majorca Dentildo Contracting for the Purchase of the years first Harvest of Sugar from Las Palmas in the Canary Islands The Governor General of the Balearic Islands has with the Crowns approval Fixed the Price And the reduced Tariff It is Your humble servants opinion that Your Emissary in Palma be advised to Secure a Favorable Tonnage

It is my most honored privilege to inform You that The Duke of Colver has Seduced the Wife of the King's Captain of the Garrison at Maracena and that there is a Threat of Armed Conflict The Duke is in Arrears to the Royal Treasury The Duchess Joana has Retired to the Nunnery at St Emeta under the Protection of Bishop Krunicanta The Duchess is a Friend of the King but Not of the Queen It is Your servants humble opinion that no steps be taken regarding this very Delicate and Embarrassing Affair

It is my most honored privilege to inform you that There has been Authorized by the Vice-Admiral of the Spanish Fleet an Expedition to the Maghreb with the purpose of gathering Information as to the Route across the Great Sand to discover the Source of Gold that the Moors sell in the ports of Alcasar and Mazagan It is Your humble servants opinion that This action would be a Violation of the Treaty of Alquerava But It is a wasted effort to which the Spanish Royals will find no Benefit And it is Without the need of Concern to Your Royal Highness Your interests are well Protected in the Maghreb by Your Soldiers under the Command of Captain Azambuja at your Fort at Jao de La Mina This is but an Insubstantial Spanish Intrusion into Your Royal Territory

It is my most honored privilege to inform you that The Kings long Convened Talavera Commission has Finally Reported They Advise the Crown of Their Rejection of the Plan of the Genoan Cristóvão Colombo. The Plan well Known to Your Highness of a Voyage of Discovery to reach the Indies by Sailing directly West across uncharted Waters of the Ocean Sea Your humble servant has received reliable information that Señor Talavera who your Royal Highness Knows to be an Honored and respected Geographer and Scientist is himself in Agreement with the plan But advises against the

Cost Your humble servant has spoken with Others of Renowned Expertise in this matter who in Secret consider the Plan to be Sound The Queen herself Favors it as well as the Person of the Genoan whom I have also Questioned directly and who Travels with a Mystic from the Island of Tenerife and whom I have also Questioned It is your humble servants opinion that such an undertaking would Now be Highly Advisable since the Return of the Lucky Eighth. Why not have a Larger Stake in the Game to India with Your Reach from the Ocean Sea as well Around Africa

It is my most honored privilege to inform You that soon a Royal Edict will Issue Expelling All Jews and Moors from Castile and Aragon under Penalty of the most Dire of Consequences It is your humble servants opinion that this Action may be to the Benefit of Your Royal Highness and I would humbly suggest that Contacts be Initiated to Señor Spilco Rabbi Eqilix and Bishop Hernandez

All This I Advise under Your Royal Seal in Absolute Truth And Confidence this Third Day of January in the Year of Our Lord Fourteen Hundred and Ninety Two Signed by the hand of Your loyal Subject and Ambassador Hieronymus Deza

Chapter 18
Granada Crostobal & Ysabela

Three days after the reunion of Santangel and Deza, January 6, 1492, the day of the celebration of the Feast of the Epiphany, the King and Queen of Spain rode from their military encampment at Santa Fe. At the Genil River, a mile from the walled city of Granada, they will receive the surrendered Andalusian Region from the hands of the reining Moorish monarch, Emir Muhammad XII, known as Boabdil. So ended eight hundred years of Muslim life and rule in Iberia.

Ferdinand, of average height with straight brittle hair, spoke in a deep-toned cadence that complimented his proficiency in deceptiveness. His wide spaced, brown eyes further mask his true motive. Royal life had been dominated by perpetual wars, and so, accustomed to danger, he practiced restraint and a discerning nature.

This warrior King of Spain is mounted on Al Khamsa, his chestnut Carthusian, the finest strain of Andalusian horse. Wearing a brocade-covered cuirass over a velvet doublet and armed with a Moorish sword, he rode at the head of a resplendent squadron of knights.

Ysabela rode on his right, draped in a sable jacket, the bodice of her dress sewn with pearls. To diminish the martial atmosphere, the Queen had insisted Ferdinand wear a purple torque and a floppy feathered hat. Behind them rode the Cardinal of Spain, the Duke of Medina, the Dukes of Sidonia and Cadiz, and the Marquis of Violana; followed in row by the Marquis of Mashkis, the Count of Valcarsal, the Counts of Nevboid and Bartlet and the Duke of Ariela. These were the men who, in the last decade, had helped King Ferdinand conquer, castle by castle, the verdant Mediterranean coastal region of Granada. All were mounted on regal Arabians, high-tailed, spirited horses with arched necks and cunei foreheads. The thunderous, imperial hoard rode under a forest of majestic banners, purple silk glittering with silver and gold, brocade pennants and multi-colored standards. The Golden Cross and the Royal Banner of Castile flew highest in the cloudless blue sky, there on the banks of the Genil River.

A cortege of two hundred Moors rides down from the red walled town in tight formation. Boabdil leads this procession that will close forever eight centuries of Islamic history and culture. They ride at a smart pace and in silence. Kursiyya turbans hood their white burnooses, the cascading cloaks that drape the Moors. The Spanish are accustomed to seeing these same white burnooses soaring like wings behind mounted fighters in thunderous gallop, charging wild-eyed horses, curved scimitars raised high, voices roaring in defiance, 'Death to the Infidels'. Not today.

The Spanish regents, poised figures of grandeur and immense dignity, wait as the conquered army rides up the hill. Their animals hold fast on the highest rise, heaving and steaming, whickering and pawing the earth. Boabdil, without dismounting, bows low to Ferdinand and Ysabela. It has been agreed that the key to Granada will pass to Spain without their leader having to kiss the hands of the King and Queen. Instead, as a sign of respect, Boabdil bends and presses his lips to Ferdinand's sleeve. The Moor's son, who has been a hostage along with four hundred Muslim captives, is released.

To surrender Granada at the Alhambra, the most magnificent of man's creations, the palace where future queens of Europe will grow up to be married into political alliances, cracks the heart of the vanquished sultan, and he says to Ysabela, "The hand of God is to be traced in all things." Neither the victors, imbued with triumph, nor the defeated, in agony over their immense loss, can hold back from weeping.

The route into the walled city is hung with tapestries and banners; the ground graveled to prevent the horses slipping. The fields are filled with a cheering mixture of rag-tag peasants and armored soldiers. Crowds roam the city like locust in search of crops. Hefting hoes and swords, they jostle for a view of the royals. They witness the King and Queen's slow ride toward the Calat Alhambra, the Red Fortress, Islam's last citadel in Iberia. Multitudes have fled the city, knowing this to be just another bloody struggle to benefit the few and leave the peasants starving. The Cross and Banner rise in the sky over the high Tower of Comares as the *Cronista de Armas* shout their proclamation, "Granada! Granada for King Ferdinand and Queen Ysabela!"

The conquering entourage circles the Tower of the Hall of Ambassadors. A hemispheric dome, adorned by mosaic stars and suns, is supported by forty alabaster columns and ten arches. Centered under the dome, a fountain rests on the back of ten stone lions. Built by the caliph Abd-ar-Rahman III, Protector of the Jews, it holds a fifty-meter pool of crystal water. The lions represent the ten lost tribes of Israel, and the invisible pool on their backs, the teaching of the Prophet Mohammed.

The Spanish regents planned this momentous event, the transfer of power, as more a spiritual ceremony than a military conquest. Absent are the usual trumpets and drums heralding victory. The Queen's chapel singers surround her, chanting Te Deum Laudamus, the Hymn of Thanks. The haunting cadence reverberates through the starred mosaic halls:

We praise thee, O God: we acknowledge thee to be the Lord. All the earth doth worship thee: the Father everlasting. To thee all Angels cry aloud : the Heavens, and all the Powers therein. To thee Cherubim and Seraphim : continually do cry, Holy, Holy, Holy : Lord God of Sabaoth; Heaven and earth are full of the Majesty of thy glory. The glorious company of the Apostles: praise thee. The goodly fellowship of the Prophets: praise thee. The noble army of Martyr : praise thee. The holy Church throughout all the world: doth acknowledge thee; The Father : of an infinite Majesty; Thine honourable, true and only Son; Also the Holy Ghost: the Comforter. Thou art the King of Glory: O Christ. Thou art the everlasting So : of the Father. When thou tookest upon thee to deliver man : thou didst not abhor the Virgin's womb. When thou hadst overcome te sharpness of death: thou didst open the Kingdom of Heaven to all believers. Thou sittest at the right hand of God: in the glory of the Father. We believe that thou shalt come: to be our Judge. We therefore pray thee, help thy servants: whom thou hast redeemed with thy precious blood. Make them to be numbered with thy Saints: in glory everlasting.

The Queen kneels and weeps.

Moving through the crowd of turbaned men and women in chadors is a tall, modestly dressed man, inconspicuous among the throng of grandees, soldiers, monks and peasants. Only three days before, he had been on the coast at the La Rabida Monastery visiting his son, Diego.

As ward of the Queen, Colón has received a modest stipend of *maravidi*. Surprised by her summons to Granada, he ponders if this means redemption, that the Crown might finally support his cause. He walks aside the yellow stone-wall that encircles the city. Rows of orange trees line the narrow streets marked by columns of green and purple marble. Looking into the sky in a sun-baked plaza Cristóbal imagines a day when the crowds might be cheering him.

Cristóbal Colón did not expect a call to Granada at a time so critical for the Queen's attention. He was prepared to wait several weeks for an audience, but she called for him the day after his arrival. Nothing had, or ever would, dissuade him from believing his plan was divinely inspired. Yet somewhere in his heart Cristóbal Colón knew that he was before the Queen because of a woman — actually, two women.

In 1484 Colón had been introduced to Eleanora de Bobadilla, whose older sister, Beatriz, had been the Queen's childhood companion. Now Beatriz was the Marchioness of Moya, Ysabel's devoted lady in waiting and best friend.

Cristóbal cultivated a relationship with the younger sister, intoxicating the impressionable young woman with stories of adventure. He told Elenora of his survival in battle, how he swam miles to shore after being shipwrecked off the coast of Portugal. He whispered mysteries of the gold trade in North Africa, the Maghreb. Perhaps he exaggerated a bit. Perhaps he embellished the exotic nature of the Island of Celos on the eastern Mediterranean Sea, and being closest port to the Silk Road, filled with Turks, Hindus, and Chinese.

Everywhere he went, everyone he spoke to, had an opinion about the shape and size of the earth. Every sailor he met believed the world was as round as the moon.

Eleanora fell madly in love with the Genoan and entreated her sister, Beatriz, to promote his cause to the Queen. Beatriz told Queen Ysabela of the gold, silver and precious stones, the spices that would flow into the kingdom from Japan and China. The fabulous riches first described by Marco Polo, the trade of these treasures on the Silk Road now ended since the fall of Constantinople to the Turks.

The thought of Spain being the apotheosis of world scientific knowledge delighted Ysabela. What honor it would bring to solve the puzzle of the earth's shape and size. And what more exalted beneficence than to shepherd the holy word of Jesus Christ to countless pagans? She reveled in the vision of glory these twin triumphs would bring to her reign.

Beatriz praised Cristóbal's pious nature, his charisma, his handsome features, a man of courage and taste for adventure. The Queen summoned him.

Cristóbal Colón knew that despite her interest and favor, Ysabela's power in this regard was limited. Many of her most trusted advisors in the Talavera Commission, even the King, were opposed to the project as risky, and of doubtful reward. The Commission had kept pushing back his arguments, farther and farther, like the promise of the horizon that a ship never reaches.

Colón enters the room high in the Cromarte Tower of the Alhambra, his worn leather boots squeaking his presence on the intricately tiled floor. Ysabela reaches out a regal arm to greet him, glad for that day in Cordova in 1486, when, because the Ocean Sea was within the jurisdiction of Castile, she, rather than Ferdinand, had first received him. She sits on a cushioned sofa. Royal rings adorn her hands as she strokes the ermine trim of her yellow silk jacket. As Colón walks in and bows, she recalls him from his last supplication. Tall and handsome, but dressed like a shop-keep.

Ysabela and Cristóbal are close in age, and like her, he has light blue eyes and a fair complexion. Elanora calls him stubborn and silent, but the Queen is attracted to his religious fervor. Accustomed to unsure people, she finds no insecurity in Cristóbal Colón, a man of reflection and action. The Queen bids him to state his case.

Colón's presentation is organic, always growing in depth rather than length, evolving with new information for fresh listeners. He begins each rendition with, 'To free the Holy Land of Jerusalem'.

In an inviting manner, Cristóbal says, "I pray that this holy mission brings freedom to Jerusalem. Observe your Majesty," and unrolls a chart on a table near the Queen.

"This chart was made by the master cosmographer, Paolo Toscanelli of Florence and sent to the court in Lisbon. King John requested it 15 years ago and asked one question, 'What is the shortest route to the spice regions?' The maestro's answer was *'brevior via ad loca aromatum'*, 'to cross the ocean.'"

The Queen settles into her travelling throne, attentive to the presentation, her lips a flat line, with one eye higher than the other, as if her mind holds a very stubborn question.

"The chart is a compendium of all that the ancients knew. Here, the new discoveries of the African coast. Here, the Ocean Islands. Using the accepted computations of the Persian, Alfraganus, and the Phoenician, Marinus of Tyre, I have placed the Great Island of Japan and the mainland of China here, closer to Iberia than Your Majesty's great scholars place them."

Ysabela follows Colón's finger, now pointing to an island labeled Japan far from Portugal. In between a multitude of smaller islands are scattered in the 'Unknown Seas'. Beyond Japan and China and through

India is the entire continent of Asia to the eastern shore of the Mediterranean Sea.

Cristóbal Colón's hand sweeps the chart tracing the alternate route. "The Portuguese have advanced down the coast of Africa to here," indicating a point just below the bulge in the continent at their settlement of Joa de Mina. "Just how far they must go to round the tip and retrace themselves north is unknown. It may take years. But the shortest route to the treasures of India lies in sailing west, from here," and pointing to the Canaries, he flourishes his hand across the chart, "straight over the Ocean Sea."

The Queen interrupts, "Yes. I know of the Portuguese efforts and the treasure they've spent searching for gold on the coast of Africa. It's been fifty years and without much to show for it." Her shoulders tighten and she waves a hand dismissively, her fingers bouncing like spider legs. "Oh, they say they're looking for the path to India, but I don't believe it. It's gold they want."

The Queen pulls at her handkerchief, her once delicate fingers now twisted from the worries of a monarch. She knows the challenges facing Colón and is silent for a moment, measuring what to say. "Many learned men have told me that perhaps some land may indeed exist to the west. But they say that no ship can return once it has passed the farthest line of the known waters. That there is a zone of calm a thousand leagues west. Is there not great danger in failing to find land? Wouldn't you be unable to return?"

"Your highness, I believe, as most do, that there is land to the west. Every sailor who casts off into the Ocean Sea risks his life. I have been to sea for twenty-five years, sailing the waters of the world. I have crossed the Mediterranean many times from the Pillars of Hercules to the furthest Greek Islands. I have explored the coasts of Africa, Europe, and Asia. I have sailed in the great North Sea, to the English Islands, and beyond to Ultimate Thule, the Land of Ice. I am at home in the Azores and the Canary Archipelagos. Everywhere, I have sought the counsel of thoughtful men; sailors, scholars, priests, cosmographers, Christians, Jews, and Moors. All who have the slightest sense of geography understand and believe that by going west one rounds the earth's sphere, and arrives at the shores of Asia and the Empire of the Great Kahn."

The Queen withdraws from studying the chart. Unsure what she wants to hear from Colón, she needs a conclusive argument to take to the King, something irrefutable. Her hands are clasped, as in prayer. Thinking how Ferdinand will respond, the Talavera's Commission's report in mind, she says, "And in your voyages and encounters, have you heard no doubts? My advisors say that there is little reason to support such a risky venture."

Ysabela was being kind. The report in fact had called his hypothesis 'mad' with 'colossal errors', that the distance across the Ocean Sea was far greater, the majority of the earth's surface being water, not dry land.

Cristóbal replies, "They say that I am not learned in letters, that I am an ignorant sailor. As the Lord is my witness, what I have encountered are facts of validation. It is by sailing, and at the water's edge, that I've heard confirming stories of living fact. I was told by the brother of my dead wife, God rest her sacred soul, that on the Isle of Flores he saw the dead bodies of men with yellow faces and straight black hair, the same as the people of Japan and China."

The Queen interrupts. "But what can I tell my advisors besides rumors and salty tales?" She stands and walks to within his arm's reach. "You tell us that the Earth is round but I see it with my own eyes and it is flat. And even supposing it to be round, how can a ship descend on one side and return? Water does not flow up. You cannot sail up a waterfall."

Cristóbal Colón, pauses, his head turning slightly to the left seeming to listen to an unheard voice, and responds "Your majesty, the sun that shines on us now will do the same in China while we sleep in the night. In the morning it will return to greet us in the East, having crossed the great continent of Asia. By sailing west we do the same as the sun. With enough time we can traverse the earth and return to Iberia from across the land of the Persians and the rest of Europe."

The Queen paces, stroking the furniture, twirling a curl of her hair around a finger, a sure clue she is agitated. Colón pivots, his body turning to face her as she worries the room.

"Your Majesty, *mare totum navigabile*, all seas are navigable. Between the edge of Spain and the beginning of India the sea is short. All seas are peopled by lands and every country has its east and west. In all the world there is nothing that has only one side. The ancients, whose comments we revere, when they speak to the question, say the same. The Ocean Sea can be crossed to land."

The Queen leans in, clutching her lace handkerchief in one hand then the other, her countenance deep in judgment. Her troubled eyes look to Cristóbal Colón. She has no real questions for the Captain General, but seeks to measure his commitment.

Cristóbal Colón knows that his moment has come. All the mathematical calculations, all the pronouncements of the world's great thinkers, all the predictions of size and shape, all the myths and sea stories, all are to no avail without the Queen's belief in him and his vision.

"Your Majesty. It's not just me. It is Aristotle and Eratosthenes. It is Seneca. It is Microbius. It is Bacon. The greatest minds for a thousand years have been saying the same thing; 'The world is round'. Travel at its broadest and you must go approximately fifty thousand kilometers over four continents. As the Lord revealed to Pythagoras in the 6th century, we live on a sphere. In the 8th century Virgilius, the Bishop of Salzburg, taught a doctrine in regard to the 'rotundity of the earth'. It's not just me, your majesty." Stepping forward, arms extended, his voice rising, "If the great ancients, Aristotle and Ptolemy, Cardinal Pierre d'Ally and Pliny were to speak to the royal commissions, if Plato were to stand here before your Highness, would there be a moment's hesitation?

"Your majesty, my mind has considered nothing else for nearly two decades. I saw the truth early and it has occupied my mind. Even in my sleep. I see China shining like a brilliant star and am willing to risk body and soul to reach it. My absolute certainty of success comes from my dependence on God. I am but his agent, chosen for the accomplishment of great ends. I cannot fail. God has decreed it."

Colón detects a change in the Queen's expression, a lowering of her chin, and her eyes less challenging.

"The men who scoffed at these great thinkers, who called them fools and dreamers, as I am called now, you know not their names. They are forgotten to us. Why, your Majesty? It is because those men who they derided, who they funned, the men history reveres as the great thinkers of the human race, have blessed us with knowledge. With God's guidance they have shown us the way to organize our lives, to govern our peoples, to build our cities. Let them be your commission. Your Majesty is destined to stand with those giants, and Destiny will not be cheated. Lead your great nation and carry the word of God as commanded by Jesus Christ, our Lord and Savior."

Ysabela exalts her regal posture, waves her hand high, smiles and says, "I am with you Cristóbal. You are my knight."

Chapter 19
Santangel & Ferdinand

Three days after Cristóbal Colón's audience with Queen Ysabela, the excitement of conquest has not diminished. In the Comares Tower of the Alhambra, the King of Spain preens. He considers his reflection in the mirror, seeing himself taller, his hair fuller, and his wide-spaced, deceitful eyes warmer. Resplendent in his red satin breeches and yellow doublet, a laced brocaded vest covering his white satin blouse, he admires his splendor and celebrates his royal magnificence.

Having ruled for thirteen years, the king has come to certain conclusions. He and Spain are one and the same. All men are his vassals. He might grant protection, exercise his grace, or he may not. His word rules. It is possible to appeal to the king, but impossible to appeal against him. The birds sing his glory and animals deliver their bodies for his table. The grains yield his bread and the grapes his wine. The forests grow to build his ships, and the Ocean Sea and the rivers flow to carry his emissaries and armies. The sun and moon exist to provide light for his conquests and trade. The stars and planets are placed to center on him on Earth.

His arm sweeps high, his hand reaching out to greet his Royal Treasurer, Luís de Santangel. There is comfort in the King's smile, his bloodless lips, for these are his days of glory, when his very majesty is being enshrined. He has ridden his battle horse, Al Kamsah, through the gates of the walled city as crowds cheered his path, although he starved them under siege for more than a year. Granada and its surrounding region, its back to the Mediterranean and across to Morocco, has been the final battle of a ten-year blood-bath, in which famine, disease, death, and hatred were the lot of the people. He has crushed the Muslim population, forcing them off the Iberian Peninsula, their homes for over eight hundred years. And then, at the foot of the sacred Alhambra, he has received the sword of surrender from the Emir. The victorious King, defender of the faith, wielder of the Sword of God, feels immaculate. As an act of cleansing, he orders the burning of over ten thousand Arabic manuscripts.

Santangel bows, sweeping his soft hat to his side. He surrenders to the King's hold on his shoulders, a gesture well received, and which unseen eyes will note and report. The crown has been the avatar of safety and well being for the Santangel family, and Luís has been in audience with the King in various capacities throughout his life. In royal favor as the King's Treasurer, men petition Luís with gifts of silver and gold, fine wine, and invitations. A man could hold no greater status than Ferdinand in Santangel's eyes, and he himself could be no humbler. Yet, his awareness of being humble holds no humility. He feels an overwhelming sense of esteem for the King. Still, why does the King not protect his subjects? This man before him has united their kingdoms of Aragon and Castile, a centuries old dream. Now, victorious in his decade long crusade against the Muslim religion, he is blessed by Rome, loved by his subjects, feared by his enemies, and envied by the crowns of Christendom. What more could a King ask?

The King releases Santangel's shoulders, guiding him to a chair. Sunshine fills the tower and reflects off the high blue mosaic walls designed in riddles to illuminate the faithful. Santangel's courtly manner is exaggerated, executed in slow motion. He is careful to avoid arousing Ferdinand's suspicious nature, and understands that the King will not reject topics for consideration out of hand. Rather, there will be an easy, practiced turning aside of things His Majesty does not wish to discuss.

The King says, "It is good to see you here, Santangel, you look fit. How are you enjoying Meli's hospitality?"

Santangels's speech is measured, his tone moderate. "The Duke is most generous, sire, and he sends his warm greetings and again congratulates you and the Queen. And if I might add my own humble congratulations, this is truly a spectacular and blessed moment for your kingdom."

Ferdinand breathes deeply; every compliment offered is well received. They toast a French wine to God's grace.

"Now Santangel, you know that I know you met with John's ambassador, what's his name. How did you find that visit?"

"Yes sire, I met with Hieronymus Deza three days ago across the Jalon River in Perivilla. I was traveling with a man from your Canaries as my valet. It will very much interest you, Your Majesty."

Ferdinand has long admired the detailed accuracy in the reports of his royal treasurer. It is one of many attributes the King credits to Santangel's fine mind, the quiet force of his focus, a persistent push of each thought to the very end. The King trusts his treasurer and arranges himself in comfort to devote attention to the story. He strokes a fresh beard on his usually clean-shaven chin, and rests his royal side against a cushioned velvet arm.

"It was good to see my old friend, Deza. He's a bit larger than before, but retains his wit and discriminating insight. He was quick to convey congratulations from King John, and he adds his own humble salutation. Beyond the topic of the war, his interest was centered on the gold trade from the Maghreb. However, I detected a note of displeasure. Knowing the man's genius at masquerade, it was probably intentionally communicated. Most likely referring to adventures made by mariners out of Your Majesty's port of Palos and into their African territory."

"I'm not surprised, they've begun to coin gold reals for the first time. He has ships scouring the black coast for the 'river of gold'."

"Yes, Your Majesty. And they are using their African settlement at El Mina not far from the Canaries as a base of operations in search of it. In any event Deza let it slip that there has been a substantial increase in treasure ships. Of course it was not a slip. I believe King John directed the news, perhaps as a taunt."

"Most likely so, Luís. And what else?"

It is Santangel's moment. The efforts of many, and perhaps their lives also, depend on what he now says, and how it is received. With the end of the war there will be land and power allocated. Those nobles who had contributed most to the cause of the *reconquista*, in treasure or on the battlefield, will be rewarded. The order will shift. Other matters will take precedence, matters of politics, power, and rank. Many in the court have found it expedient to ridicule Cristóbal Colón's plan of sailing west to reach the east. Those that favor it lack sufficient influence. A royal chip to their side would upset much, and more so if the voyage was successful. He knows that Ferdinand has an eye for risk, the way some men have an eye for a horse's heart.

"Well, Your Majesty, I was traveling with a Canarian, a man called Gotzun, as my squire. Deza inquired about the man, and I saw him speaking directly with him out of my hearing. Immediately after, out of the blue, he asked about Cristóbal Colón."

"That's very interesting, Luís. Was there more?"

"Yes, Your Majesty. He inquired as to Your Majesty's opinion of the Genoan's venture."

"I just today dismissed that man on advise of Talavera. John knows my attention has been on Granada."

Santangel carefully comments, "Perhaps King John is concerned that your attention will shift to exploration."

"And so, you believe John has a plan? That he intends to encroach himself on my realm in the Canaries?"

Santangel wonders; 'Is it time? Has he taken the bait? Should I risk it all?' "It is not a faint possibility, in my humble opinion. They have for decades pursued the goal to round Africa as a route to India. King John is following Prince Henry's unremitting exploration of the coast. As you know, their man, Dias, has rounded the tip of Africa. If Cristóbal

Colón is correct, and there exists a shorter route to the spice, it would undercut and render useless their long and costly efforts. It would be a catastrophe for the Portuguese."

Ferdinand warms to the thought of a disaster for his rival. He enjoys a game that ends in a win or loss. He thinks 'Oh how I'd love to fuck that cross-eyed pimp.'

The King says, "My admiral in Majorca tells me Dias's crew mutinied. Threatened to slit his throat if they continued to the edge of the world."

Encouraged by the King's interest, Santangel closes his eyes briefly to calm himself. "That's true. The Portuguese have been seventy years trying to round that cape of storms. But the next voyage, which is sure to happen, will bring them around the southern tip of Africa, into the Indian Ocean and the sea to the Indies. To Calicut and the Malabar Coast. To the spices of Celon and Goa. Only a step away from India and its riches."

"My astrologers say that Colón's plan is an illusion, derived from his wish that it be so. They tell me that he dreams it, that a dream misleads him. They tell me he has conversations with himself or with some phantom. I don't know. And what do my nobles say? The last I heard they thought that by sailing west, the Genoan, would sail with a ship of fools, men who would never see port again."

Santangel was ready for this challenge. "The Dukes for the most part are opposed. I have compiled a list of your loyal subjects who would encourage your assent." He hands a sealed folio to the King. "As you can see there is support from a wide variety of your Court. The merchants from Sevilla, Pinelli and Rivarolo, seek expanded markets."

The King is all business now. "Yes, the Genoese have a genius to make a fine profit in new markets, without the cost of conquest or administration. What is that ditty?" And he recites:

> *"So many are the Genoese*
> *And so sure-footed everywhere,*

> *They go to any place they please*
> *And re-create their city there."*

Ferdinand surveys the list of fifteen names. "Who else is here?"

Santangel has been meticulous in his selection and says, "Of course those with sugar revenues from the Canaries are included."

"Yes, I see, Medina Sidonia and Celi, they have already made their wishes known to me. The Queen's confessor, Fray Juan Perez at La Rabida, as well as Alonso de Quintanilla," then to himself, 'They support the plan?' "Who is Dr. Gegorio Fernandez?"

"Astronomer to the court, your Majesty. As well as Hernando de Talavera."

"Talavera? What is his name doing here? I thought his commission declined support?"

"Yes, they did sire, Señor Talavelra objected to its price."

Ferdinand, sharing his royal opinion says, "Talavera is a man who measures out his life in terms of what each minute cost."

Santagel says, "However, the Commission did say that possibly the effort was feasible. Actually, Talavera, whose perspicacity is well known to Your Majesty, is whole-heartedly in favor of the voyage."

"But, have you heard what the Genoan wants, Santangel? Colón wants a title here, and a large part of everything there. And he wants to be Viceroy of all he manages to stumble across. What arrogance from a family of petty thieves.

What do you think?"

Santangel recalls Colon's Uncle Nuncio, how Cristóbal would like to evaporate that blemish on his family name. He says, "It seems, like the childhood pox that marks you for life, one is never finished with one's family. But titles are cheaply granted Your Majesty. Viceroy, Baron,

Duke, words that cost you nothing. Terms can change. On the other side, if the voyage is successful, the rewards will be glorious."

"I don't know, Santangel. Cristóbal Colón is a strange man. His hand is unnatural. An arrogant hand, so full of dots and dashes. And he speaks a stilted tongue, not only in a foreign accent, but almost in an archaic language."

"That is true sire. But what are the King's valiant knights and hidalgos to do now that the war is over? Perhaps it would serve the king's purpose if Your Majesty had more titles and promises of wealth to bestow on those warriors that pursue this voyage. For the glory of God? Also, many with large debts might prefer another chance to serve Your Majesty, rather than burden your goals."

Ferdinand adjusts his collar finding it uncomfortable in this time of conquest and glory to consider a possible future conflict in his kingdom. Santangel continues, "And then, sire, there is the question of protecting your rights under the Treaty of Alcáçovas. His Holiness did a great service to secure Portugal's pledge to honor your sovereignty in the Canary Islands, as well as all isles and lands to the West. Even if the Genoan fails, the voyage will serve to strengthen your claim of title should any others follow him and seek to claim that which is rightfully yours alone."

The King's eyes brighten. He thinks how clever he is to have Luís in his service. "That's a fine point, Santangel, I had not thought it."

"You are aware, sire, that the funds are available. There would be no cost."

"Cost! The cost is but a fraction of what I paid last year for Inez's wedding. But you're right, the problem of what my Dukes' barons will do must be dealt with, and the soonest is best. Left alone it is certain that they will fight among each other."

Santangel watches the King calculate and asks, "Would not the Pope encourage your efforts to spread the sacred word of Jesus?"

His Highness mutters his royal logic to himself. 'Ysabel wants it. That sailor knew what he was doing when he said it was her destiny to be called 'The Catholic Queen'.'

Then, "I'll give it more thought, Santangel. You're certain that Deza will advise John to fund the sail?"

Santangel thinks, 'as I know the sun will rise,' and responds, "I believe so, Your Majesty. Deza has just sent his recommendation by currier. The Canarian, Gotzun, told me that Deza suggested he accompany him back to Lisbon."

"Has that happened? Did he go with him?"

"No, sire. He remains with me at the Duke's castle. The Genoan, having failed to receive your royal permission, has just left to return to La Rabida where his son lives."

The royal treasurer measures his next comment, speaking in a voice of utter confidentiality, "Elenora Bobadilla, who rules in Gomera, is at the castle also, Sire."

The wide brown eyes of the King flinch. Santangel measures the effect of mentioning the beauty's name, but continues as if he hadn't. "There is another matter, sire. I hesitate to mention it because it is but a mere feeling, a sense, I had. An impression."

"What's that, Luís.? By all means tell me."

The King's breath stops. This is the sweetmeat on the bone that Ferdinand has been waiting to hear, the kernel that Santangel always holds back, as if to say, 'This is it. What you must know'. Ferdinand leans forward to the edge of his chair, his eyes narrow in concentration.

Santangel speaks in a hushed tone. "As you know, Sire, since '27 with their discovery of the Azores, the Portuguese have made several attempts at voyages further west, using those islands as a jumping off point. They have referred to them as 'excursions'.

"Yes, excursions, so quaint. I know of them. They number eight, and they all failed."

"Perhaps not all, Sire."

The king's eyes light up.

Ferdinand struggles to keep his thoughts coherent. 'The damned Portuguese and their infernal 'excursions'. Now with the fall of Granada, my reign at its pinnacle of glory, and that moron, John, a man who has opposed my every effort for the glory of Jesus Christ, would like nothing else than to divert the attention of the Holy See. After all, with the war ongoing for ten years and the city under siege for more than a year, this triumph has been a foregone conclusion. News of a water passage to India would spread like wildfire and there would be a rush to capitalize by the Florentines and Genoans. Hmmmm. The 'lucky eighth excursion'.'

Ferdinand had not expected to deal with these complications. This was to be his triumph and his alone. Except for Ysabel, of course. Yes, the Queen. His wife, the woman who still grinds him for every indiscretion. Elenora, a dalliance so long ago, yet was it not just last week when Ysabela called her a scum-whore? How repulsive to chastise me, the King. To punish me. I don't need these peccadilloes now during my great triumph.' He is calculating, pressing into service his formidable powers to put things moving in the right direction. Perhaps there is a way to resolve several circumstances.

He sighs and his fingers roll the edge of a yellow linen parchment, as he considers, 'If Ysabel knew of Elenora's presence here, and she probably does, life is to become much less pleasant. That bitch will foment trouble, that's certain. The Genoan's plan may prove to be very convenient. If this voyage was to proceed, and Colón's plan is to leave from the Canaries, from her very castle, she would be the last to have the Genoan's ear. A distinct advantage for an ambitious woman. But she would need to be there for that, and so she must return to the Canaries in order to posture her claim. An idea I could make happen for her.'

Ferdinand cannot help but remember the woman. He sighs again as he recalls Elenora Bobadilla, her kohl lined eyes, the taste of her full lips and the firm nipples crowning her ample breasts. He permits himself a lingering moment in the poetry of Aeschylus, 'Her soul as serene as the calm of the seas, her beauty adorns the richest finery, her flower of love fatal to the hearts."

On the parchment he is holding, now with a well-curled corner, is a copy of the very letter written three days ago by Deza and Santangel in Perivilla, and sent under seal to Portugal and King John. Ferdinand congratulates himself on his efficient web of informants, so often the source of his prescience. The King considers the phrase, "the lucky eighth" and mouths the salient words in the report, "why not have a larger stake in the game to India with your reach from the Ocean Sea as well as around Africa?"

"If there is nothing else, I thank you for your service, Santangel. My best to all our friends."

Dismissed, the royal treasurer smiles cordially, bows, and without turning, withdraws, whispering to himself, 'pic-poc, pic-poc'.

Chapter 20
Good-Bye

Home on his island, on Tenerife, Yoggi wants attention and nuzzles Revela's side. Instead, she fumbles over her brother, brushing back his hair, pulling at his clothes. She clenches her teeth to make the tears stop, swallows a choke and thinks, 'how quickly his little boy face has changed.' The wound on his cheek from the soldier's ring is now more like a continuation of his smile. 'It's kind of attractive' she thinks. 'And his eyes are playful, no longer drowsy'. She pulls at his collar, worried but hopeful.

"You've got to take care of yourself now brother. This sail wasn't much, you know. It's a big ocean." She knows that nothing has changed the fact that Dante is a wayward, skinny child in terrible danger.

"I'll be fine sister. You're the one who... you've got to be careful. Stay with the Jews." And Dante thinks of David, certain he will protect Revela, as if wishing it would make it so.

For a moment, Revela's face is a vacant stare, betraying the dark psyche of a woman in panic, as if she has realized a danger too late. She holds Dante's gaze, a lifeline, thinking how one's fortune can turn so quickly, so completely, in a moment. She tries to quiet her mind, but her heart throbs in her chest and pulses of fear run through her. Then, as quickly as her life has changed, Revela does what's necessary. "Be careful."

"I will...you too. It's all right."

They stroll down the beach, tiny figures beneath the towering cliffs that the Guanches call 'Los Gigantes'. Yoggi chases gulls that are chasing sand crabs, his tongue flapping, his paw prints disappearing in the sand.

Brother and sister, arms circling each other's waist, head toward Gotzun who waits on a skiff rocking in the surf.

Revela stops to kick off her shoes and Dante asks, "What do you think is happening on the farm?"

Revela shrugs, bobbing her head. Unlike Dante she has often thought about the life they left behind, wishing she could burn the past and everyone in it.

"Oh, you know. The pigs, the chickens, the stink. Father is probably swearing at Segundo for not latching the south pasture gate."

Dante walks with his head down, thinking about their footprints, the way they disappear as soon as they pluck their feet from the watery sand. He remembers his life and knows what it will no longer be, but not what it might become. He says, "Can you imagine if they hadn't tried to rape you? If we were still at home and we never left? And when old, in our forties, our hair gray, our teeth yellow. And I smell like Juan Abreu. We'd be sitting on the porch, talking about our lives and I would say, 'Oh, if only we were young again. I would sail away across the Ocean Sea.'"

She looks up and smiles at him, pauses to consider what he's said, then glances higher. The sun's glare prevents her from seeing the top of the cliff. "And what about me? You'd have left me to feed and clean for your brothers for the rest of my life?" Then to herself, 'there really is more to him than even I thought.'

"I remember once when we were walking on the beach together. I must have been about seven or eight. So you were very young. We played a game and I was a princess from far away. And you were the prince, King Ferdinand's son. You tried to save me from a terrible dragon. But you couldn't. And you told me that you had to die."

They wept as they spoke, spoke as they wept, and then embraced, their cheeks pressed together and their tears mixing. Holding tight, she kisses him twice, the second with all her strength. She lets go, then looks at him and kisses him hard once more, as if this last embrace will cancel her loss. Heartbroken, each retreats to that circle of solitude when one must face the world alone. She turns away. What else can a brother and sister do?

Dante wades into the water and boards the small sailboat. Yoggi remains in the shallow surf with Revela, knowing his duty, whining at the separation, his triangle ears standing straight up. Gotzun raises the sail. Standing in the stern holding on to a mast-stay, Dante waves good- bye, and on a puff of wind the skiff heels to port and sets course on a tack northwest towards Gomera.

Watching the skiff sail on the infinite plateau of ocean, Revela cries silent, unstoppable tears.

Ship's Log

Friday, 17 August 1492:

"Two weeks have passed since our departure from Palos, and the crew has become restive. I am beginning to fear for the safety of Doña Elenora. I am also wondering why Martín is taking so long."

Sunday, 19 August 1492

"A special mass was said today for the safe return of Martín Alonso and Doña Elanora. My enterprise is in God's hands."

On Friday morning Elenora Bobadilla returns to Gomera from Gran Canaria. On the Santa Maria, Cristóbal Colón watches her caravel slip into the bay to anchor where her small castle overlooks the most favorable passage into the harbor.

The Captain General has selected an entourage to present to Elenora Bobadilla including Luís de Torres, Maestra Bernal, and Dante. Colón keeps the boy at his side. As they approach land Dante is again in awe, marveling at the huge rock formations reaching high into the cloudless sky, and imagining their frightening mass under water. While provisioning for the voyage they have all been ashore several times and experienced the exquisite courtesy of the island peasants. They make the pier and tie off the skiff. The small group climbs the broad earthen steps that wind up the promontory.

Wide maguey cacti guard the narrow road that leads to the arched stone entrance of the compound. Rows heavy with harvest ready dark grapes line a large vegetable patch spotted with guava and papaya trees. There is a rising smell of fresh cut hay. Bernal guides them through the gardens. It is near sunset and the cliff-birds swoop, swifts and gannets skimming the evening meal of insects that swarm over the blackish-green grape vines.

A welcoming party, four women and three men, Elenora in the center, is waiting to greet them in the late afternoon light. All have previously met the sailors before her return. They stand like chess pieces, between two tall Canary Palms silhouetted in the blue sky.

The Governess does not hesitate. Holding aloft the trail of her dress she approaches the Captain General, her extended hand pressing his with an excitement and anticipation matched in the Captain's eyes.

A sultry, "Captain". He bows, and fully grasps her hand to kiss it. "Governness."

Maestra Bernal, the ship's doctor, makes the crew's introduction to Elanora. Each sailor stiffens in expectation of her gaze and she does not disappoint, making eye contact with each man. Her eyes linger on de Torres, more so than the others, assessing him. The Captain General has the luxury of watching her. Here, framed by the pristine garden with lush greens and splashes of yellow hyacinth, he remembers Aeschylus, writing of Helen;

'Soul as serene as the calm of the seas, beauty that adorned the richest finery, gentle eyes piercing like an arrow, flower of love fatal to the hearts.'

The servants dressed in black skirts and white blouses bow, affirming the privilege of servitude, the grateful oppressed. They cross themselves as they were taught good Catholics must, the oldest with burnt-out eyes, repeating the gesture many times as if she were a spider weaving web on her chest. The sailors enter the foyer and the shy Gomeran women dip their heads, drawing in their underlips as they serve trays of red-orange papaya and sun-warm peaches.

Dante is last to be introduced to the Governess. She has been told of the boy, and that he looks like her own son, Hernand. Intrigued, she awards him a friendly smile, more than an easy grin. Pulling him by the arm she says, "Come. Let's go into the garden." When Dante hesitates. "You're not afraid of me, are you?"

Dante has heard talk of the Governess and has practiced how he might greet her; a sweep of his arm and bow from the hip, or perhaps a snap to attention and salute. But no rehearsal could have prepared him for Elenora's beauty. His knees buckle when she chooses him above all the others to receive her attention. In the presence of a Muse, radiant beyond his boyish imagination, the boy falls.

They stroll the manicured grounds. "You must be very proud to be shipmate with so great a man as the Captain General."

"Yes, of course. He is a master sailor and navigator. He even showed me the ship's log. I read your name in it."

The Governess almost blushes. Her long black hair falls forward as she dips her head and widens her kohl-dark eyes. Appearing impressed she says, "Really. How fortunate for you. And where do you come from?"

"We're from the Mouger region, a small farm near there."

An expert in projecting an illusion of feminine trust, her eyes encourage his confidence. "We? Is your brother with you?"

Dante realizes he is about to reveal information that perhaps he shouldn't, but he has no defense to this woman.

"No... My sister, Revela. She's on Tenerife now, with....friends."

"I see. Well perhaps I'll get a chance to meet her also." She brushes a lock of Dante's sun-bleached hair. The Governess has raised three children and genuinely appreciates the company of young men and women. Dante does bear a resemblance to her oldest, Hernand Peraza, next in line to inherit rule of the island but whose patrimony has been threatened by a noble.

"You are a handsome young man, and on such a dangerous voyage. I admire bravery. Have you enjoyed my island?"

As Dante's eyes fix on the woman's inviting look, his foot snags on a large root and he stumbles. He reaches and holds tight to the Governess' arm.

Embarrassed by his boyish clumsiness, he gushes, "Oh, sorry." He gathers himself and stammers, "This is a wonderful place. The people are so friendly, and everything grows here. And the ocean is much warmer and clearer than Spain."

"Oh, but this is Spain, Dante. You are at home here."

They circle the grounds, Elenora naming the various fruits, commenting on their ripeness. Gaining ease, Dante slips into his La Sirena sociability, laughing at his own humor, luxuriating in the Governess' attention. As a parting gesture Elenora extends her hand to him, perhaps inviting a kiss, then excuses herself. With a last look over her shoulder, she smiles and enters the house.

As the sun sets, candles are lit in the castle. The Captain General enters a barren room, void of any adornment except for a table and chairs and two large urns each holding a hibiscus bush of yellow flowers. The faded walls are a soothing yellowish white, softer than the flowers. An exquisite freshness dominates the air. A water stain on the tile floor circles one of the urns, the result of a year-old crack in the red pottery. A carafe of the island's wine and two crystal glasses sit on a table.

Looking out through an arched window as if searching for a sign, Cristóbal views a courtyard and a small chapel. Beyond are the waves of the Ocean Sea, lazily rolling landward. The light pours through the window sparkling on the faded walls. The sun on the horizon and magenta sky reminded him of the Azores where he had lived a happy life, married for 5 years to the governor's daughter, Filipa Moniz Perestrelo. They spent many days with their son Diego playing on the island's beaches. He thinks, 'when things are wonderful, how wonderful they can be.'

Standing next to the table, Elenora's long nailed hand rests on the head of a lion carved on a tall-backed chair, its clawing paws curl from behind either shoulder. Her eyes embrace the sailor. She walks toward him, the very picture of determination, and he bows taking her extended hand to his lips.

"Captain Colon. It is such a pleasure to see you." "I am at you service." She tightens her grip.

The Governess tilts her head and narrows her eyes in familiarity. "And fortune has smiled on you, as has the King and Queen. But mostly, I understand, the Queen."

Cristóbal acknowledges the game. "Their royal highnesses have been most gracious and generous. The Queen sends her regards, and the King would, I'm sure, if he could."

"And how is the Queen, and her friend, my sister, Beatriz? Did you have occasion to spend much time at court?"

Cristóbal smiles, brushing aside the false inquiry. It is as if he can see right into her, know her in an unveiled way— the way she never utters the first thing that comes to her, but rather the third or fourth, after it has been examined for defects and errors. He thinks, 'You do not know me. I am not the same man.'

They enjoy skewering the royals and the hypocrisies of court. When the banter ends they stare at each other and their hands entwine. Although she believes she has ownership of his affection, Elenora can see a change in Cristóbal. She has often admired his commanding presence as he came off a sail, the swagger and the conquering attitude. Now there is more to him. His awkward courtly manner and self-deprecating naïveté is gone, as is the walk of a supplicant. On his divine mission, now validated by the King and Queen, his face glows a serene confidence.

She grips his arm as they walk out into the palm-shaded courtyard, enveloped in a perfume of gardenia. He says, "You've taken an interest in Dante. I saw you together in the garden. The boy was walking on air."

"Yes, I do have 'an interest'." She whirls to face Cristóbal, then as if she suddenly had a marvelous thought, says, "Why don't you leave him here? I could give him a worthy education."

He pauses, his head a slight lean to the side as if listening to someone, thinking, 'she will deceive you', and in a voice that admits no argument, "The boy comes with me."

His tone of command in claiming the boy checks the Governess from insisting. With a palpable indifference she turns the topic to another in his party.

"That man, de Torres? He has a strange look."

"Yes, he is obsessed with his own death. That's all they've left the poor bastard. To love his own death. And he wants to do it properly. In a way it's like sailing with a dead man."

She nods and congratulates herself on her perception.

This meeting satisfies a great yearning, one that each held in secret for many years. There is an awkward silence, charged with possible disclosure. Then Elenora says, "Tell me something, Captain. Tell me your thoughts."

The Captain General thinks, 'a woman's question', and says, "I'm certain you've heard of the contract I've made with the Crown, the Capitulations. God granting success, my life will change. Nobility for my family will be assured."

"Oh, yes. Very impressive for you, Cristóbal. But let's not talk of that right now. Tell me how much you've thought of me."

"It is all coming to pass, just as the Lord told me it would." Then realizing what she's just said, he checks himself and laughs, "Though the days have been demanding of my time, my thoughts always return to you."

His hand slips around her waist, and she rewards him with her arms encircling his shoulders, the press of her body. She whispers, "I knew that nothing would stop you. Nothing would keep you from me."

Earlier this year at Meli's, in Granada, the very day Ferdinand agreed to sponsor the expedition, Cristóbal told her he would need her help. Since then he has dominated her thoughts, obsessed with an intense awareness of him.

Being the widowed Governess of Gomera, she has full power over the exports and imports in this last deep water port. She assumes, mistakenly, that the riches of the East will pass through Gomera on return voyages. What would be an appropriate levy on the trans-ocean trade? It is simply a matter of a number. Certainly a small tax will be acceptable to Cristóbal. And there is the matter of her son, who she must protect. Title and power must be passed to him. Surely the Captain General will use his influence at court to assist her.

Elenora calculates that it will require two weeks for repairs to be made and the fleet supplied. This should be ample time for Cristobal to grant her desires before he leaves. It will be unsure, but she knows the man must go away in order to return. What Elenora is certain, is that she will hold him in her arms, bathe in his command, and when he does leave, her heart will break.

Cristóbal Colón is certain also. Certain that God has chosen him. His every thought is centered on his divine mission. He believes that before a dream is fulfilled it tests everything along the way, so he lives unafraid of danger, confident in success. He envisions his name spoken with those of the great world philosophers, Aristotle, Malmonides, Ptolmey.

Each day is a blessing he feels entitled to, and Elenora is his current reward. He could take her or not, surrender to her or not. It makes no difference to him. As they embrace he makes his choice.

Chapter 21
Ygnacio & Lily

To Lily, for some unknown reason, Ygnacio has not visited her for over a month. Only Debrun has any contact with her. For the young girl it is like being awake and dreaming at the same time. At the slightest sound she becomes paralyzed with fear, yet, despite the startle, something in her remains calm. Perhaps it is her innocence, perhaps an utter lack of understanding, but something has kept her from plunging off the precipice of sanity.

When Debrun brings the daily gruel, Lily senses waves of his demonic breath before he arrives. As if to reverse her world she wonders, 'Could he die? How would he die?' And she considers the strange ways she now knows to embrace the end of life. But she does not foresee Debrun's future, the chase by a mob of neighborhood children, many the off-springs of his victims, run off a cliff, landing far below on the shoreline rocks, face first.

Each day Lily cries until she gags. The former blossoming farm girl is now a skeleton with terror filled eyes popping out her gaunt face. Although she cannot tell day from night, and although the words burn her lips, she asks Debrun, "Has the captain sent for me?"

Debrun is bored with her. Despite his dementia, he is expert in estimating the life force remaining in a body, and he's listed Lily for quick disposal. That requires the consent of the beneficent father Baragio, a permission that is never unreasonably withheld.

Debrun enters Lily's alcove and motions her to follow him. He stands in the doorway, backlit by the passageway's torch, his scraggly hair matted in an upsweep to either side of his devil-head. Lily sees his face distorted in an idiot's grin with a few brown teeth, stammering as if an insect inhabits his brain. Panting, he brings her through the dank passageway to a favorite toy, a simple device designed for children. He straps her in, singing to her in the monotone of a madman imitating a madman.

Flowers on the hill
Water in the river
I'm a little sailor
Floating in the sun

Lily's awareness of being tortured is torture itself. With eyes held shut she loses awareness of her own screaming. It takes no time for the pain to reduce her to mere flesh. Debrun knows that the holy father would not be pleased with the girl dying and he thinks, 'I'd better not 'dunk' her. Better to wait.' So Lily is saved for the stake and fire. Could death have a heart?

November 3, 1491, is a sunny but cold day at Palos de la Frontera. Arctic winds sweep the coast of the Iberian Peninsula heralding the arrival of another brutal winter, a season to be shaped by starvation, disease, and intolerance.

Icy gusts howl through the weathered boards of San Loretta, the ramshackle hospital behind Saint George's. The deficient infirmary is quiet; no visitors comfort the disease ravaged bodies that lie on blood stained platforms, those who will soon be called to embrace the end of life.

Next to the administrator's office, in a private room where the air stinks of bitter medicine and a pungent smell of rot, Ygnacio de Silva is delirious. A cyclical fever has left him emaciated, lying in a pool of putrid sweat. He is near death, hallucinating, reliving a jumbled confusion of memories, fears, and fantasies from his childhood that pour through his mind like volcanic lava. He envisions himself playing by a creek with his cousin, Leo, catching frogs that burst in his hands, their blood and organs spattering him. Leo laughs. This image morphs into burning animals, then to a murder of blackbirds, wings flapping in a crackling crescendo of caws. Then the scene he hates most, his father in a maniacal, laughing rage, beating and raping Marta, Ygnacio's younger sister. As if Ygnacio consciously wills it, his hallucinations devolve into his father cursing in savage anger and writhing in agony, consumed in fire.

Three days of delirium later, Ygnacio wakes from his macabre visions, gagging in bile, his tunic soaked with sweat. The wound in his abdomen has closed and the bacterial infection defeated, victim to Ygnacio's inner wrath. He has received 'last rites' twice, but the tenacity Ygnacio cultivated in his rancid childhood has saved his life.

He hears the heavy rumble deep in his chest and shudders, his lungs trembling as he struggles to breath. Regaining consciousness, he begins to remember the series of drunken, bizarre mishaps that led to his own knife being shoved into his abdomen by that idiot farm boy, Dante. The moronic whelp who thought he was saving his sister from rape. 'Hah!' thinks Ygnacio, 'I'll provide the end of life for that strumpet of a wash girl and her warbling little brother. I might need to wait, but my time will come.'

Ygnacio is tall, over two meters. Unchanged are his lifeless shark's eyes, his long nose with high, permanently flared nostrils, and the nervous tick that curls his lip. New are the lumpy blue veins in his temples, and his sallow, jaundiced cheeks. The hardness around his eyes and mouth suggest the hardness in his heart, a heart that pumps darkness through him as it pumps blood.

His thirty-year old bones are infused with rage and contempt. Now a stiff spined man with a brittle gaze, he has cultivated cunning to pursue his lifetime passion, inventing ways for others to suffer. He relishes murderous constructs, going to them like a tongue pushing at the tender hole of a missing tooth. Damning all life's comforts, diabolical ideas weave through his mind in search of life through a death.

Learning that the despised pair, Dante and Revela, have fled, Ygnacio begins his search at their farm home. That fateful night, the Osorio family relied on the pretense of sending Pepe and Josephina north to Mogeur by mule. But the contrivance was plausible to mislead only if chase had been made within a few days. Now three months later, suspicious of the story, Ygnacio questions Juan José as if jabbing a tied-up dog with a stick. He resists the urge to deal severely with him. True to his cunning nature, the soldier avoids the false trail and heads south instead, to the port, seeking the person most likely to provide the information he wants — the gravedigger.

It is a moonless night. Ocean wetness invades the coast, a creeping fog from the sea, fog over the docks and in the alleys, fog in Ygnacio's brain. Under a dome of utter dark, he lurks through the streets of Palos, spider like. "I am back," he thinks. Skulking through the muddy streets, his eyes hard and gleeful, a man returned from death's door, he knows where to look for Juan Abreu. He smiles at his remembrance of the grizzly salt with stick out ears, the geek like man with the broken, wine stained teeth and high pitched whistle voice.

Ygnacio spots Juan Abreu alone on the pier, and moves toward him in a mean slouch, a slide in his step. He weaves crab-like, one arm tucked in close to his side to guard his wound, all the while his eyes fixed on the gravedigger.

Abreu's body cools, sensing danger like a surprised animal, sniffing the air, considering which way to run. He stiffens in a giddy sort of terror as Ygnacio's gaze freezes him. The fine hairs on Juan's neck stand at attention and a sensation of heat grips his throat, warning of something wicked on its way.

Watching Ygnacio, Juan Abreu can't be sure he is moving toward him or sliding away, as if the soldier is wary of an attack from behind.

The captain is excited. Hailing Abreu with a wave, in the voice of an old friend, he shouts, "What can you tell me, gravedigger? Where have my little birds flown?"

Juan had heard of the captain's recovery and knew that this day was coming. Although selling information was his chief source of money, he had already reasoned that Captain Ygnacio de Silva was no man to shake down for a few *maravedi*.

The gravedigger whistles through his broken teeth, "Whys I can tell you what I knows, sir Captains. Everythings I knows."

"Good Juan, and what would that be?

"Those stew murdring devils smanaged to get on a boat that very night they cowardlys struck you down, sir."

"And what boat was that, my friend?"

"Whys it was a Pinzón boat, sir, the 'Gallega'. One of the sree that left the next day for the voyage to the Magrhib for slaves. The brothers' sboats. Do ya know em?"

"Yes, Juan. I know them." De Silva's eyes narrow, and he speaks in a deep voice as if drilling into Abreu's throat, searching for the answer. "Where did they go, gravedigger?"

"The Canaries, sirs. The Canary Isles off Afrik was their sport o calls. So helps me, that's swhere they went. Thasall I knows."

A smirk crosses de Siva's face, quickly followed by an expression of malice, revealing his true deformed character, and he says, "Well, that's fine, Juan. I appreciate your help." He reaches into his half vest and says, "Here, I have something for you."

Abreu relaxes, certain he has made a wise choice. Juan has always thought it fruitful for a smart man to seem foolish, so he has thoughtfully traded his hope of compensation for the safety of the Captain's good graces. He sees something shiny come from Ygnacio's vest and is doubly encouraged. A small gold piece will be his reward after all.

The goat-head charm Ygnacio carries in an inner pocket, his keepsake since childhood, is snug in his palm, the horns extending a thumb's width through the middle fingers of his fist. His curled lips tighten and a distinct redness boils up in his face.

The sparkle excites Abreu and his eyes widen. 'Gold' he thinks. Then they widen larger still, as the charm slips into the soft tissue at the side of his neck where it finds his carotid artery. Juan smiles, showing his broken teeth, his face looking desperate to remember something critical. He reaches up to grab de Silva's wrist, readily surrendered, its work finished. The throat slitting makes a muffled, disgusting sound and leaves a gash that gives Juan the look of an extra mouth. The grave-digger feels a crush of misery as a geyser of his blood spouts an arch over Ygnacio's shoulder. The thickset fluid gurgles out and Juan Abreu hemorrhages into oblivion, called to embrace the end of life.

Somewhere at the bottom of Ygnacio's soul a fathomless resentment festers, a raw wound, a hatred of life itself. The devil could not have made him meaner. The strike, the stab into a living body, the twist of the wrist for the killing jerk, the sanguine liquid smell — for him this is the best. No lust for a woman could equal his surge of delight as the blade strikes in and the blood spurts out.

Now Ygnacio can plan. A ship, Lily, several trusted guardsmen, letters of transit, perhaps a commission from Father Tomás, the Inquisition Council's secretary. Oh, life is going to be fun again, with glorious days of reckoning to come — and soon.

Returning to Palos, Ygnacio wastes no time in contacting Father Baragio. Debrun's plans for Lily are thwarted, but it matters little to this executioner, for there are many souls to correct. At the prelate's instructions Lily is returned to her home. It is an unexpected turn of events for the San Pedro family.

Nine days later, Ignacio appears at Lily's farmhouse. The girl looks emaciated, almost invisible. Still, she has improved, her face reddened by its recent return to the outdoors, and her skin, though not healthy, no longer decaying. Her eyes cast an aura of frailty. Her thick black hair has been chopped short, exposing abscesses flourishing on her neck.

Lily never had any particular aspiration to be happy, but now she believes she is unhappy, that the little shudder in her head must be unhappiness. She is a shadow of the magical girl always just come in from playing. Simply 'dressing up' had been her greatest pleasure. Naïve to a fault, she once believed that if a word existed, such as 'troll', then there must be trolls. But now certain words that might attach to various common meanings, words like tight, or hard, or burn, have only one meaning, and that is pain. Where once she thought being herself too good to be true, now she is steeped in humiliation, her spirit obliterated by depravity and perversion.

Lily cannot remember in detail any specific moments of her imprisonment. It bewilders her that she cannot recall the fear or the pain. She knows what it represents but this is not a true memory, perhaps what she remembered was the impression of the memory. She has suffered the domination of her spirit and flesh, and learned the lessons that fear and pain teach; to not make eye contact with the torturer, to not plead for mercy, to not expect the agony to stop, to not anticipate the crack of the whip or the turn of the screw, to not smell, to not look at those places on your body throbbing with abuse.

Her mother tried to comfort her; 'the reward of suffering comes in the world to come', but Lily knows that the tortured stay tortured. No longer truly alive, she will carry death with her forever. She waits for life to betray her, to prove what she suspects, how little there is for her except more misfortune and a life of undeserved misery.

She sits in the rocking chair on the porch. If only she could be alone forever, if only no one would speak to her, if only no one would come near her. Her reality is so utterly without desire, her spirit gone in deference to death.

Lily hears a low heavy breathing, a familiar deep rumble, and senses a darkness. De Silva's tongue swipes his lips and he greets her with a cheery, "Hello Lily", as if they've last been on a picnic. Seeing him, Lily trembles and gags on the familiar taste of bile. She bites her lip hard.

She senses him peering inside, under her skin, that peculiar warped half smile on his face, a smirk of ruin. Her stomach knots and a warm trickle rolls down her legs.

Inside the house, Lily's mother, Maria Teresa, stands to the side of the window, invisible to the pair on the porch. She grasps the window frame with her fingers and her eye crawls around the corner. The view of Ygnacio is enough to send a chill of fright down her spine and a knot of anger to her face. Terrified, unwilling to interfere, she withdraws slowly.

Lily knows Ignacio to be a man with more than a touch of strangeness. He is no imitation but rather a lunatic of inevitable menace. Standing before her is no less than death's apprentice living the cunning of the insane, and well aware of his power to destroy the virtuous.

"Lily, my little bird. I have often thought of you while I was away on the King's business. Father Baragio tells me you have done well. You've thought of me often, haven't you Lily?"

She clenches her jaw, and again bites her lip hard to stop the tears. A deep sob comes out, and then, "Yes sir."

Ygnacio pays no attention to her distress, certain Lily is overjoyed to see him. "Fine, Lily. I'm glad to hear that. We must go on a journey Lily. Soon I will come for you, so prepare some clothes and things you might need. It will be soon Lily."

She tries to smile but cannot, "Yes sir."

Ygnacio, ever feeling important, and bringing important news, says with an air of edict, "It is necessary that you accompany me. Essential to your family. Do you understand Lily?"

"Yes sir." And she does understand.

Seeing Ygnacio jars Lily back to her corpse like existence. She is certain that her wounds will not sleep, her life will never return. Perhaps her life is a dream that she will awake from when she meets death. She hopes that deep inside her something timeless remains that only death can release. That in the wreckage of her existence there will be something she leaves behind, a life in her death.

Two weeks later as promised, Ygnacio returns for her. He knows that if the seas are rough, Lily, so fragile, might not survive the ocean voyage to the Canary Islands. Fortunately, he hears of a trick to avoid the ills of sailing. He was told that if the mind does not lose its visual perception of the horizon, the movement of a vessel will be accommodated by the brain. Ygancio interprets this wisdom incorrectly and the unintended consequence finds Lily locked below, amidships, where the motion is felt least, a favorable thing. But she never sees the water, the sun or moon, the deep blue waves, the distant coast, the stars at sea, or the endless horizon. Everything in the small space allotted to her stays in place. Nothing moves except when everything moves together. Somehow her inner ear balances the angles to permit Lily to dream of ending this sail. Although the ride is a grinding, claustrophobic terror, it is far better than the nightmare of Debrun's hospitality.

Cloistered below deck, good at being alone, Lily pretends she is sitting on the farmhouse porch in the blissful comfort of her mother's rocking chair. True to her nature, yet perplexing, out of love and kindness she tats a lace handkerchief for Ygnacio, a grief in white linen. She passes the time inventing stories to match the different patterns she has learned. She uses a silver thimble and a lace-maker's tool, a pin vise, alternating the small crisscross tracks of birds with the shy holes of rabbit tracks, two close in front then two larger behind. But her unsheathed fingertips are raw from needle pricks. Lily closes her eyes seeking a scrap of sanity, and accepts that her life is one of unjustified suffering. 'After all', she thinks, 'if nothing else, I have the good sense to die'.

Chapter 22
Guanches

On Tenerife the exiles set off from the beach led by Doramus ben Como. Tall, older than Revela but younger than David, ben Como's face betrays the sorrowful burden of witnessing his friends and family enslaved and killed. Like many Guanches, Doramus is fluent in the Spanish language, brought to the islands by Emmetak, one of the twelve Guanches to have escaped slavery on Majorca Island over a century ago.

They ascend the imperial cliffs on the lee side of the island. Far below the ocean blasts and sucks and thunders; it swirls and ebbs and falls over itself, but it cannot move the mountain. The group climbs through iridescent air, heavy with the odor of salt, as white gulls with blood-red beaks circle, screaming 'trespass!'

The Guanches, dressed in animal hides, climb effortlessly, setting a harsh pace for the Jews. It is hard going up a low slope of the volcano, through the chaparral of thorny bushes, desert plants contending for land no one wants. The Jews wear heavy dark cloaks. Most shoes have given their best during the long trek to the coast and now only scrap leather defends against the jagged rock. They scramble in pain under the brutal noon sun. Arching arms of maguey cacti rise like claws of creatures trapped in the earth. Long legged tenants lurk in the giant plants, netted in milky spider webs.

Nothing had prepared the exiles for this mountain. They do not know it, but their senses are heightened to the extreme. The sting of sulfur jars them out of the stupor of the climb. There is a constant low rumble, almost imperceptible, a zen-like tone. If they were to watch closely they might detect the movement of spider webs or a slight shifting of the sandy volcanic ash, not from any wind, but emanating from the world shaking power beneath them.

Yoggi trots off the trail and back again, dog-alert, disappearing for long periods. On his home ground, his ears straight up, his back arched, he barks at shadows and chases lizards.

That first night on the mountain the Jews sleep closer to the star filled sky than any of them have ever been. In slumber, transcending time and place, they look no different as when they last slept at home in southern Spain.

Rabbi Moises is awake. Merosa stirs, inching into him. He kisses her hair, and she asks, 'You've seen them, haven't you?"

His graying beard flutters with his sigh, 'Of course." She murmurs, "And?"

"And nothing", he says.

Merosa slides away content that the subject has been broached. She wonders if the girl is intelligent, if she could have a meaningful conversation with her, the kind of talk she might have had with her cousin Edit.

The rabbi wonders what his wife is dreaming. He forgets about sleep and thinks the night away tying to fathom something he had heard earlier by the cliff. Just before he drifts off, he recalls, it was Jerard making the common toast, 'Next year in Jerusalem.'

The next day travel is more determined. After a grueling three hours, Doramus stops to rest at a level promontory. Ahead, Teide's peak high above is patched with ice and yellowish steam rising from scattered *fumaroles*, lacunas in the earth that belch the acrid sulfur. Behind, to the west, clouds pile on the horizon; below, the sea and the distant island of Gomera, where the Santa Maria holds at anchor.

The children look to Revela, accepting her into their world to share each new experience. The adults watch as first the smaller, then the older, demand her attention, never doubting her genuine warmth or competence. She readily reciprocates their affection and accepts her responsibility, hoping to gain David's confidence.

Stopping to rest, the men and women drop rather than spend energy searching for the smallest comfort. The children sprawl in the shade of scattered scrub acacia. Birds hidden in the upper branches of the high pines, zip and sing. Tiny finches and kestrels, friends to the children, come and investigate the newcomers.

"See, I told you there were birds" Yva chides Jacob. "You don't see them if you walk around looking, you have to stop and wait for them."

Revela is thankful for the break. Chavery leans into her leg. "Here, why don't you go play with the other children?" The youngster shakes her head 'no' and buries her face in Revela's waist. She picks her up, cradles the girl in her arms, and then swoops her side to side. Chavery giggles, her head bobbing as Revela sidesteps toward the group. The older children include the shy youngster, joining hands in a circle and singing.

"Ring around the rosey a pocket full o posey.....

David watches Revela, admiring her easy manner. The song's tempo increases, and as Revela smooths her auburn hair, David takes in the shape of her mature body.

Ashes ashes, All fall down.

The children drop to the ground laughing, then scramble back up for another round. With each rhyme's interval, David stares at Revela, and Revela allows herself to be stared at.

As they climbed higher out of the southern desert, the land changes into blankets of daisies and white and pink broom flowers, growing close to the earth, as if there is danger in growing too far from it. A young Guanche boy with a serious demeanor metes out water and *gofio*, a pasty barley gruel. The Jews discuss the Canarians, relying on impressions rather than evaluating behavior, measuring these natives by their tolerance. Trustworthiness will be determined later.

The Guanches, on the other hand, are reticent concerning their guests, and for good reason. Canarians have seen their fill of Europeans, their trail of betrayal, enslavement, and murder. Still, youth finds its own. David asks Doramus, "How long a journey remains?"

Doramus, his eyes green as leeks, squints while he calculates what would normally be a two-day journey, then speaks slowly. "If we can get over the ridge today, then about twenty parasangs, three or four days more. The heat will end when we reach the forest. It will be easier for everyone."

It is not necessary to reach the summit of Tiede in order to get across to the north of the island, the windward side. They pass through a ravine-like channel, a jet-black tongue of recent lava flow cut through foot hills of deep beryl green on one side, iron red on the other. The multi colored ground appears almost artificial to the travelers. Doramus explains how the hills have been formed over centuries from the volcano's exploding ash. The magma, minerals deep in the earth, has showered the mountain as if rained upon from different colored clouds.

Descent of the northern slope begins away from the western sea, into the *bosque*, the dense forest of pine, cedar, and juniper. Seasonal layers of needles and cones blanket the ground. The atmosphere changes from dry desert to an air of vitality, a cool caress to support life in the decaying underbrush. The children and Revela, Chavery by her side, walk grouped together like a school outing.

In mid-morning David says to Doramus, "The men would like to stop for a short time to rest and pray."

Ten Jews create an unclosed circle in a flat expanse surrounded by towering pine trees, a cathedral like glen, and read from prayer books held chest high. A short distance away Revela sits with David's mother, Merosa. They watch the laughing children chase each other then disappear behind trees.

Revela says, "It feels good here, doesn't it Merosa?"

The woman knows Revela and Dante's story of escape from Palos. "Yes, Revela, finally a breath worth taking."

Revela asks, "Are you homesick?"

"What is homesickness when there is no home to go to?"

The girl gulps. "They're praying now, right?"

"Yes. Today is a holy day." The woman laughs to herself thinking,' there are so many', and says,

"These are the first days of our year, when we reflect on the past, and atone. They're honoring the new year."

"But who are they praying to? And why are they standing? Shouldn't they be on their knees?"

"The prayer is called the 'Amidah', Revela. It is prayed silently, deep in one's hearts. They stand before God in obedience ready to do his will. But, no child, it would be against the commandments to kneel. They pray to our God, not to an idol."

Merosa realizes what she has said, and how all her life her lips have been sealed to any comment on Christianity.

Revela says, "Is that one of the Ten Commandments?"

Some of the children have joined them. Merosa laughs, thinking, 'What a strange feeling, this freedom to speak'. It is as if something kept locked in a world of fear is now set free. "Yes, I suppose so, Revela. But there are many more than ten commandments. Many more. Many things a Jew must and must not do."

"Yes, like, not to stand by idly when a human life is in danger," says seven-year-old Sofia.

"And, not to take revenge", shouts her younger brother, Noah.

Others join the game. "To love the stranger."

"Not to commit incest with one's sister". They giggle.

"Not to eat a worm found in fruit."

"Not to be afraid of a bad man."

"To save someone."

"Not to consult ghosts"

"Or wizards."

"Not to intermarry with gentiles."

Revela blanches. Merosa regards her with soulful eyes that say, 'You can come and talk to me, my child, as if I were your mother.' and then to the children, "That's enough now. Victoria take Hannah and go with Edmundo. Let's go Revela, that boy Doramus is motioning us."

They set off together, Revela reflecting on of her own religion. That Jesus died and suffered for her holds a pride and thrill for her, but she resents those who insist on his humanity. After all, did he point to his wounds and say, 'Look Revela, I bled for you. Now obey the priest?" To think of Christ as a man with arms and feet, and a face with teeth, is vulgar to her. It denies the mystery. She prefers him extra-human, not of this world. She wants a sense of the eternal in her prayers, rather than an everyday list of rules to follow. She knows the miracles are not real facts, no more than Gotzun's stories of mountains fighting. She believes that what one cannot experience is probably not true.

Farm work and the daily struggle of family life and poverty, had made it hard to find time for the Church. So to please her mother Revela memorized a little Latin; an Ave Maria, a Pater Noster, and she set religion aside to be used only if necessary.

"Ave Maria, gratia plena, Dominus tecum Sancta Maria nunc et en hora mortis nostrae.... Amen

As they walk together, Merosa continues. "Revela, our faith not only provides each person with spiritual guidance, but also promotes a harmony within our community. We are bound by others, like a tree that can flourish only with the cooperation of all; the leaves, the branches, the soil, and the roots. You understand child, don't you?"

Revela nods.

"Our religion is thousands of years old. Its laws have evolved over years, even centuries of argument. Many rules may seem obsolete, even silly. But our people have been persecuted and deprived of their own land for hundreds of years. Yet we have survived. And this is because of our laws. You see what I mean, don't you?"

"Yes, I think so. You just don't believe in Jesus, right? Not that it's a reason to kill you."

"Well, you'd think not. Yes, you could say that is the essence of our difference with Christianity."

The group pushes on. The world looks different to the exiles in the spell of deep summer on this charmed island, its forest of dark acacia and light green juniper. Cones and chestnuts cover the ground and moss curtains the old growth trees. The sun's radiance embraces Revela through the leaves and branches, yet she is shaded.

Her thoughts drift to her mother. Of all the children she looks most like her, tall, rosy cheeked, wide brown eyes and with the same deep-throated laugh. Revela smiles to Merosa, grateful for the companionship of this older woman. 'This is like The Garden of Eden isn't it, Merosa?" the girl says.

"Yes, it is. So exceptionally brilliant." Merosa is distracted. She doesn't wish to provoke a situation, yet a mother knows when her son is smitten. She believes the girl to be intelligent and thinks explaining more of her faith will help Revela understand.

"Revela, what do you know about us?"

"Not that much, I guess. You've always just been there. I do remember when Dr. Koyn, he was a Jew, he saved Stuvro Breir. Stuvro fell from a tree and no one could wake him. They thought he was dead. But Dr. Koyn knew what to do, and he fixed him."

"Do you know your Bible, Revela, the first part, the part about the Jews?"

"Well, I know that God created heaven and earth and said 'let there be light.' Then he created Adam and Eve, but Eve ate the apple and God expelled them from the Garden of Eden."

"And what of the Jews, Revela?"

Well, God spoke to the Jews and gave Moses the Ten Commandments. And there were ten generations to Noah when the flood happened to punish man. And there were ten generations to Jesus. And then the Jews killed Jesus. They did do that, didn't they?"

"No, Revela, they didn't. The Romans crucified Jesus, as well as thousands of other Jews. Not unlike what is happening today."

'How true the words of Maimonedes.' Merosa thinks, "It is always easier to close a door than to open it again. It is always easier to maintain a cleverly constructed lie than it is to find an unclear truth."

She says, "But you have the basic idea. That part about God speaking to the Jews is important. For you see when Moses led them out of Egypt and slavery, they all heard God's voice at the same moment. Not just Moses. Like everyone they had prayed to many different gods. But they experienced together the existence and oneness of God. Do you understand, motek? One God. That's where it started. There on Mt Sinai."

Revela listens, and is startled. 'This is a woman talking!' Never before had she heard a woman speak of anything but babies, cooking, and washing. Even the nuns at St. George spoke only of praying and the disgusting excesses of men, and, of course, of burning witches and Jews.

Merosa is concerned she might have gone beyond Revela's understanding, but not her ability, so she continues.

"Our spiritual ancestors are the same. Abraham and Sarah. Jacob and his twelve sons. Hundreds of years before Christ, ten of the twelve tribes, Jacobs sons, were forced from their home and transplanted thousands of miles away by the Assyrians. We are a part of that scattering. In a way, we carry our land with us. We've never given up hope of returning. That's what it means when you hear, 'Next year in Jerusalem'. We've never forgotten our lost brethren. Our star of hope, our longing, is that someday the ten lost tribes will emerge from the darkness of history to be masters in their own land. Not temporary guests, like us. Perhaps the ship we sailed on will find them. Perhaps Dante will be the one to make that connection."

Revela's heart quickens at the sound of her brother's name and the thought that he might play a role in history. "But how could so many people get lost?"

"They were lost to us, Revela, only in the sense that we lost contact. Remember, they were taken away as slaves. Sent to Mesopotamia and Greece. Who knows where else."

The desert heat has lifted, invigorating the mountain air. Behind Teide the sunset illuminates the sky with melting lines of red and orange. Merosa sees Doramus motioning that it is time to make camp and says, "Perhaps we will talk more about these things later, motek."

On the third night the small group rounds the mountain, beneath the constellation of Scorpio. Revela's perception is distorted by the silhouette of Teide, an immense blot in the sky, a cave like opening in space surrounded by a shower of stars. Stumbling, she reaches for David to steady herself. Below, in a caldron enclosure, she sees movement.

Doramus motions them to wait and says, "We are at Ucanca."

Below, they see a natural amphitheater, bathed in torchlight. A ring of men sit around a fire, necks bent slightly forward, appearing headless. Their naked bronze torsos convey a serene power, a slumber like consciousness. Sitting in silence, skin glowing in the firelight, a peculiar beauty messages something ancient.

Crouched in the earthen cradle the men form a human wall. They seem to be people not fully created, outside the nucleus of life. Reptilian in the torchlight, Revela fears that if she averts her eyes for only a moment, they will become invisible.

At the muffled sound of a drum, the men rise and begin to tread the earth, each man in profound concentration, stomping the ground in unison. Then, turning clockwise, they all pivot on their left leg in a five-step dance; *thump, thump, thump... thump, Thump*, each footfall a statement; thump, thump, thump... thump, Thump. Then in a sidestep, the men slowly revolve around the fire, the rhythm unbroken, thump, thump, thump... thump, Thump.

Revela feels David's breath on her neck and slides her hand into his. "What are they doing, David?" He shakes his head.

From a distance, David's parents can see them, David and Revela, nearly leaning on one another, with Doramus standing close.

Doramus says, "We must wait."

Directly above is a full moon. The circle of Guanches treading the earth breaks into a long undulating line, like a giant serpent. Men spin slowly to form a gyrating circle around the fire, then once again brake into a twisting line, treading the ground, thump, thump, thump... thump, Thump.

Then the shadows, which are not truly shadows, surround the human wheel and move inward to reveal the smaller shapes of women. Stepping forward as one, they create their own circle, ringing the men, humbly thumping the ground.

Both men and women tread the earth, the men advancing in sidestep, the outer circle of women dancing in place. Then a song is heard, a music without rhythm, an eerie, elemental sound, as if it held the universe together.

Now, the men link, each placing a right arm on the next man's shoulder. The outer circle of women revolves, in reverse from the inner circle of men. Still thumping, these rings, one within the other, spin in opposite directions.

Simultaneously, the circles break open into undulating parallel lines. The men and women spin, and then sway, to the drum's savage rhythm, forming a double line in mirror image, an endless, curling human thread.

Suddenly Revela shudders and cries out. "Oh, David, look." She sees the dancers move through the fire, in pairs, a man and woman joining hands at one end of the flame and releasing at the other, oblivious to the inferno that engulfs them.

Revela envisions them passing through the blaze and then a great combustion. The gyrating columns leave the earth, stretching into the sky. Revela sees human pillars rise like comets, circle the full moon, rejoin, and return to the cauldron.

The girl swoons against David. The dancers are again treading the earth in concentric circles, singing inwardly. Then silence, and the Guanches sit in place, save for one diminutive, very old man. His ivory backbone is hunched, his stalk like arms hang loose. From absolute stillness, with deliberate bird steps, he lifts his skeletal legs and returns them to the ground, knees bent, springing, almost jumping, from one leg to the other. His arms whirl, and then he suddenly stops, staring out with a fearsome gaze.

The drumming stops and the shaman sings in a discordant, jarring tone. Watching this primitive ritual, Revela feels outside of time. What she also feels is fear, not her own, but everyone's, and bewilderment at their indifference to it.

The savage bird step dance and impassioned song end. The shaman's body is smeared in dark red with black beastly eyes, while his own eyes stare as if sightless. His face, reflecting the flames, seems to be on fire.

The men and women sit motionless in an aboriginal silence. The aged shaman speaks in a raspy voice that reaches deep in his memory.

"Listen humans. I am the one. I have lived forever. I have just been born. But I am weary. What are you without me? I hold the water of life and the shadow of death. Is it time? Wake up and listen Vincheni. Beware! Fear will crawl into your soul if you let it. Don't be afraid. Don't seek to know how you will die. Must you leave Chineche and go to the sun beyond the sun? Look to your dreams where your noble soul waits for you. What a man sees in his dreams is real. When the world began the Raven created Earthmaker and he was called Eraoranzan. He was without consciousness. He was of good nature but his two hands fought each other. He saw what was needed and he made the earth. He turned himself into a woman and bore children. His tears became the waters. His feelings became things. Salves and curing plants came from his penis. He dove into the earth and came back again as if out of water. He walked on water without sinking, as if on earth. He went through mountains as if they were empty space. He embraced the sun and the moon in his hands. He shaped the earth. Hungry for food, he wandered. He committed many sins. He did mischief but his good heart redeemed for all. He treated the Vincheni in kindness. Yes, men steal and lie because of him. Yet one thing he never did — he never warred. He roamed around the world and loved all things, calling all brothers. He was a builder, not a destroyer. Is it time for Eraoranzan to leave?

Is Eraoranzan the God of Yesterday? Are the Vincheni closer to death than to life? Does the Christ Son of God need our blood? Must the Jesus God be welcomed? These Christers, they are not complete. There is a hole in them. I have seen it. They cannot fill it. They are unfinished in their inner places and they will go on taking till the world will say 'I have nothing left to give you'. How many Vincheni are now dust? Is there not a monster at large? Is there a dream dreaming us? Look to your dreams Vincheni."

In the sheer depths below, the earth was invisible; In the vastness above, the sky could not be seen. When I looked, my startled eyes saw nothing; When I listened, no sound met my amazed ear. Transcending inaction, I came to Purity, And entered the realm of the Great Beginning.

'Yuan you', The Songs of The South, translated by David Hawkes, Ch'u Tz'u

A cloud crosses the moon, the fire dies and in the chilling darkness the Guanches fold into the night. Revela turns to David and thinks he has somehow aged, as if he sensed his own death. Unable to rationally absorb the experience, she enters a moment of profound silence as witness to something sacred. Tears streaming, she turns to David and embraces him, hoping with all her being that there might be something for everyone on this cruel earth, even for her.

Chapter 23
Departures and Arrivals

Landfall is uncomplicated, an event any eye can find and accommodate. Departure is more difficult, more distinctly a process, a ceremony of navigation, a sense of occasion. You must know where you are on the wide ring of the earth's horizon and consider movement — of the planet, the water, the wind, and yourself.

After a thirty-day layover, the Niña and Pinta join their flagship at Gomera. On September 6, 1492, following the church's blessing, and with all apparent obstacles surmounted, the fleet sails from the Canary Islands, westward, slipping from the known world into uncharted waters.

Dante is unnerved, afraid he might do the wrong thing, or worse still, embarrass himself by being clumsy. With no opportunity to learn or practice, he simply must follow any order given and hope he understands. He promises himself not to act on his own, not to be impulsive.

Despite the sail's potential for disaster, the crew is as calm as the harbor water. Haul and stow Esmerelda, pull the sweeps, unfurrow the sails and raise the booms, set the runners, and settle in on deck. The voyage is underway without mishap.

Harana fixes one mariner's eye on the sea, calculating the ship's speed, the other on Dante. The marshal is bald, 'plucked clean' he says of himself, and it suits him. A dedicated ship's officer, he makes it a point to find out what he hasn't yet heard. The crew respects him, many signing on because of his salty reputation. He knows that de Torres had suggested to the Captain General that Dante remain aboard as an able seaman in exchange for a pardon of his crime, the same as Juan de Moguer.

The recruitment of sailors for the voyage was not as difficult as might be supposed. Just a few obvious questions were asked. Could they carry enough supplies, particularly water, to reach their destination? They were told the distance to travel was approximately 3,700 kilometers, so thirty-days supply will be sufficient. Given the wind systems pushing them across the Ocean Sea, could they return on a beat or tack against those winds? Cristóbal Colón and the Pinzóns' own experience, not theory, told them that by sailing back east at a more northern latitude with a prevailing wind behind them, they could easily return.

What could be more persuasive to a sailor to join a dangerous adventure than knowing the ship owners, and their families, were on board? The owner of the Santa Maria is its master, Juan de la Cosa. Cristobal Quintero, owner of the Pinta, signed as able seaman on board his own ship and Francisco Martín Pinzón is its master. The Niña is part owned and captained by Vincente Yanoz Pinzón, and its master, Juan Niño, also part owner.

These are not just any owners and sailors. These are the Pinzóns, known to be an exceptionally resourceful, fearless, and experienced Paloan sailing family. They captain men of the sea, those vulnerable to visions of fortune and discovery, men of courage and loyalty, the virtues that knit a ship's company together. Seduced by the promise of gold and adventure, a titanic attraction, its lure was the power that kept sailors from the common occurrence of jumping ship in the Canaries.

Cristóbal Colón resumes the voyage routine begun in Palos. The mariner's day starts at high noon and continues in three four-hour shifts. A daytime prayer schedule is adhered to, two meals provided, and night prayers said. All participate in this devout protocol, or pretend to. After the evening meal, as the sun sets ahead and to the north, Luís de Torres approaches the Captain General on deck near the tiller.

"I wish to extend my apology to you Captain General, for my behavior the other evening. It was most unfortunate and inexcusable of me to express myself in such callous, inappropriate terms."

"I understand, Luís, you have suffered greatly. I'm gratified that you feel free to speak your mind. A man should be straight forward." But he thinks how blasphemous the man's words were — 'a religion of death!'

"Thank you for your tolerance, Captain. I am so completely overwhelmed with grief. It is greater than I, so how can I command or fight it?"

The Captain General examines the new astrolabe used to determine latitude. But his eyes are focused beyond the instrument, as if searching for an exit. He feels obliged to comment. "The reconstruction of your life has to begin somewhere Luís, and what better time then now? A man's life has many outrages, all you can expect are small moments of justice. Here, look at this new device from Zacuto."

Luís takes the sphere shaped device and examines it, nodding with a familiarity he does not possess, accepting it in lieu of further discussion.

As the Voyage of Discovery sails west from the Canaries coming close to the New World, a steady wind pushes the caravel Scrimshaw over foamless waves past Gibraltar, southwest, down the coast of Africa toward the Canary Islands. Lily is confined below, rocking in her cage-like space, wondering if seasickness could be fatal. She is tatting a handkerchief for Ignacio with particular care. She works the white linen cloth with delicate holes for the crisscross tracks of birds and rabbit tracks. In a burst of imagination, she runs a wispy, red thread along the border that drops into the center hole. But it is not a hole, rather it is a thick stitch of black.

When properly folded in pocket it appears as an eye dripping a slim stream of blood. Lily smiles as she works and when finished, she soaks a corner in a drop of a gardenia scented oil.

Ygnacio stands in the prow of the ship, enjoying the experience of sail, riding the waves, the occasional spray of salt water on his face. An ordinary man might be contemplative of his life and consider his successes and failures, his loves and losses. But Ygnacio is not an ordinary man. He looks at the ocean, but there is no water in his thoughts. If he could think past hatred and revenge, if he were capable of thinking about who he is and what he's done, if he could see the ocean of his mind, what would be there?

After nine days of sail, they have arrived at Gran Canaria, the large island east of Tenerife and Gomera. Ygnacio and Lily are seated in the Scrimshaw's skiff as it slides across the calm harbor waters. They round a huge outcropping of steep, volcanic rock covered with a rash of moss. The late afternoon sun reflects a yellow sparkle off the porous, solidified lava, as it has for millennia.

The garrison at Gran Canaria has been alerted to the arrival of Ygnacio, a member of the Cronistas de Armas, the King at Arms. Approaching the narrow dock, Lily gasps, "Oh."

Standing tall in a perfect circle, framed against the blue sky, is an oasis of Canary Palm trees. The trunks are thick with diamond-incised, coarse, bark. They support a lush canopy of arching, green fronds with bunches of red, grape-like fruit hanging beneath starburst leaves. Behind the trees, a blood red and white carpet of bougainvillea cascades downs the black rock cliff. The flowers camouflage tall, skinny trunks of papaya trees. Globes of the yellow fruit sit in the shade of clownish scraggly leaves. Behind, as if a trail out the tops of the trees, is a wall of broad steps, hewn in the rock, curving down the cliff to the pier where soldiers wait in welcome.

The skiff settles next to the narrow pier and its painter is flipped to a soldier who tightens it hard against the bollard. Ygnacio and Lily disembark.

"Bienvenido a Gran Canaria, Don Ignacio. Bienvenido Señora." says Julio Clavere, a lieutenant in the Las Palmas garrison. The soldier salutes and nods a bow to Lily. "We have your quarters prepared. This way your Excellency.

Careful your step."

Ygnacio de Silva presents the quintessential vision of a Spanish soldier. His gaunt, sharp-bearded face is chin strapped to a plumed caballero's helmet. He wears his most formal uniform, a burgundy, pleated doublet emblazoned with Aragon's coat of arms, string-laced black breeches, and high leather boots. Sheathed in an elaborately tooled leather belt slung across his chest, is his short-bladed *basilard*, the very knife so unconventionally returned to him by Dante.

With the end of the ocean passage, Lily's faculties are somewhat restored. The roar in her head and her double vision has diminished. Her sequestered voyage to the Canaries has given her time to wonder about the future. But, like Ygnacio, she is no longer ordinary. Her spirit has been crushed in Debrun's lair. Survival has demanded she escape from rational life to a numb limbo. She can tat lace, and that is all she does.

The newly arrived pair's perception is disoriented during their first moments on land. Like newborn colts, each step forward requires two quick sidesteps to maintain balance. Comically, they reach for each other, but misjudging the distance, grasp only air. Surprised to be so muddled, yet aware the other is experiencing the same confusion, they stumble, clutch at each other, and laugh in embarrassment. Lily, her eyes on Ygnacio, is grateful for his attention, and she mumbles, "Thank you."

Wearing her change of rough peasant garb saved for the arrival, climbing the winding steps, she walks behind Ygnacio and the soldiers. They are escorted to a palm shaded courtyard, the center open to the sky.

The air is heavy with the biting aroma of roast goat. Members of the garrison are being served their evening meal by Guanche slaves. They rise to attention, and bow to the arriving guests. Ygnacio and Lily sit at a corner table shaded by two magnificent pear trees, heavy with October fruit.

Ygnacio weighs the bargain these ranked soldiers have made. They serve their King in the Canaries without pay, compensated by land and titles. Each year of service earns them fifty hectares on the island of their choice, plus twelve slaves from the local population.

For the first time since leaving her home on the farm, Lily is hungry. She devours a plate of grilled fish and barley. Strengthened, she works up the courage to ask, "What are our plans don Ygnacio? Will we be here long?"

Ygnacio has also feasted on the food and local wine, and is in an uncommonly convivial mood. "This does seem a pleasant place. Perhaps we will stay awhile. But I have some business to attend to. I'll consider our future after that."

Mustering all her nerve, with head bowed and both hands extended, Lily presents the lace handkerchief to Ygnacio. Her shy eyes look to Ygnacio and he pauses, then takes the gift. Lily's trepidation prevents her from even muttering, 'This is for you.'

Ygnacio is confused, unaccustomed to un-coerced generosity, without a single memory of someone showing him kindness. Bringing the delicate cloth to his face he inhales deeply and the odor of gardenia fills him. He raises an approving eyebrow and tucks the gift into his chest pocket where he keeps his golden goat's-head talisman.

Fixated on a single thought, Ygnacio holds his mental focus the way children absorbed in play do not hear calls for dinner. But he is also haunted by memories. Incidents of carnage and slaughter, pleasant enough to him when occurring, get twisted in recall, the roles reversed. When this happens he is overcome by a dry panic. He suffered these hallucinations during his recuperation in the infirmary, when he was consumed by images of himself as victim. Dante and Revela have become his anchor, real live people who wronged him. His vengeful focus on the fugitive brother and sister keeps him sane.

A soldier approaches Ygnacio, a towering brute who salutes in a carefree manner, and introduces himself, "Berecillo de Arbolluvia, at your service." Berecillo removes his hat and stares inside it as if the words he has to say are there. "I understand you wish to travel to Gomera, correct?"

Ygnacio's head jerks back like a snake ready to strike and he gives the soldier a stony look. He stretches his legs under the table and sips his wine. His lip curls and he says, "Perhaps. And of what concern might that be to you?"

"Sire, I only wish to advise you of the goings on there. I just returned from La Palma, an island near Gomera. But I did stop there."

Berecillo de Arbolluvia has the cold, furtive eyes of a predator. Known to be a sadistic bully, he recently escaped punishment in Sevilla after setting fire to an inn that served him a bad meal. Unfortunately, the Earl of Culver's brother was dining at the time, and ended up as well done as the venison. Like many fugitives, Berecillo fled to the Canaries where he energetically joined in murdering the islanders.

Ygnacio thinks, 'A stroke of luck'. "And what news have you?"

"Good news, captain." the uniformed thug says in his oily voice. "These heathen have had their fill of Spanish steel. I had their chief in front of me. Begging to be baptized". He turns slightly to see if others are listening. "Of course that was impossible after we lost three men to those swine. So I asked him if I could try out my new sword. When he said 'yes', I ran it through his middle. It worked fine." Berecillo, beside himself with a vulgar laughter, his eyes disappearing into creases slaps, the table, and looks to the other soldiers.

Ygnacio gauges the man standing before him. Berecillo's wild beard intensifies his air of domination, his booming voice magnifying the fear he enjoys instilling. The soldier laughs until he finds it almost impossible to breathe, then composes himself, "These ignorant pagans are slippery. They do not fight like men," and he turns to nod to his men. "They are vermin, eaters of rats. They run and hide in foul holes in the mountain. They're not worthy of baptism. They're good only as slaves."

Ygnacio deplores this crudeness, yet feels a kinship with the soldier's depravity. "This happened in Gomera?"

"No, no. It was in the island just north. La Palma. The savages ambushed us in the mountain passes. We'll be after them soon with a force of fifty. We ship out next week. No, Gomera has been tamed, sire. The savages there won't raise an eyebrow where Doña Elanora rules."

Ygnacio knows the name, remembers that she is the sister of Beatrice de Moya, the Queen's friend. He's heard rumors of her, the kind of rumors that travel mouth to mouth among barmaids and stable hands.

"Tell me did you happen across a young Spanish couple newly arrived? A brother and sister, perhaps?"

Berecillo bends closer. "Ah, looking for someone? Who might they be?"

Ygnacio sniffs. "You will answer me. Did you?"

Berecillo huffs a shrug. "I saw no one other than dead savages. Many dead savages. No pubescent hidalgos. But I can tell you the fleet that left three weeks ago for the horizon, a voyage of which I am sure you are aware, both provisioned and disembarked at San Sebastian Harbor."

"Disembarked what, soldier?"

"Jews, captain. Fresh from the Peninsula. *conversos* and old Jews. But they didn't stay. They went on to Tenerife. That will be their last stop." He laughs again, turning to the plaza.

A flash of good fortune leaps up within Ygnacio, a foretaste of his vengeance. He curbs a grin of satisfaction, feigning little interest, as if his thoughts are elsewhere.

He orders Berecillo, "You will secure my passage on the next ship to Gomera." He turns to see Lily half concealed behind a palm tree. Both her hands rest on the short palm and he thinks, 'She's praying. She had better.'

Lily bucks, and vomits her first Canarian meal.

Chapter 24
Crossing the Ocean Sea

Sunday, September 9th, 1492, three days after departing the Canary Islands, the Voyage of Discovery is beyond the sight of land. Each day the Captain's log records little more than the weather, the course heading, an accurate account of the distance traveled, plus a lesser distance that he reports to the crew. The subterfuge, his log explains, is meant to dispel thoughts of such a long voyage and the diminishing chances of returning home.

Cristóbal Colón has long wondered if the sea has rhyme or reason, or is it truly unfathomable? The surface offers shine and sparkle, but the depths only an impenetrable darkness. Tiny bubbles rise from where unimaginable creatures breathe and feed on each other, lurking sea-beasts without eyes or appendages.

Land creatures are the same. They feed on one another under a merciless sun that can crisp life to a finish. As one descends deeper either into the fathoms of the ocean or into the caves of Teide, both get colder and blacker and are equally terrifying. On land or at sea, when mystery transcends the boundaries of perception, time can pass with agonizing slowness, challenging one's sanity.

Just as the earth struggles to accommodate all living creatures, so does the ocean desire limerence. Its waves and currents cradle life and cultivate harmony, but on its own terms. Men who go to sea learn that sailing is as mysterious a puzzle as is living in the ocean of infinite time. Just as time will never be conquered, the sailor will never conquer the celestial winds. A roaring blast may come from anywhere, shrieking as if loosed from hell, destroying the sails, obliterating the course. These tempests will panic a man, but it is the sea the sailor needs to fear. When the wind conjures towering waves, a sailor must breathe like a fish in the spume blowing off the crests. In the fierce and relentless swells and troughs he feels blood drain from every cell. Then comes a moment amid the ceaseless rise and fall when, with no decrease in danger, a sailor moves beyond fear and he understands the sea knows only two conditions, afloat and beneath.

After evening prayers Cristóbal Colón and Luís de Torres go below to the Captain General's cabin.

Cristóbal says, "Some wine, yes, just the thing." and in a short time the *malmsey* has them both light-headed. These after hour conversations have become a routine escape from the monotony and anxiety of the sail. The Captain General, who seldom speaks to ordinary sailors, feels especially fortunate to have found an articulate companion of intellect.

Colón is a man of impressive accomplishments, well known in the courts of Western Europe. The intelligentsia discusses his ideas, even if in ridicule, no small triumph for a common man in a time and place where status is rigidly fixed at birth. A network of thoughtful men and women, people of character, have taken up his cause, despite exposing themselves and their families to grave danger in a society reeking of superstition and cruelty.

Colón and de Torres have been in each other's company three times before, always with Santangel, most recently at a meeting in Granada at the start of the year, when the Spanish Crown again rejected Cristóbal. Colón left the court intent on taking his case to the King of France, or even once more to the Portuguese. How he hated the humiliation.

De Torres had recently avoided the clutches of the Inquisition, thanks in no small part, to the intervention of Santangel and the Duke of Medina-Celi. Having survived the murder of his entire family, consumed by an oppressive guilt, ashamed to have escaped, ashamed to be living, he savors the only thing left to him, his grief.

A shaft of light enters through the hatch of the cabin and magnifies the Captain's shadow onto the bulkhead, his bony knees awkwardly cramped under the chart table. An oil lamp illuminates the ship's log next to de Torres. The interpreter sits on a small stool, his arms akimbo for balance, and his face contorted in thought. Breaking an extended silence, the Captain says, "Another?" After several drinks they are intoxicated and the boredom becomes bearable.

Luís de Torres holds out his mug, and Cristóbal Colón pours from the half empty bottle. Luís takes a long drink, the edge of the mug bumping against his front teeth, and as if in the middle of a conversation, words burst out that suggest a continuation of an angry interior monologue. He says, "I wanted to say, but I don't know about what. Would you please ask me something. I must be able to say what I feel."

The Captain General, unsure what Luís means, refills his own mug and hesitates, considering the best response. "Then say what you feel, Luís. Of course." The captain's arm makes an exaggerated, sweeping gesture as if all topics are permitted, but he thinks, 'Please, not the Inquisition again'.

Luís remains quiet, pondering, undecided, as if he was under the influence not of alcohol, but of himself, his grief, his dread. Then he jumps up as if suddenly remembering something he has to do. "Well time... I don't really know. It just kind of popped up in my mind. Is it wrong?"

"Is what wrong?"

"What I said. Is our true nature beyond time, or isn't it?"

The Captain General stretches his arms above his head seeming to push away his fatigue at his friend's vagueness, and says, "What are you talking about Luís?"

"Well then. It has happened. Not often. But on occasion. For a moment I get dizzy. A recollection of something overwhelms me and I lose any awareness of the passage of time. Like the instant of pause when the sun is dipping below the horizon. Time stretches. I feel I'm there now."

Cristóbal, his forehead resting in his right palm, asks, "How so, Luís?"

"I had a strange experience last night. I woke up and did not know who I was. I looked around, and really, for a minute I didn't know who I was. I didn't wonder where I was. I wasn't afraid. I was simply someone other than myself. Like a visitor. Did you ever feel anything like that?"

Cristóbal Colón sighs and fully aware of his condescending tone, says, "Time is a mystery, Luís, to the rabbi as well as to the galley slave. Their answers are as good as mine. Clearly it changes everything. In fact, it is everything. Each man has his own way to cope with it. After all, Luís, we are totally in error about so much, do you really think we can understand time? The greatest mystery of all?"

Luís snaps, "Don't be a pompous ass. You know perfectly well what I mean."

Their eyes lock, their faces contort, then both explode in unrestrained laughter. They laugh so hard they both begin a fit of coughing. At that moment the ship rocks and they fall into each other's arms. Off balance and off guard, they roar, back-slapping and guffawing. Cristóbal bangs the table with his fist, braying and fighting for breath, laughing as if all the irony and humor in his life has burst in one unexplainable, supreme moment of buffoonery.

The Captain General is first to regain a modicum of composure, and sputters, "You should heed those wise men you studied so diligently. You know the ones who say 'all knowing is simply remembering'."

Luís cuts him off, "Yes!" He raises a finger in the air, "And 'to remember is the same mystery as to foretell.' You see, that's your Genoese arrogance that seeks to solve all questions by not thinking. I've read about people like you. I've studied Aristotle, Maimonides, Thomas Aquinas. Did you know that Mo Tzu propounded the theory of universal love four-hundred years before Christ? Captain, you have before you a learned man." He bows deeply, swaying so far to the left he must catch hold of himself on Colón's chair.

Luís is relieved by this play, it takes him to a place of no judgment. He puffs himself up, grips his lapels, fingers the air and continues.

"Some lives unfold by guideposts with simple rules of thumb, the flow of life directed by a reliable filter. A distinctive sense of reality provides these fortunate ones with a delightful knowledge of how to live." He turns to the Captain, then stumbles forward and in that deliberate way of a drunkard, presses his hand to his chest and confesses, "I am not one of them."

Raising both hands, Luís entwines his fingers, "The incidents in our lives are linked by unknown purposes. Interconnected by a million little strings tied to everything we do." His fingers wave in the air. "It's impossible to know the turning points, the hidden decisions that direct our lives. In essence, everything, everywhere is linked with all other moments in time. Don't you see?"

De Torres doesn't wait for a response. The floor is his. His hands dance as he improvises. "The moment of both the present and the past. That exact, fleeting, frozen instant."

The Captain General, also more animated of late, stretches his arms, splays his fingers wide, and says, "Oh you are such a sorry prick, Luís. You've got my mind muddled. Do we really need to take time to think of time?"

Luís smiles. "Actually Captain, the awareness of the passage of time has no time in it."

Cristóbal sees no exit. "Very well. We agree. We agree. Nothing is more certain and unchangeable than time. Let's not waste it, it would be lost forever. Now is now. It doesn't concern itself with the future or the past."

De Torres pounces, "Aha! I know who you are. I know what you do. You're fundamentally different, my friend, in a strange and wonderful way." He's leans into the Captain General, inches from his face. "Everyone looks to the past for the way to be what we call 'here'. It's obviously our natural perspective. There is a veil to time that curtains the future and forces the mind to live in today. But, Captain, your natural perspective is the future. It's your trick. And you probably don't even know it."

"Perhaps Luís." To himself, Colón muses, 'my guidance is divine. A dream sends me.' Then aloud, "But I can tell you that sometimes, when I am alone, there is a stillness just before the arrival of an idea. An idea of consequence. I can't explain this anymore than I can explain why water is wet. It just is."

Luís drops the playful affectation and says, "You see Captain. It's more. It's deep in our nature. We don't really feel the power of time. We resist it believing our inner lives eternal. Think of our passion, our urge to live longer. In fact, to live forever. We can't fathom the question, let alone solve the puzzle. As we pass time, we yearn to increase it. It's like Alighieri's Hell, a starving man dining on food that makes him hungrier."

"I must say, Luís, you actually sound like a sage at times. Is this common with Jews?"

The Voyage of Discovery sails on. False-dawn charges against the spin of the earth, bringing a cloudless gray sky. The sea changes from puce to blue as the rising sun makes a pinhole on the horizon. To starboard, dolphins hump the waves and lung ahead of the Santa Maria as the sunlight reflects a green sheen off their backs. Tuna glide twenty fathoms beneath the dolphin.

Sancho Ruiz leads the crew in morning prayer. The sky remains uncertain as early winds pick up. Every man is silently grateful for friendly waters, for a sea that tolerates their presence. Always in mind are the specters of friends who suffered the sea's wild torments, now at rest in watery graves.

Harana, coughs hard, and in an unusually affable tone and welcoming nod, asks Dante, "And how's our new sailor?"

"Fine, sir. Good morning to you." Dante is delighted, believing Harana has crossed the line and now favors him.

For Harana, a deep-water sailor with a draconian character, there is no unmerited discipline. No rough treatment without cause. Ships sail under a long evolved code based on authority, consistent in its definition and severity of punishment. Harana himself wears well-earned scars for transgretions. The marshal believes that the administration of hard rules saves men's lives. Although he appears mercurial and is often called shrewd, he is a patient man, and well able to set things in the right direction.

Harana notes the morning wind, it will be the best of the day. Amidships, Orkon the Turk calls out, "Here Dante, have ya done yer duty and tipped the Pope's hat?"

"Right," says Harana, without pause, but coughing, and with a hidden wink to Orkon. "Have ya done that yet?"

"Well, I don't think so. What does that mean?"

Orkon looks up and points both fingers of his left hand skyward. "There boy. Ya need to get to the 'truck' at the top of the mast. It's the rule."

Dante's eyes crawl up the mast, measuring the space between yardarms. He's developed a proper respect for anyone going aloft, and has measured himself by climbing shroud-ladders. Anxious to step further into the seafaring brotherhood, he fingers the fuzz above his lip, then hitches his pants. With a glance towards Harana he swaggers toward the mainmast.

Several sailors hear the exchange, and gather round as Dante approaches the mast. The men pat his back, encouraging him, acknowledging his rite of passage.

Harana coughs hard and spits. "There ya go lad, right up."

Cristóbal Colón and de Torres watch from the poop as Dante grasps hold of the belaying cleats at the mast step and boosts himself onto the nubby steps of the mainmast. The crew cheers. Harana looks over his shoulder to the Captain General and de Torres, and then to the sails that have begun to belly out.

Luís says to Cristóbal, "What is this? Some sort of initiation?"

"Yes. First sail out, it's required of able seamen."

The wind strengthens, the Santa Maria picks up a knot of speed, changing the rhythm of the ship's roll, deepening to starboard. Dante begins his assent. The waves swell and the ship rolls upright. The force of gravity draws Dante away from the mast, and he pauses to secure a tighter grip on the mainsail halyard.

Coughing hard now, Harana watches. The ship's carpenter, Unai, says' "He'd better make it quick, that wind won't help."

And it doesn't. Dante claws up in ever slowing spurts, then rests. The roll to starboard deepens, increasing the pressure of gravity. The waves swell and the ship and mast roll nearly twenty degrees. Then, as the ship uprights, the mast springs back. Dante barely has a hold on the halyard, and his surprise yields to worry. He continues, inching up now, his stamina ebbing, until he can no longer lift his body. Half way up, his strength spent, he clings to the post as if he will fly off should he relax even a finger's grip.

Another roll to starboard and Dante's knees let go their hold. His body swings out, one arm flailing the air, the other clawing to grasp the mast. The crew reacts to the challenge. A sailor grabs a float in case the boy should fall in the sea, which would not necessarily be dangerous. However, should he fall with the mast's upswing, Dante will hit the deck and most likely break his neck.

He does neither. As the mast swings back to perpendicular, it leaves Dante unattached in mid-air. At that moment, the loose halyard smacks him in the face and he grabs it. Before being snapped back, Dante wraps an arm and leg in the line. This stops his descent but carries him crashing into the mast. His arms cushion the impact, but his head hits the Palos pine hard and he falls. He falls almost two meters, his own height, when the line still wrapped on his leg pulls tight. He hangs, unconscious, dangling upside down like a Serrano ham.

Edmundo grabs Gotzun's arm and says, "If he's swinging the wrong way when she rolls back, he'll be like a knot at the end of a whip. It'll break him in two. Or snap off his leg."

Another cycle begins and the ship's mast dips to the sea, dropping the dangling boy as deep as the previous wave's trough. When it rebounds up Dante separates further, the mast and boy about to repeat the dance. Dante's unconscious body narrowly misses the mast as it swings a short distance beyond to port.

In the tense silence the entire crew realizes the next turn will swing the halyard and Dante far out over the sea, and then violently snap the boy back like a slingshot. All eyes scream open. Lorenzo, the helmsman comes off the wind to starboard in an attempt to steady the ship, but the sea is in control. Watching the boy in danger, the Captain General grips the rail, his knuckles white, his tongue dry, his throat closed. His mind screams 'the boy'!

Men scurry on deck, occluding one another as they rush to station themselves, tracking Dante's changing positions. The crew scramble for a man-overboard, and spare sails are dragged to a spot on deck to cushion a fall. Two young seamen, Jacobo and Joshua, carrying coiled line begin climbing the mast as if their toes were fishhooks.

Just before the whip crack, Joshua, part way up, grabs the halyard below Dante and holds it fast against the mast. Jacobo somehow levitates himself, leaps over Joshua like a hopping bird, grips the mast with his ankles, and stretches to grab the tunic draped over the inverted Dante's head.

Harana shouts, "Ah, those monkeys got em!" and the crew cheers.

Chapter 25
Merosa

In 1485 Rabbi Moises and Merosa sit together at their home in Huelva, near the banks of the Guadalquivir River. The meal is finished, the children in bed, the evening fire reduced to embers. Side by side, they fit just so on the worn, hide covered sofa. They earn the necessities each day but life is hard and often dangerous. Holding hands, they feel safe.

Merosa often thinks of her cousin, Edit, in exile, wondering what life is like for her, if she's found a new home, whether she is bitter. Knowing Edit well, Merosa is certain that wherever she lives, she feels only the singularity of coming from another place, not inferiority.

Often, Merosa and the Rabbi discuss long standing controversies. A small knot forms in the center of Merosa's brow as she fingers her dark hair, a forewarning to the Rabbi of a serious discussion. On occasion she takes a position hoping Moises will oppose it, and then she capitulates. The rabbi returns the favor. When unresolved issues leave them both frustrated, in order to calm the air, the Rabbi recites the poetry of Judah Halevi, which calls out to every Jew to return to the land of Israel.

O Zion, beauty and gladness of the world,

Thine is all love and grace,

and unto thee In love and grace we are forever chained.

We who in thy happiness were happy

Are broken in thy desolation.

Each In the prison of his exile bows to earth,

And turns him toward thy gates.

Scattered and lost, We will remember till the end of time

The cradle of our childhood, from a thousand seas

Turn back and seek again thy hills and vales.

Now, beneath the great volcano, Teide, under the constellation of the traveler, Sagitarius, the Rabbi arranges a make-shift bed. The unspoken loss of their previous life and their exile, that bone of banishment, is forever lodged in their throats. Why say what does not matter? Better to be silent. What is broken will never be whole again. Because of this, they miss each other even when they are together.

The Rabbi lies on the laurel leaves covering dry palm fronds. Merosa brings a gourd of fresh water and places it on the rock beside her husband.

"Why not?"

"Why not what?" Merosa asks as she covers him with his coat.

He repeats to himself. 'Why not?'

"What?"

"Next year in Jerusalem."

Merosa looks at her husband as if she has not seen him for a long time. There are new grey hairs, and longer, deeper creases in what has always been his worried face. He looks older, much older. She wonders if he sees the same in her. She strokes his head and thinks of that city.

Jerusalem. Ever since King David made Jerusalem the capital of Israel a thousand years before Christ, Jerusalem has been the spiritual center of Jewry, the place where Adam lived all his life, the place named by Abraham, the place where their ancestors built the Holy Temple.

Throughout the centuries of Jewish diaspora, the daily prayer of liturgy, the Amidah, is recited facing the holy city. 'Next year in Jerusalem'.

The phrase resonates among the Jews as another pillar of identity, like the Ladino language. Its roots are a deep seated wish of collective consciousness symbolizing everything – the end of exile, a homeland, the fulfillment of the prophecy, and the honoring of their covenant with God. 'Next year in Jerusalem' came to express endearment and reverence as it passed from generation to generation.

Merosa says, "Why not? Why not a castle in Tuscany?" The words of Judah Halevi burn in her heart and she thinks, 'Oh for peace and rest. To be safe.' Under her breath she recites her favorite verse.

My heart is in the East, tho' in the West I live,

The sweet of human life no happiness can give,

Religion's duties fail to lift my soul on high;

'Neath Edom Zion writhes, in Arab chains I lie!

No joy in sunny Spain mine eyes can ever see

For Zion, desolate, alone hath charms for me!

The next day, guided by several young Guanches, Merosa, Revela and the children traverse a switchback trail winding down a cliff side to a beach. The Saharan sun burns, sparkling off shards of silver mica in the black volcanic sand. Revela shades her eyes, "It's so bright."

Emerging from the spikes and spines of the chaparral onto the flat beach, the children run for the shoreline, some stripping off their heavy tunics, others not bothering. Crashing waves leave a thick mist, a watery prism of looping rainbows, rollicking colors spiraling just above the surf and down the long beach. Waves pound the cliff walls, echoing and amplified into a mighty rumble. The children stop to inspect long tubers of tangled brown and green seaweed wrapping a jellyfish spread on the hard sand like a flattened peony. Ringed in ocean foam, the slimy plant teems with miniature crustaceans. The youngsters are thrilled by everything they see, happy to be free of adult presence. They race back and forth between beach and sea, washing off the stuck-on sand as the sun dries the sticky salt on their skin.

The smaller children are swamped as waves cascade over their heads. Running, shouting, spitting what they don't swallow, they forget time and circumstance. The older children dive under the surf. They sputter commands, their faces glowing a swarthy red from the island sun, their screams and laughter blending with the cries of resident sea gulls.

Merosa and Revela sit in the shade of a promontory's overhang, basking in the intoxicating, briny air. Merosa says, "They look like children again, don't they? Children. Not exiles."

Revela sweeps her long hair back with both hands, ties it up off her neck and brushes the sand from her feet and legs. "As far as I can see, life in exile is an awful lot of waiting. Here. I've never seen black sand like this before. I'm not sure I like it."

"It is different. But then, we are different here also. Aren't we?"

The fresh salty air, the serenity of perpetual waves, the children's open laughter, combine to take Revela a step outside her situation. She releases her guarded attitude and warms to Merosa's sensitivity, perhaps even more to her intelligence. Feeling safe, even allied with the woman, wanting her approval and friendship, yet aware of a risk, the girl takes a quick breath and says, "David thinks this place will make a wonderful home."

Men in the face of danger might understand one another without the necessity of a spoken word, and in the same manner two women can establish an unspoken emotional connection. A simultaneous moment of female insight, a view through the same eyes, binds them with a common intuition. Revela and Merosa clear their throats at the same instant.

Merosa's eyes widen. She thinks, 'Love is so simple', and says, "Yes, David is very perceptive. Let's talk about David, Revela. You like him a great deal, don't you?"

"Yes, I do. But I know we could never be together, that it would be against your commandments." She says this easily, as if her not being a Jew is a convenience, and stands in place of the guilt she feels that makes her not worthy of love.

Merosa shifts her position in the sand and says, "Oh, our lives are very different now. We have no choice but to break commandments every day. But just as the breaking of a wave does not destroy the ocean, one broken commandment does not make a person wicked or sinful. And if we feel we can love a person, and they can love us, we make them a part of our family."

Revela squeezes her entire body tight, her breath stops, trying to contain as truth what she has heard. Her eyes look into Merosa's with a sanguine silence, a quiet promising trust.

Merosa, says, "You've lived near a port. Have you ever seen a ship in a bottle? You know what I mean? Sailors make them. I guess it's a hobby."

"Yes. Yes, I know them. Juan Abreu, a man who helped us get on the Santa Maria makes them. And he sells them too. I could never figure out how he does it."

"Well, we are like that ship. It doesn't know where it's sailing. The wind cannot blow it. It cannot sink. Do you see what I mean?"

"Well, not really."

Merosa leans forward, her hand sinks into the black beach, then lifting handfuls of the fine sand, lets it pour through her fingers. The mica sparkles and sticks to her skin. The woman's face, lined with worry and faith, moves closer to the girl's. She stares into Revela's wide, brown eyes and says, "We are a community, Revela. No matter what happens, that does not change. Our lives are bound, infused with tolerance. What is different from us must be understood, even accepted, but never feared."

"Isn't everyone afraid of something?"

Regaining her upright posture, Merosa says, "Yes, that's true. But fear must be faced. Being frightened of what is different is the same as being frightened of the truth. It's important to try to conquer fear."

"I think I see what you mean."

"Do you, motek? Let me explain. A fearful person does not think logically or act with kindness, much less mercy."

"Uh huh."

Merosa continues, "We mourn our past but put fear aside. We trust the future will bring opportunities to build a new life. Oh, it's a problem, the old sour insults and hates. The humiliation and spite that bring a pain hidden inside us. They say, 'when you leave your country you are like a plant taken out of soil'. But this world is all we have. It's our duty to one another to make the most of it." She thinks, 'Enough. This takes time. Our greatest enemy is that we never believe what is happening to us.'

Suddenly Merosa's attention goes to the ocean. She springs up, kicking out the black sand, and shading her eyes from the glare, exclaims, "Oh look! That's too far!"

With Revela scurrying behind, Merosa leaps on tiptoes through the burning sand and churns several wide sweeps of her arm high in the air, calling into the wind, "Aidan! In! Come closer. In!" Then louder." Aidan! In! Come in!"

The boy is treading water off shore where the waves first break. He disappears into the white curls crashing over his head, then reappears. He sees Merosa calling and begins bobbing his toes off the bottom, slowly returning to the safety of shallow water.

Seeing the two women on the water's edge, the younger children splash through the surf, wiping their eyes, talking all at once. "Did you see us? We're playing sharks. Baruch is the shark and he's trying to get us. Watch me! Watch me!" And they turn, splashing back into the water, squealing in excitement.

Chavery can't resist staying close to Revela. The youngster collects tiny shells rolling in the receding tide's shallows. Revela scans the shore looking for the sheen of dying jellyfish, the stinging kind that look like bloody veins on the beach, common to the Spanish shore.

The women walk, the orphaned girl trailing. "It's almost like things are normal," Merosa says.

As if she's wanted to speak for days but did not have the courage, Revela suddenly blurts "I think it's terrible what they've done to you Jews. You know. Everything. You don't deserve it."

Merosa shakes her head at the girl. "Deserve has nothing to do with it. You would think that all men could not bear seeing women and children suffer." She sighs and says to herself, 'May the torments of the past no longer weigh on my heart.'

"Do you know about our King and Queen, Revela? Who they are? Who they really are?"

"Ferdinand and Ysabela? What do you mean?"

"Well, you know about the Estatutos de Limpieza de Sangre, don't you. The 'blood laws'?"

"Yes, I think so. They decide if you're a true Christian don't they?"

"Well, yes, in a way. The laws declare that you need to go back five generations with no Jewish blood in your family. That means everyone for the past hundred years or so, those Jews who chose not to be tortured and burned. They call them 'New Christians' and they persecute them as they do us."

Revela nods, wondering where this conversation is headed, fearful it might threaten, even cancel, what Merosa previously said about the commandments and David.

"Those laws have been used to force generations into exile, destroying their lives. Just as it has ours."

Merosa leaves the shoreline and wades into the water, reaching down to splash herself. She refreshes her face and shakes her hair out in the water, soaking her clothes. Revela mimics her, luxuriating in the cool ocean.

Merosa continues, "Well, the irony— you know what irony is don't you motek?" The girl nods. "Well, the irony is that Ferdinand, our most Catholic King, his great-grandmother was Jewish. And that's maternal great grandmother, something that means a great deal to us."

Revela stops her splashing. Her face squinches as if she's arrived at a locked door. Perhaps this is just another story like Gotzun's.

"That's right, motek. Ferdinand's great grandmother was Palomba from Sos. And our queen? Three of her great great grandparents had Jewish roots. And by the way, do you know anyone who doesn't know the Virgin Mary was a Jew?

Revela shakes her head.

"And you know the name Torquemada?"

Revela shakes her head again.

"Well, no matter. But, him also. So, you see what I mean?"

The information about the King astonishes Revela and she thinks, 'This must be a secret that only the Jews know.' She sees an opportunity to unburden herself of her own secret, the way close friends, especially women, trade intimate thoughts. Or perhaps it is simply that she wants someone to confide in. She asks, "You know why Dante and I are here don't you? About the fight at La Sirena Taberna?"

"Yes, I know."

"Well, you know Dante thought he was saving me. But the truth is... he wasn't."

Merosa jerks to attention. "What do you mean, motek?"

"Well, I knew those men from before. That night they were drunk and we were kind of dancing.' The girl is fumbling for words. As she recreates the scene in her mind's eye, she throws her head back and raises her arms to let the oppressive memory escape.

"There was a lot of noise and I guess I might have screamed a little, but not for help. I didn't cry out for help. But Dante thought I was in trouble and he tried to save me. It all happened so fast, I couldn't stop him. Oh, Merosa," she pleads, "I'm so sorry for it all."

PART III

Chapter 26
Bencomo

The seven Canary Islands are isolated from one another, all visible on the horizons, but with little communication between them and much intolerance. Numerous competing fiefdoms exist within each island, governed by counsels and kings, known as *menceys*. A powerful kinship prevails, but languages, customs, and gods vary from island to island. Still, 'tomorrow' is the same word as 'today' in every tribe, and all view the spiritual and physical world of man as one entity. Plants, mountains, animals, rivers, all have souls.

But division into hostile tribes leaves the Canarians powerless to the onslaught of European Royals and the Catholic Church. A fear of horses, their deadliest weakness, is fully exploited by the invaders. They have suffered a century of strife, first as an ebb and flow, then a spiraling escalation, of slavery and murder.

Doramus is the son of Bencomo, *Mencey* of the Vincheni of Taora Region in Tenerife. The *mencey* is more a personification of his people's collective consciousness than their ruler. Should he show signs of growing weak or become ineffectual, this signals the tribe that their spirit requires rejuvenation. A new *mencey* is chosen and installed. Or, if he defies the gods, who send a plague upon the land, the king is deposed, or even executed.

It has been three weeks since the Jews' arrival in Tenerife. Doramus, David, and Revela, Chavery always at her side, enter the Guanche village overlooking the lush Orotava Valley. The rest of the group remains at the narrow entrance to the defensive enclosure, situated on a plateau beside a steep rise of the volcano. The visitors are unimpressed by the flat-roofed dwellings, low shelters of mud and stone. A low fire near the center of the compound yields wisps of smoke like a genie emerging from a bottle. There are several scrawny, swaybacked dogs, hunkered down, with scruffy fur and yellow teeth. The islanders have been told the Jews are religious exiles escaping the Spanish. Despite their fear and hatred of Europeans, they accept the exiles as victims-in-common and watch indifferently as they pass by.

The small group approaches a man seated on a flat rock in front of a shelter. His long, wrinkled face is frozen in a tragic, toothless grimace. Whitish hair droops from his high forehead and chin. Doramus places his hand lightly on the old man's shoulder and says, "This is Bencomo, *Mencey* of Taora, and my first-father."

The *Mencey's* mirthless eyes are undaunted by the look of fear he sees everywhere these days, and now again in the faces of Revela and David. Without pause Bencomo says, "Is there anyone chasing you?"

Revela lies, "I don't think so."

David says, "We are but a handful of many fleeing the Catholic Church and the Spanish."

"Like us, then," the king bemoans. "What do you want?"

David answers, "To live freely in your land and be true to our God."

Bencomo considers the request. Chavery lets go of Revela to stroke the king's white beard, and then hesitates at the musky odor of elderly flesh. The *Mencey* regards the sad faced girl who responds with an impish smile. The burden of fighting ruthless invaders, this struggle for survival in his own land, has left him bewildered. He has searched his dreams, the dreams of a king, unlike those of ordinary men. But he's found no answer. He has lost his hope that the adversities of the honorable are a test, not a penalty. His tribe needs justice, but what he wants is vengeance.

Watching Chavery's fascination with his beard, he pauses, puting his thoughts in order. The Mencey thinks, 'someone should get what they want', and says, "You can stay but you must build your own shelters. You must take care of your sick and not leave dead bodies around. We will share our food but you must help gather and prepare it. You must not fight us or ask your God to kill us."

The young Spaniards nod their heads in agreement, and the *Mencey* in turn nods to Doramus, dismissing them. Doramus observes how his father has begun to mumble incessantly, his hands shaking and body trembling. 'Perhaps', he thinks, 'the *Mencey's* time is over.'

Revela has not fully accepted her change in status from fugitive to exile. She never doubted the Canarians would honor their request for asylum. But true to her nature, what she doesn't know concerns her. Just that day she had heard the Rabbi and Merosa almost arguing, and was certain she heard her name. 'What was that about?' she thinks, lamenting how far away from home she is.

She says, "Then we can stay, right Doramus?"

"Yes, you are all welcome."

David reports the news of the *Mencey's* consent to the exiles, and Rabbi Moises leads the group into the compound. Despite an overpowering scent of starvation in the camp, the Jews are grateful for the benign welcome and the luxury of a semi-enclosed hut. A fire pit borders a long table and benches in the space where two walls meet. The floor is dirt and a low flat roof rests on the half-open structure.

That evening under a full moon and star-milky sky the Guanches assemble near a cliff's edge, their site of sacred ceremonies. An ancient *drago* tree, revered as a source of magic and wisdom, dominates the space. It takes the extended arms of nine men to circumscribe the massive trunk. Tube-like arms stretch upward where the branches divide and thin, thin again and again, like a purse seine, so dense they blacken the sky, a labyrinth that appears time itself could not penetrate. At the end of each arm is a cluster of long, pointed, green leaves.

The Guanches sit in the moon shadow of this primeval tree, creating a casual semi-circle around the Jews, affirming their acceptance and protection. Yoggi, missing for days, appears with his rough dog's tongue hanging out, investigates the group, and then settles between Revela and David.

Young girls serve guava and tiny green and yellow lemons, no larger than walnuts. Doramus offers Merosa a basket woven of spruce withes filled with cactus fruit. She turns to him and says, "It's very good. Is this an ordinary meal?"

"No. This is a feast meal. We gather and listen to storytellers. Our daily meal is there in the pots. It's not much. You see our bodies. Ground barley mixed with onions. Maybe some mushrooms or turnips. Sometimes sardines."

During the meal, conversation is short, kept to low tones, mixed with the muffled laughter of children. The two groups are utterly dissimilar. The natives wear animal skins they've cured and coarsely tailored, while the Jews are dressed in their traditional dark tunics. The Jews mistakenly regard the primitive shelters as a temporary makeshift encampment. The Spanish and the Church of Christ are their common enemies, but the Guanches are pagans, so the Jews feel no brotherhood with them, only victimhood.

Life has never been easy for the Guanches. They live in a physical paradise but remain subject to the universal assortment of human foibles; jealousy, pride, illness, and a hardscrabble existence. But until the Spanish came, their island was never so totally plagued by evil.

Bencomo stands, slowly lifting himself from a throne-like seat of stone. The cooking fire lights him from below and gives the translucent skin of his anguished face an otherworldly look. The sharp crack of conifer branches splitting in the fire are accompanied by a shower of sparks. Above the Mencey's delicate chin, his thick lips knit together like crossed arms. He knows it is too late. His eyes, usually wrinkled with sagacity and humor, are enraged in accusation. He raises his skinny arms and calls out:

"Hear us Eraoranzan. We suffer our terrible, rotten lament. The Spanish hunt us with the eyes of a predator to enslave and kill us. They go on butchering and butchering. Why? Are we not their brothers? Is not our blood the same? We are not a great civilization but we too are human. Our life is now changed. Strife has made us weak. We cannot tend our animals or our crops, and they fail. We get sick and die. Perhaps these Jews will prove useful. I hope so. Help us to put fear out of our minds. Our young men die by the hard sticks. What becomes of their unlived lives? Where do they go? Are they lost to the Vincheni? Does humanity have a destination? Help us, Eraoranzan. Protect your children of Chineche."

The old *mencey* sits, then motions to a younger man who stands. He is tall with yellow hair, a square face, and a child's immature features. He closes his blue eyes and says, "I am Tetrenta. My story is new. A half moon past, Doramus led the Vincheni across the water to La Palma. There they met and joined forces with *Mencey* Tanausu of the Auaritas to fight the Spanish."

Revela looks to Doramus who has lowered his head. She thinks of Gotzun.

"We came down from the great mountain, Taburiente. We were two-thousand fighters. Brave Doramus, son of Bencomo, challenged the Spanish chief soldier, Pedro de Vera. The coward would not fight. He sent another, Juan de Hoces, a man who had killed many Vincheni. He was huge. As tall as an alder tree. He wore hard garments so that his body did not show and carried a shine-stick and a shield that wrapped around him. His eyes were wild, and his face twisted as he charged with his weapon held high, screaming his battle cry, 'Jesus and Ysabela!' Doramus stood his ground in the center of the green field with his back to the charging warrior. Yes, his back to him. When the giant was almost upon him, Doramus saw in the tail of his eye a blue finch-bird fly from a thicket. He spun and whirled his dart with all the might of Earazonan. The missile flew like a seabird diving into the sea. When it struck, the giant's shield burst into flame and shattered. Then the dart pierced the brute's armor and entered his heart. He fell dead."

The Guanches sat stiffly silent, listening intently to a story that would forever be revered in their history. They wanted to cheer but they knew this victory was like others before, ephemeral, and a harbinger of a terror to come.

"But the Spanish were not honorable and did not accept defeat," Tetrenta continued. "On his horse, Pedro de Vera charged Doramus. He wounded him with a long stick. Then they all attacked and Vincheni fell. My brother, Adargoma, was made a prisoner along with many others. Many Spanish also fell. Bodies lay as close as raindrops. This did happen."

David leans into Doramus and says, "How can you fight steel swords and horses with sticks and rocks?"

"Yes, I know."

"How many men did you lose?"

"Three hundred Guanches died and two hundred made prisoner. They were put on a ship and told they were coming here to Tenerife. It is a short sail from La Palma. But it was treachery. In truth they were going to Spain to be sold into slavery. So when the ship passed Teide, Adargoma led a revolt and they were all put ashore on Lanzarote, the isle closest to Africa."

"And what will you do now?"

"It has been decided that we must move to higher ground." He points to where there are no stars, the volcano's silhouette blotting out the night sky. "There. Up closer to the peak. Teide is where we must make our stand.

Chapter 27
Luís de Torres & Cristóbal Colón

Luís de Torres, steeped in fatality, befuddled by smothered secrets, walks toward the poop-deck high off the water. A mild breeze from astern pushes the square rigged ship in the following sea. The translator is wobbling, not quite sober, clutching the rail for support. His thoughts are drifting between his own childhood and that of his children, confusing time and images, combining Hebrew and Arabic words, forcing Spanish idioms into French phrases. His unhinged mind struggles to express his sorrow, as if needing a language he has not yet mastered.

Cristóbal Colón sees de Torres approach. As he wobbles forward he is muttering, startled by the slightest movement, constantly rubbing his hands together. Sensing a lecture coming, Colón thinks, 'he's going to make a speech'.

Luís' internal thoughts are in the middle of conversation. Slurring his words he says, "Surly you agree, Captain, that our great lords are demented. The prelate Fray Richard, a treacherous man, decorates his residence with the bodies of his tortured enemies. Rather demented, don't you think?"

Cristóbal runs a hand through his hair and remains silent.

De Torres continues. "A completely corrupt tyrant, with a criminal mind. However innocent a thing may be, this 'churchman'," and he grimaces, "will discover some illegality, and solve the matter by killing the poor bastard. And of course, hangings readily solve all financial matters. What do you think, Captain?"

The Captain General shrugs. "Yes, Luís. He is a ruthless man, a monster of arrogance and insolence and a toady to those in higher authority.

There is no doubt that contemptible, brutal men, moral dwarves loyal to nothing, rule us. They recognize no limits to their avarice. To their privileges. They claim everything."

De Torres is anxious to agree. His rising voice shouts to the ocean, "Oh, do they ever! Nothing would satisfy them. The abbey cellars filled with fat priests, lounging in the ineradicable stink of power, thick as rats, gorging themselves, devouring every crumb of bread, swilling every drop of wine, while their congregation starves."

Colón has surprised himself. Long ago he had compromised his integrity to patronize those who might advance his cause, spending years in supplication to the hidalgos in the courts of Europe. But those obligations have ended.

His hands flailing the air, the Captain General closes in on de Torres' face, "Yes! They own everything. Every hill and lake. Every plant. Every insect and animal. Every man. And when there is nothing left for a child to eat, they feed their animals the last remaining crumbs. They are Church members, but not Christians."

It is Luís' turn to be startled. 'What has happened to the demur, unflappable Cristóbal Colón?' he wonders. The man whose stern face never loses an expression of caution. The Captain General could be expected to be cynical after decades of imploring their favor, but it's unthinkable he would actually malign the aristocracy!

Speaking as if having discovered a kindred spirit, Luís says, "Yes. Exactly. And they worship cruelty. Men will go along with any sort of myth, no matter how preposterous. Without their churches, their crosses and bones, their blood-wines and body-wafers— what is left? Nothing except fear. Fear drives their religion. Fear of the mysterious. The fear of anything different, anything even unfamiliar."

As the ship rolls out of rhythm, Cristóbal Colón leans against the binnacle, careful of the *bitacora*, the little oil lamp's protective hood for night sailing. He is unsettled, but composes himself to reply, "Yes, to spend a night without the fear of day. To completely forget fear, might make life perfect."

"Remember Luís, we all have a dark side. The Greeks say even the Gods have a dark side. There are more things to admire in men than to despise. In both our religions many great men have heeded the call. Thinkers you admire. True Christians whose acts of charity and love for all men make the world a better place. You know that Rome has condemned the excesses of Torquemada."

De Torres purses his lips, "Oh please!"

Colón could hear the grief in de Torres' voice. "Luís. Your circumstances. The past. You cannot go there so often. Don't think you can. It will choke you. Free yourself from memory to visit your soul, not your past."

"Forget my past? Forget that? I've got to die to forget that."

What could 'put the past behind' promise to a man hoping to erase himself, to leak out of the world and fade completely away? Each day finds Luís less substantial, more weightless, like the last drops of dew on a flower. The world has gone on moving without him. His bitterness leaves him with a certain satisfaction, but no answers are provided by his religion. His heart is embittered, but all hope has not left him.

At one time he had playfully debated his father concerning the Jewish religion's failure to address the question of death. He would ask, 'Abba, what is it that continues after we perish? What is the point of a religion offering no explanation for what happens after life ends?' The rabbi would quote the Talmud, answering with a question or a parable. Nor could Luís find an answer in the part-thoughts one thinks to oneself. Knowing nothing of death's demands, yet unable to accept mortality, the Jews, who make so much of life, seem doomed to live in its shadow. Luís envied the Christians, the way they structure death into the circles of hell, purgatory, limbo and heaven. But the Jew, who for five thousand years has discussed every possibility of the social and spiritual life, argued the minutia of every issue, investigated every question concerning life on earth, still has no sustainable concept, promise, or hope, of what happens after death. Instead, he acquiesces in silence to the cryptic question deep in everyone's mind, 'What's next?'

Colón continues, "Luís, death does not nullify a life. It is one thing among many. No, if that is the solution, if death is all that lies ahead, then we are on the wrong path. To seek death is to seek nothing. After all, death comes to all. There are no survivors." And he laughs out loud. "Better to mourn the past, but take the road that leads to building a new life."

Facing astern into the wind, the interpreter attempts to focus through his wine-fog. Already believing in nothing, his wish to die rises closer to the surface. He has lost all sensibility of being alive, having already committed a partial suicide, killing the aspect of his personality that nourishes contentment and laughter. He is awake in his own death. Bunching his hair back, he ties it with a worn black ribbon, thinking, 'We may die but the past is never dead.' Had not his father told him that because death stalks us the world is a mystery, that without our consciousness of death everything is inconsequential?

Cristóbal responds to his friend's boundless sadness with a soothing voice, "Luís, when God created the world he assigned death to mankind, but not life. He reserved life to his care. We must accept the suffering and sacrifice of innocent women and children in the same way as we accept the sacrifice of Christ."

De Torres responds, "But Captain, everything we know about Jesus was recorded by followers. Christ is not known to have written any of his thoughts down, except by tracing figures in sand. The scriptures, the sayings, the miracles, the messianic prophecy, all are filled with contradictions and make-believe. All were written about him two hundred years after the fact, written to prove true what had happened when none of it could be disproved."

The Captain General has released his grip on the rail and he turns to de Torres as if he has just finished a conversation with someone else. His hands search for a place to rest, his voice strains. He says, "Every religion inspirits ritual. Every religion unfolds a mythology of miracles. The experience of God connects you with what is timeless. It is a mystery that man will never fathom. The meaning of life, it's not words but experience, Luís. *'Credo in Jesum Christum, filium Dei unigenitum'* — I believe in Jesus Christ, the only begotten Son of God.

"Not for me Captain. I no longer believe in religion, or God, or Heaven, or Hell. Especially Hell. How can anyone who is truly humane believe in everlasting punishment? If there is a Hell, I am certainly in it."

Colón reflects on the Bible's brutality and absurdity, the fear instilled by God's promised punishment. "Yes Luís, the Bible is filled with cruelty and impossible demands. It's true, some things just cannot be believed, but you cannot be sure about your faith unless you test it."

De Torres recalls his father's admonition never to criticize the precepts of religion. The Rabbi reasoned that cultures were built on man's faith in the truth of doctrines. If men did not believe in an omnipotent God, if they doubted divine order in the world, then they would feel exempt from obeying the tenets of civilization.

"Well, I did believe until they took away the people I loved. May the jaws of night obliterate the memory of that day. I'm sorry Captain, but Christianity is a doctrine of injustice. A violent ideology that professes love under the cloak of religion. It is the preaching of a cult of death. Fifteen hundred years has numbed us to the lunacy of it."

Cristóbal Colón eyes goggle, stunned by de Torres' audacity. He almost shouts, "And yours?! Your history tells of the Jews putting whole nations to the sword. Murdering men, women, and children. Thousands who had given them no offense. Moses, Aaron, Joshua, Samuel, David. Their lives were a tidal wave of rape and tortuous executions. The Jews made no converts. They butchered everyone. Saul's thousands put to the sword. David's tens of thousands. Children punished for misdeeds of parents. Simple people punished for misdeeds of rulers. Baskets of children's heads at the city gates as a warning!?!"

He takes a deep breath. The Captain General knows that you cannot compel anyone to live, or to love. It's useless to try. Calmer now, he concedes, "Well, my friend, you cannot be forced to believe in Jesus."

"That is a true history Captain. In the age of Jesus, most of the learned men, men of honor, whose ethics and virtue were beyond question, they were not persuaded by Jesus. They did not believe he was the Son of God. If he ever said he was. Who could pose a better argument than himself? Still most rejected Jesus. Why, after fifteen hundred years, when all that remains are words written about him, not by him, words attributed to him but never recorded until two hundred years later, arguments made by ordinary men. Why should anyone believe it?

"You are free to believe anything you wish."

"Am I free to live without the threat of God demanding my children's blood?"

"Freedom comes from accepting our mortality Luís. After that, everything is possible. When you have accepted death, the question of God's existence will be resolved. Not the opposite. After all, if living doesn't have a barnacle's worth of meaning, why live it?"

"Exactly. What could be clearer."

They pause. The Captain General notes the fluttering of the small stern sail in the light breeze.

Luís de Torres rarely spoke of all he'd lost, but a day did not pass without thoughts of his unburied family. Time had begun to dim certain images, but he was not able to genuinely forget. He'd become adept at surrendering his innermost nature, a deliberate letting go of reality; one day a friend less, the next, a mother less, one wife less, one child less. The spool of thread that tied him to life was unwinding. Yet in his awareness of being alone, he is not lonely. His heart is embittered against the world, the veil of time torn, but all hope has not left him.

After a lull of utter silence, Luís begins, "I suppose you're telling me that it's time to forget? To simply wall it up. Time to put away grudges and self-pity. To drink water from the Lethe. Is that right, Captain?"

Colón nods at the reference to the 'river of forgetfulness'. "Luís, every man is worse for holding a grudge. Guilt, self-pity, they tell us nothing. They exist to protect us from the past. Only the insane seek to suffer. Be true to your own soul, my friend. That is the best a man can do."

"The soul?" He twists and rolls the word on his tongue. He is pacing from helm to stern, touching the shrouds, the binnacle, running his hand along the rail, speaking as if remembering a lesson. "God is directing every minute detail of creation. And every soul is guided by His will. This is His plan for the world. Right?" He looks to the Captain General but does not wait. "All that has happened. To me and to you. To my family, and to everyman, is God's doing. Does God really see everything? Is that what you believe, Captain?"

Cristóbal Colón assesses Luís de Torres's state of mind. He believes that, unlike most men who long for eternity while fighting the inevitability of death, Luís longs for death and fights the eternity of his life. "I do not attempt to understand that which I nor any man cannot. Understanding is a small matter. No man can completely know the world in its perfection."

Exasperated, Colón scowls. "Many facts support the soul's existence, Luís. Without the soul it would be impossible for these facts to exist. Since there is no such thing as an impossible fact, the soul must exist."

Luís eyes flash, challenging the point. Secure in his thinking, he quickly responds. "By reverse reason you fool yourself into believing something proven, which cannot be proven. Facts do not follow opinions. It is the other way around Captain. You could claim anything to be real if the only basis for believing it is that no one has yet disproved it."

244 • PHILLIP SPOLIN

"But Luís, look about you." He steps away and sweeps his arms skyward. "Consider the course of the heavenly bodies. The creation, and the passing of life. Everything follows well-ordered rules. The universe is eternal and holy. Our souls long to be with God. You are an enlightened man of culture. You've studied civilizations and philosophies. You've had children and understand the miracle of birth. God's presence is revealed in nature's design. It can't all be an accident, Luís. Our dreams and desires exist. They came from somewhere. Someone gave us the tools to realize them. You see that astrolabe, there on the table? It is neither a stone nor a vegetable. Someone made it. Now look around." Again the sweeping arm. "Did this beauty all just 'happen'?"

De Torres shakes his head, and opens a hand, "Captain there is no logic to your argument."

"Luís. Think. Reason cannot possibly account for everything that happens every day in the world. Reason is only one star in a sky full of stars. Why confuse yourself with riddles when we won't ever unravel the secrets, the mystery?"

Luís' eyes are softening, his jaw relaxing. Despite the interpreter's words of denial and rejection, the Captain General senses a turning in his troubled companion. The wind shifts slightly, fluttering the sailor's hair. His cheeks cool. "No one is truly at ease in this world. Struggle is all we have. Isn't it Luís? And isn't it better than nothing? Be grateful. It is God's will."

"Be careful Captain. To assume to know the mind of God, well, there is no greater sin."

"My friend, be encouraged by your pain and confusion. Embrace it, for it means you are alive. Human! The wonders of life and the glory of the world are at your pleasure. You will be dead and in your grave soon enough with ample time to ponder the stars as the worms slowly eat you."

De Torres considers the many ways of being alive, and the singular way of death. He had been told that if he survived prison, he should promise himself the right to live, but Luís could not do that. Nor could the Jews fathom rumors of their pending annihilation. Because they could not imagine it, they failed to believe it possible. How could a ruler foment the destruction of his society? How could a fog of evil envelop their entire world? Then it was too late.

The Captain's eyes trace a loose halyard, causing the mainsail to shake. At that moment Harana booms, "Rodrigo! Pedro! Here, ya bastards! Get over an' put that sail right." He slaps the rail with his whip handle and glances astern to the Captain General and Luís de Torres.

Chapter 28
On Board

The instant the creature shows just below the surface, Rafrid yanks the long gaff under a forward fin. A heavy pool of blood slaps the hull as two men drag the catch on board.

The large head is gray-green and off-white underneath, with a long snout.

Victorio says, "It's d'lfin. Let it go." Pedro says, "What? 'At's good meat."

The struggling animal flops and quivers, then stills. Breathing heavily, its roving eyes seem to greet each man. How often had this dolphin wondered about 'men'? Did he swim close to the shoreline with his mate and calves to watch the gathering humans?

"It'll be a while fer im to die," says Victorio, "they're not like the other fish."

Dante asks, "Why? What's different?"

Despite growing up near a seaport, Dante is a farm-boy. He has birthed calves and sheep and lambs and dogs, he has sowed and fenced and planted and harvested, he has baled and fed. But off the farm he is ignorant of most things. What he knows about fish concerns mullet and sardine mixed with animal manure to spread on the fields for spring planting.

Victorio steps back as the others club the animal. Its eyes close.

"There, ya see, did you ever see a fish close its eyes? They're differnt, like the nat'al. Even the humpback and right whales. They 'ave families 'n protect their yungs."

Dante can't take his eyes off the streamlined creature. Victorio says, "Pedro was after tuny. They swim deep, followin' the lead of them d'lfin hunters that sweep out 'n circle fish. They don't eat tuny, so the tunny's safe. Some say d'lfin ain't evn fish. And they talk ta each other. Makin' clicky sounds. It's true."

Dante says, "You've heard them talk? Really?"

"Well, I've heard thur noises. Squeals and clicks. You will too. Night's the best time fer that. They sleep on top a the water, all t'gether like. I tell ya they act like a team and they kill sharks. I knows a man who swears a d'lfin saved 'is life when he went o'erboard in a storm. A group of 'em ther animals drove off the sharks. They even pushed 'im along in the water to shore."

Dante listens, at the same time watches intently as Pedro and Marco gut the animal. Its viscera steams and slides on the deck, sloshing to the gunnel and overboard.

"And looky there," Victorio says pointing to the soupy organs. "Ya see. It's hot inside. Ya know any other fish like that? Hot inside? I tell ya them are friend to man and we oughtn't be killin 'em.'"

Cristóbal Colón, stands with Gotzun on the poop, listening to Victorio. He turns away and shrugs his shoulders, the corners of his mouth turned down. His eyebrows raise and he tilts his head as if to ask the tall sailor's opinion

"An unhappy omen," Gotzun says.

Captain's Log

Monday Sept 24, 1492

I am having serious trouble with the crew, despite the signs of land that we have and those given to us by Almighty God. In fact, the more God show the men manifest signs that we are near land, the more their impatience and inconstant increases, and the more indignant they become against me. All day long and all night long those who are awake and able to get together never cease to talk to each other in circles, complaining that they will never be able to return home. They have said that it is insanity and suicidal on their part to risk their lives following the madness of a foreigner. They have said that not only am I willing to risk my life just to become a great Lord, but that I have deceived them to further my ambitions. They have also said that because my proposition has been contradicted by so many wise and lettered men who consider it vain and foolish, they may be excused for whatever might be done in the matter. Some feel that they have already arrived where men have never dared to sail and that they are not obliged to go to the end of the world, especially if they are delayed anymore and will not have sufficient provisions to return. I am told by a few trusted men (and these are few in number!) that if I persist in going onward, the best course of action will be to throw me into the sea some night. They will then affirm that I fell overboard while taking the position of the North Star with my quadrant. Since I am a foreigner, little or no account will be asked of the matter, but rather, there will be a great many men who will swear that God had given my just desserts on account of my rashness.

Harana stands in the shadow of a ladder. Having heard enough, he steps into the middle of the group and announces, "Ya know he came over the bows, not through a cabin window, for his command."

As if their brains were trained to freeze at his voice, all turn to the marshal. His eyes accuse, 'a mutiny?'; his stance dares, 'on his ship?'

"The Captain General, he's got the grace of our king n' queen, and many men whose boots yer not good enough ta 'ave yer asses kicked. An the capt'ns of those other ships? What about them? Can anyone here stand as but farts in their shadows?

"If any man doubt that fact, it best he speak now for I won't take it kindly anytime later." A meek voice is heard, "Where are we going?"

Then louder from behind, "When will we get there?"

Harana winces at the grunts of approval and smiling faces. The marshal turns and walks straight to the fool, like a harpoon, and spits overboard.

He fingers his scourge tucked in his belt, his knuckles hard like little men. He pulls out the whip, red welts at the quick of his fingers, and digs the ivory handle into Blanco's side. Angling his face against the fleshy skin of the tall man's neck, he growls, "Ya be thinking about being captain, do ya? You be the man ta follow when our lives be in the balance, are ya?" And he jams the whip deeper into the sailor's ribs with a forceful twist.

Harana doesn't wait for an answer. He pivots so each man can feel his gaze. He knows that strength and cunning confer the right of leadership. The crew are already turning away when ship's bells hurry their pace.

Chapter 29
Guanahani & Tenerife

Aboard the Santa Maria beneath a quarter moon at 2:00 am on October 12, 1942, Rodrigez de Triana, on watch with eyes fixed on the horizon, sees the stain of land and cries, 'Tierra! Tierra!"

Luís de Torres enters the Captain General's cabin dimly illuminated by a flickering candle. Dante is cradled on the floor, scrunched in against the hull with his legs half under the chart table. The two men face one another, Luís barefoot in open shirt and sagging britches, his hair loose of the tie. Colón stares expressionless, his threadbare tunic hanging from one shoulder.

Incongruously, he wears his winged crush-hat. Then standing in the indistinct shadows, they reach out, embrace, and slap each other's back while bouncing like children.

Luís proclaims, "You've done it! It's real! Your dream has come true!"

'My dream?' thinks Cristóbal, then with a gratified grin, "Well, let's say this is a good start."

Typical of the man to be cautious about success, Cristóbal has had so little, and always with a caveat. But never has he felt such exhilaration. Reaching for the malmsey, Cristóbal laughs at spilling more than fills their mugs. They drink and laugh, howl and cry. Raising his arm in celebration, he says," To the future."

Luís lifts his mug and repeats, "To the future."

Luís de Torres has not had a conversation during the past two years that wasn't dominated by the inequities of his life, the cruelty of society, or the murderous tyranny of those in power. This man who has denied the existence of the soul, who has concluded he has no reason to live, this man whose belief system has crumbled, now salutes the future.

Luís and Cristóbal feel a great sense of shared meaning and they toast allies, colleagues, supporters, friends, and well-wishers. They toast enemies, rivals, backbiters, informers, defamers and betrayers. Cristóbal credits those who have stood by him, encouraging him to persevere, none more earnestly than King Ferdinand and Queen Ysabela. He acknowledges the contribution of the converso community, their hope that this is a biblical voyage, a part of God's plan, as the Captain General truly believes it to be, but in a different sense than the Jews.

"You see, Luís, how this new land is the holy revelation that exalts the glory of God's mystery?"

The vision he holds for his future drifts to Cristóbal; nobility, respect, a world renown name, and wealth. Luís, despite the crippling burden of his memory, feels swept into something beyond his own circumstances. He muses, 'Perhaps this brutal world does have an order, and I a place in it.'

The Santa Maria groans, straining at its anchor, hooked into the earth ten fathoms below. De Torres stands beside the Captain General, his head bowed. Dante is agape, thrilled but hesitant to join their celebration. No banners or flags are flying, no despotic religious symbols displayed, no maniacal crowds cheer.

Kneeling in the cabin's cramped quarters, humbled by the immensity of his triumph, Cristóbal Colón recites a childhood psalm, praising and thanking God for this deliverance:

Non komo muestro Dyo, non komo muestro Senyor, Non komo muestro Rey, non komo muestro Salvador. Ken komo muestro Dyo, ken komo muestro Senyor, Ken komo muestro Rey, ken komo muestro Salvador. Loaremos a muestro Dyo, Loaremos a muestro Senyor, Loaremos a muestro Rey, Loaremos a muestro Salvador. Bendicho muestro Dyo, Bendicho muestro Senyor, Bendicho muestro Rey,

Bendicho muestro Salvador. Tu sos muestro Dyo, Tu sos muestro Senyor. Tu sos muestro Rey, Tu sos muestro Salvador.

There is none like our God, There is none like our Lord, There is none like our King, There is none like our Savior. Who is like our God?, Who is like our Lord?, Who is like our King?, Who is like our Savior? Let us thank our God, Let us thank our Lord, Let us thank our King, Let us thank our Savior. Blessed be our God, Blessed be our Lord, Blessed be our King, Blessed be our Savior. You are our God, You are our Lord, You are our King, You are our Savior.

Because the words of Cristóbal's prayer are familiar to him, Luís does not immediately comprehend what he is hearing. The prayer is intimate to his childhood. Then his breath catches and Luís realizes that Cristóbal is praying in Ladino.

Prayers not withstanding, Cristóbal's profound faith that he has obeyed God's plan is unshakeable. This voyage and its sacred charge to spread the word of Jesus Christ was received in prayer and sanctified by the Church of Rome. Even in his dreams, especially in his dreams, his destiny is to fulfill God's will.

Their prayers of gratitude ended, Cristóbal corks the flagon of sweet wine, puts his arm around Luís' shoulder, and says, "Being amphibious animals we must sometimes go ashore, and that we will do tomorrow. Good night, Luís."

Cristóbal Colon stands with both arms raised holding a beam to steady himself. He stares at Dante for a long moment, thinking intently, wondering.

Under the keel of a half moon, the night of the monumental land- fall passes. At five o'clock the island emerges in false dawn, as a white bird crosses overhead and the sun brightens a steely blue sky. The eggshell thin horizon merges with the ocean leaving little distinction between heaven and sea. The water is still, as if anything living near the surface has dropped into the depths. Sailors line the rail, facing due west into an off-shore breeze that carries a musty smell of land, the scent of a continent. The decks are quiet, but the sailors' minds are not. At anchor before this new world, the crewmen consider the morning turquoise water. They silently celebrate the exquisite thrill of reaching land.

These sailors on the Voyage of Discovery have heard the call of the sea. They are coarse, harsh, superstitious men, likely to read an omen in a bird's flight. Like their Captain they believe they have reached shores that will lead to the Indies and each fantasizes his future wealth and status.

Harana's sharp rasp interrupts. "Now don't get too anxious. You'll get yer chance later. Let's see what's out there. Ya don't want to end up in a cookin' pot."

The men survey their view. "I've ne'er seen an ocean so clear, er so warm."

"Aye. Ya can see the bottom like it wer a cupa water."

"It ain't the water. Ya mates ar missin' it. Don't ya see it? Can't ya feel it? Open yur eyes and look. Just to port thar. It's the light. Ya fish-bait av ne'er seen a sunrise like this un."

And there it was, a new dawn, a yellow streak rounding the earth, shooting rays over the water farther than any of these men had ever witnessed. The power of dawn at sea is like nothing else in nature. It summons men to the awakening world, as if the rising sun is a rebirth of creation, a promise of new life and mystery. Surely now is the moment to capture where one wants to be in life, to mark when one is happiest; for Luís, the past, for Cristóbal, it is right now, for Dante, young and inexperienced, it is the future.

Dante stands beside Luís de Torres with the men at the rail. He stands tall, chest puffed out, cheeks flush above his pursed lips. He says in a murmur to Revela, as if she were beside him, wanting to share this with her. "It's here just like he said. The beaches are golden and there are palm trees and jungle like the Canaries. Everyone's afraid of cannibals. Rodrigo de Triana, they call him 'Baruch', saw land first. So I guess he gets the prize. There are lots of naked brown people on the beach. The Captain General and Don Luís and the other captains, and even Rodrigo, are going ashore. They took the big flags. I wasn't permitted to go, but maybe tomorrow. The Captain says the natives seem friendly. Gotzun says he pities them. Everyone's happy."

The Santa Maria's sailing dingy carries the banners of their King and country. Aboard are Cristóbal Colón, Luís de Torres, Maestra Bernal, Maestra Nanfilips, Rodrigo, Jacobo. They have rowed to the Niña and Pinta to collect the Pinzón brothers, the notary of the fleet, Rodrigo de Escovedo, and Rodrigo Sanchez, of Segovia. The gentle, morning waves carry them to the shore of the New World. Cristóbal Colón is first in the surf. As anyone might after 30 days at sea, he slips, and goes to his knees.

Ship's log:

As I saw that they were very friendly to us, and perceived that they could be much more easily converted to our holy faith by gentle means than by force, I presented them with some red caps, and strings of beads to wear upon the neck, and many other trifles of small value, ... they seemed on the whole to me, to be a very poor people.

They all go completely naked, ...some with scars of wounds upon their bodies, ...there came people from the other islands ... who endeavored to make prisoners of them, and they defended themselves. I thought then, and still believe, that these were from China.

After only a day the Santa Maria lifts anchor leaving the island he has named San Salvador to explore other islands.

... They came loaded with balls of cotton, parrots, javelins, and other things too numerous to mention; these they exchanged for whatever we chose to give them. I was very attentive to them, and strove to learn if they had any gold. Seeing some of them with little bits of this metal hanging at their noses, I gathered from them by signs that by going southward or steering round the island in that direction, there would be found a king who possessed large

vessels of gold, and in great quantities. I endeavored to procure them to lead the way thither, but found they were unacquainted with the route.

.... This is a large and level island, with trees extremely flourishing, and streams of water; there is a large lake in the middle of the island, but no mountains: the whole is completely covered with verdure and delightful to behold.

The natives are an inoffensive people, and so desirous to possess anything they saw with us, that they kept swimming off to the ships with whatever they could find, and readily bartered for any article we saw fit to give them in return the gold, also, which they wear in their noses, is found here, but not to lose time, I am determined to proceed onward and ascertain whether I can reach Cipango.

... I do not, however, see the necessity of fortifying the place, as the people here are simple in war-like matters, as your Highnesses will see by those seven which I have ordered to be taken and carried to Spain in order to learn our language and return, unless your Highnesses should choose to have them all transported to Castile, or held captive in the island. I could conquer the whole of them with fifty men, and govern them as I pleased...

...the natives whom I had taken on board informed me by signs that there were so many of them that they could not be numbered; they repeated the names of more than a hundred. I determined to steer for the largest, which is about five leagues from San Salvador; the others were some at a greater, and some at a less distance from that island. They are all very level, without mountains, exceedingly fertile and populous, the inhabitants living at war with one another, although a simple race, and with delicate bodies.

Before that same dawn when Rodrigez de Triana cries, 'Tierra!", far east back across the Ocean Sea, the sun sets in the Canary Islands. On Tenerife, above a small fishing village in the Orotava Valley, in the shadow of Teide, ancient stone walls terrace the ground where Revela and David walk on a promontory cliff.

Sunlight reflects a lavender and orange radiance off patches of ice on the great volcano's peak. Below the young couple, waves crash into a lacuna in the rock wall, then, high up, blow out a small fissure through a narrow passageway. A column of water shoots a hundred feet in the air as if from a whale spouting and David and Revela playfully tug and shove each other into the waterspout. Soaking, salty and panting from their game, they collapse in a cushion of white and pink periwinkle. Steam rises from their clothes as they survey the radiant sky.

Revela looks past the field of thick nespora bush that runs to the cliff's edge. Hovering over the yellow fruit she notices a ghostly darkness, an out of focus mass, the silhouette of a swarm of flying insects. Mostly aphids and flying ants, they are food to the sea birds that nest in the ledges of the cliff face. Over the ocean, beyond the cliff, a second obscure image catches the tail of her eye. A crescent shaped flock of birds advances from the north, soaring in tight formation, urged on by the setting sun. Their piercing whistle, an accident of beak and throat shape, travels ahead of them, the sound of a two-note flute. They are swifts, small-bodied birds with tapering swept back wings and scissor like tails. They ride the wind currents in the dark blue, last light of day. When they reach the insects, their song ends in a sudden silence. They dive, a foraging funnel of open beaks scooping the bugs. The air is so thick with insects, the birds leave no clear path behind. They surge high, circle above Revela and David, then sweep in a return dive over the bushes. They feast, again and again through the swarm. Then, in a final ascent, they follow an oblique trajectory, pivot over themselves, and plunge down the cliff-face. As they disappear, the sun spears the western sky a golden apricot, then magenta, and finally, as it dips into the Ocean Sea, a ruby adieu.

Revela and David lay beside each other, listening to the crash of waves, watching the sun nestle into the elbow where Tiede rises from the sea.

Sunset, the close of day, when the mind surrenders to savor the day's allowances and mark its rejections and fears.

Revela says, "Doesn't the sun look good going down over the sea? It's beautiful, isn't it?" She thinks, 'I am so very far away from home and friends. Still, I feel my heart sing.'

"Yes. So intense. Nothing like home." David winces at the word. "What were you talking about with my mother?"

She feels his yearning, his physical longing, and it makes her shy.

"Oh, just about the sail and this island. It's so beautiful. She says it's God's blessing that we are here."

A sly smile, almost a smirk, dances across his face. "Yes, according to her everything good is God's blessing."

Revela, anxious to show her interest, says, "And she told me about how special the Jews are in the Bible. And about your commandments. There are so many. I'm learning a lot from her."

"Well, listen Revela. Don't believe everything she says."

"What do you mean?"

He thinks, 'I mean I'm a heretic', and says, "Let's just say that I don't believe all our rituals, all those commandments, are really commanded by God."

"Then who?"

'Who indeed!' "They are the inventions of rabbis, Revela. It's all, well mostly all, superstition. Make believe. Fairy tales for adults."

Revela bites her thumb-nail and considers what David is saying. "But didn't God give you the commandments? Didn't he tell Moses to lead the Jews out of Egypt? That's what your mother says."

"Yes, I know. It's a wonderful story, and it has done well to preserve the community. And the commandments, the laws, have kept families and neighbors at peace." He pursues his lips, "And perhaps more importantly, they preserve the power of the rabbis."

"I don't understand David. I thought you all believed in your God. That's why you're different. If you don't, why did you run away?"

David remembers as a devout youth losing himself in the cadence of the chants, the yearning for a divine connection. "At one time, for a long time, I had faith in the rituals. And because they were ancient I thought they would put me in touch with the origin of everything in the oldest part of myself. Like talking to my soul. I thought perhaps superstition was a kind of masked wisdom."

Truthfully, David had concluded early in life that all religions were basically absurd lies. The superstitious rites were childish, the fantasies of heaven and repeated invocations of obedience, meaningless. He believed people simply took comfort in the togetherness that came with the mysteries, the sacred names for God, the diets, the gathering in mosques, synagogues and cathedrals, all the symbols that come with belief and faith. But absent those contrivances, without that comfort, men were left with their fear of death.

He looks Revela in the eye. "I joined the fun, mocking the Christians. The absurdity of bowing to bits of the Saints bones, the weird costumes, the bloody statues, the 'eat this, the flesh' and 'drink this, the blood' ceremonies. You know, the things you learned and believed in church."

Revela nods.

"Then I looked around and saw that the Jews, my own people, looked just as strange with their fancy skull caps and tasseled prayer shawls, chanting prayers as they rocked and dipped and swayed." He stopped, then as if the question had perplexed him all his life, "With all that continuous prayer, why no results?" He looks to her for an answer that does not come.

"It's all madness, Revela. The Jews, the Christians, the Muslims. All of it. Presuming that one is the personal object of a divine plan is, well, the epitome of vanity. Everyone pestering God. They just do it because it's been done for so long. Not because there is anything god-like or sacred about it."

"I don't understand. Don't you believe in anything? What about the Bible?"

"Oh, it's a wonderful book, and the stories teach us much. But, Revela, it is not the word of God. Men wrote it. Pious men, but men."

"Why do you say that? I thought it was written by God."

"Revela, the Bible is filled with contradictions. Think about it. Moses supposedly wrote the book, but it says things like, 'Moses talked with the Lord face to face', and 'Moses was the meekest of men.'" Then, his words coming faster, his tone more urgent, "Don't you see? If Moses wrote it, how can he describe his own death and burial? How is it we're told of prophets that came after his death? He names places that did not exist until centuries after his death. He tells of events that did not occur in his lifetime, speaks of kings that had not yet lived. It makes no sense."

David breathes deeply to temper himself. This is not the conversation he wants to have. His examples are for scholars, better to keep it simple. "The Bible looks back in time Revela. And there is so much more I could point out. Did Adam and Eve just pop out of nowhere? Haven't you ever wondered how God could be so cruel as to cause the flood and kill everyone? What about Noah's children, with whom did they start the human race again? Did God create us just too damn us? What about the slaughtering throughout history of women and children? What about the slaughter that is going on now in the name of God? The torture and burning. Do you think that is a plan of God? If there were really a God, or a Buddha or an Allah, or a Goddess of Mercy, this bloodshed couldn't happen."

Revela is barely keeping up, but her mind echoes her church lessons; Wasn't He sent by His father to redeem mankind? Didn't He promise a new life for the world? She says, "Well, I guess I never thought about it. But what do your parents say? Your father is the rabbi."

'Don't I know.' "My thoughts are known to my father and mother but they go no further. These kinds of questions are not allowed. Reason can be used to settle arguments but not to challenge divine scripture. Superstition rules my community just like it does yours."

His body relaxes as he rolls over on his side, picks at the periwinkle and tosses tufts of blue into the air. "Superstition and reason are like oil and water. If my true beliefs were known I would be subject to cherem, excommunication. And that would mean no one, not even my family, could associate or even speak with me. I would have to leave the community. His mind flashes to the proclamation:

With the judgment of the angels and of the saints we excommunicate, cut off, curse, and anathematize David ben Violino, with the consent of the elders and all this holy congregation....by the 613 precepts written... cursed be he by day, cursed be he by night, in sleeping and in waking, going out and coming in ...the lord shall not pardon him, and the wrath and fury of the lord shall be kindled against him, and shall lay upon him all the curses which are written in the book of the law.... The Lord shall destroy his name under the sun, and cut him off for his undoing from all the tribes of Israel, with all the curses of the firmament which are written in the book of the Law...

"If I were in your community I would be burned alive. right?"

"Oh, that would be awful, David. Then it's better we keep it secret. Our secret. Something no one can take from us." Revela thinks about her own secret, and the guilt she feels, what she cannot tell him.

David's smile signals his warmth. 'I've told you my thoughts.' He asks, "And you? What is it you believe?"

"Oh, I don't know. I always liked Bible stories but they seem written for children."

"They are."

"But I do believe in God, David. I do pray to Jesus for things. I've wished I didn't believe. But I can't help it. I do."

David said, "If I thought there was a God I could speak to, I would say, 'The Jews have no more blood. Please choose another tribe.'"

Revela laughs and reaches to touch his face. His cheeks are warm. He grasps her arm and rests his head in her hand, then turns to kiss her fingers.

Revela can feel, even hear, his heart thumping, and senses he is anxious about something other than their touching.

"Revela, do you remember that first day in Palos, when you and Dante came aboard? The way the children immediately attached themselves to you, especially Chavery?"

"Yes, sure. They're all wonderful. Why?"

"Well, do you want children? I mean, your own?"

"Yes, of course I do. Doesn't everyone?"

"Perhaps. I hadn't thought of it that way. I know I do."

Still holding his hand, Revela leans close, settling her cheek against his chest. The boundaries of the past have collapsed, swept away like a foot print by the tide. Revela, a flower budding in the morning sunlight, is radiant, alluringly vulnerable. She has never felt so free, so open. Perfectly sure of herself, with no coy pretense, she tempts him and they surrender into each other's arms.

A flush rises from her neck to her cheeks, her heartbeat quickens, a riot in her chest. She tilts her head to offer the fullness of her upper lip, her tender throat. Her brown eyes flare with fire, his shine with desire.

Trembling in a kind of triumph, David's arm circles her waist, his fingertips caress her face, his mouth finds hers. Revela responds to his wanting as his hand weaves itself into her hair and he brings her down. The euphoria of their long deep kisses reaches a frenzy as he presses himself on her. It excites her to feel urged on. Weakened, she offers her lips to cushion his ravenous kisses, and bewitched, they float in timelessness. All her secrets tossed aside, Revela submits to what he might do. Like seeds buried in a wasteland that burst through the earth, despite living in a culture of death, love finds a way.

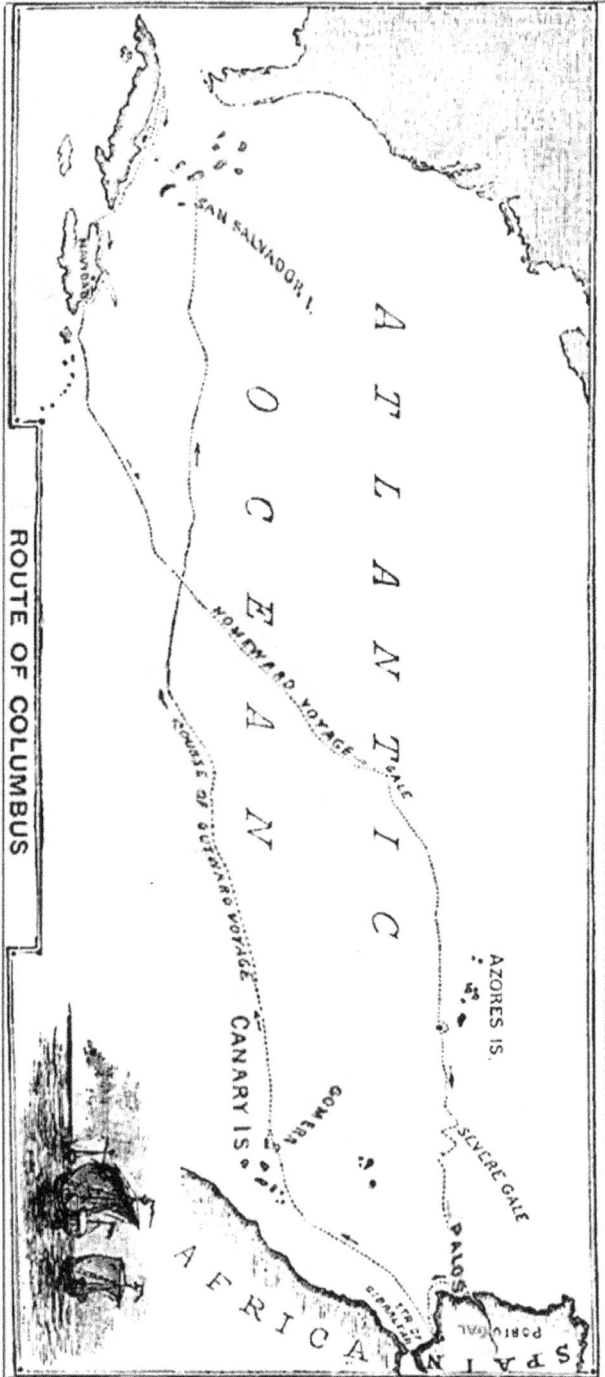

ROUTE OF COLUMBUS

Chapter 30
Dante in the New World

During the second week in the New World the Admiral designates Luís, Gotzun, Harana, and Dante along with five other sailors from the Niña and from the Pinta, to go ashore. They carry marbels, coveted by the African natives, as trade goods. Island natives, Taino, wait for them on the narrow beach, and circle the ships in canoes, hailing the sailors, perhaps believing they may be gods.

Immediately on landing the inquisitive surround the Europeans. Luís de Torres seeks the leader, who might speak a familiar language. Harana, close to him, is wary of the absence of women and children. Dante stays at Gotzun's side.

It isn't long before the initial excitement fades. The natives are unable to understand the newcomers, and the sailors are less than impressed by parrots and shells. Many natives drift into the chaparral, and the Spaniards cluster together with more questions than answers, wondering when their treasure will appear.

Dante looks down the long shoreline of powdered white sand, brilliant in the violent sun. He marvels at its sparkling softness in contrast to the golden coast near Palos or the black sands of the Canaries. A turquoise tongue of ocean recedes as miniscule marine animals disappear into the sand. The beach ends in a scalloped border of chaparral with a sharp, sudden shade.

The sun stabs through Dante's eyelids. He squints at the water, momentarily blinded by the glare. In the distance he thinks he sees two people dart from the surf and cross the beach into the jungle. He stretches his neck and flares his nostrils. Although the distance obscures size, Dante is certain the quick movements indicate someone small, or young. On impulse, he runs up the beach toward the figures.

The shore makes an 'S' curve, and when he stops to look back, Dante's sight line to his shipmates is blocked by palms. A few meters ahead, staring at him, are two natives. Walking now, he approaches a boy and girl, both close to his age. The morning sun's radiance reflects off the sea with the flash of a world just born and he squints to prevent it slicing his eyes. 'That glare again, when was it?' The same brilliance haloes the bronzed skinned teenagers. Ankle deep in the cerulean water, each has shockingly dark eyes and straight black hair. The girl wears only red and blue feathers. The boy fingers a leather pouch hanging from a lanyard around his neck. Dante raises his arm in greeting, mimicking Gotzun, and the young natives, giggling, do the same. He stops and they approach him, reaching for his arms, pulling his clothes, touching his face, stroking his hair, smelling his body, pointing at his sea-blue eyes. Confused, Dante thinks, 'this is not the way it is supposed to be. I'm supposed to be the discoverer, the explorer. What makes me so interesting?'

All three nod and grunt, uncertain what to do. Dante gestures to the horizon, to show where he comes from, and the boy and girl goggle their eyes, impressed. Then the smiling girl says something to the boy and they begin to pull Dante. The young explorer is wary. He pulls back, shakes his head 'no', scanning the beach for his crewmates. Dark thoughts flash through his mind. The natives stop cajoling, the girl takes Dante's hand and caressing it, running her hand up his arm, then lifting and placing it on her shoulder. The naked girl smiles a white, toothy grin. He nods.

Dante glances once more in the direction of his shipmates, then turns to the boy and girl and follows them on a winding path through beach scrub and palmettos. He is casting his fate on a gamble. The sound of the ocean ends, shutting out the universe he knows like the closing of a theater curtain. The duo moves quickly, looking over their shoulders and encouraging Dante with smiles and laughter.

"Jenu, jenu," they call to him.

He stays close behind, navigating the underbrush of a canopy of tall palm and cypress. The sweet fragrance of honeysuckle combines with the musty odor of decaying saw grass.

He calls out, "Wait, slow down." and the girl understands.

Across a small stream, the path widens leading to an enclosure rimmed with circular, thatched huts. A fire smolders near the center of the compound, and smoke rises from the conical roof-peaks. No one is there, at least no one Dante can see. A skinny, old dog sleeps in the shade of a drying rack, and a tethered monkey chatters. The girl takes Dante's hand and leads him into one of the huts. It is windowless, dark. The air is stale and the dirt floor hints at unseen clutter. Baskets of food hang from the ceiling on leather strips while tall poles support large cloth sacks hanging between them. Dante considers that one of the sacks contains a body. The three teenagers squat near a small fire in the center, its smoke rising through the palm-frond roof. Using a coconut shell, the girl scoops a lumpy liquid from a warming earthen pot and hands it to Dante.

Motioning him, she says, "Carg. Carg."

The boy grins encouragement as the young Spaniard forces himself to swallow some gruel. The girl presents a wooden cage. Pointing to the green and yellow bird, she says slowly, "lorso, lorso." Then she takes his hand again, and placing it just below her throat, says, "Atzi". She repeats, "Atzi".

Dante isn't certain if this declares her name, or that she is a girl. His hand settles just above her breasts, and he repeats, "Atzi."

The boy slaps a hand to his own chest and says, "Jayjo".

Then both regard Dante with inquiring eyes, and as the girl taps his chest he announces, "Dante – boy,", and again, "Dante."

"Dante – boy", they respond in unison.

Proudly, Jayjo shows Dante a club with a heavy, burled end. Dante hefts the weapon and admires the force it promises. He shows them his knife, the farm shank, his singular reminder of home. The shiny metal is magical to them.

Dante mimics cutting as Jayjo fingers the sharp edge. They insist Dante take off his shirt. He does, demonstrating how the wooden buttons open and close.

Atzi tries it on with Dante's help. Jayjo laughs as she struggles with the sleeves. She connects the top button with a middle hole and the boys bellow. Dante reaches to help her unbutton the shirt and his hand brushes her breast. Pulling back, he blushes and says, "Oh, sorry." Atzi blushes too, not from his contact, but because her nipples have hardened and she sees his embarrassment. Jayjo then tugs at Dante's pants. He fully removes them, a moment of astonishment for his new friends, who find another skin, his undergarment. They both pull at the braies, he resists, but bends his bottom toward Jayjo. The boy puts on Dante's pants, backwards. The half-naked teenagers join hands pulling the circle, laughing, understanding each could be the other.

Jayjo begins to point and name eager to show Dante the artifacts of his life - not much even by 15th century European standards. Hand woven mats cover sections of the dirt floor where they sit, and cloth sacs hang from support poles. Small candles, woven baskets, and lengths of rope are scattered around. Dante thinks, 'Not even a table. Not even a chair.'

Jayjo shows Dante his personal treasures mostly relating to survival in a dangerous world, defenses against poisonous land and sea creatures. Outside the hut, he produces a well-crafted, feathered arrow, tipped with a thin stone. In one fluent motion the native boy nocks it onto the waxed string of a short bow, draws, and releases. The arrow shoots in a low arch across the compound, and strikes a short post. Jayjo puffs up. Atzi grabs the bow from him and strikes the target higher and deeper.

Jayjo, makes an elaborate gesture and empties his small leather pouch onto the ground. He displays the contents to Dante; a long pointed tooth, but Dante cannot imagine the mouth of a jaguar, a beak shaped bone, an egg shaped stone, an arrowhead and the scar it left.

Atzi speaks briefly to Jayjo and they each grab long pointed poles. Pulling Dante, they race out of the compound on a path opposite the one coming in. They move quickly, leaving the jungle at the edge of a small, nearly beachless, horseshoe bay. One hundred meters out an exposed coral reef contains the flat water. Atzi leads the boys, running ahead into the water. Dante feels giddy, wild in play.

Atzi and Jayjo dive into the deep, magnified and slowed in the silky liquid, highlighted in the brilliant sun. Dante marvels at the time they spend submerged and then surfacing with glittering fish spiked on their poles. He can clearly see the bottom but impossible to judge the depth. It could be ten meters or ten fathoms. He attempts to spear a fish but cannot stay deep long enough. The young European luxuriates in the water, moving through, so much more than just wet.

The afternoon sun dries the ocean off Dante as he ambles on the shore. His body moves through space, the air as real a substance as the water. He strokes the new soft fuzz on his face and lays in the fine, white, powdered sand that sticks to his salty skin like the pollen of a yellow hyacinth.

Watching his new friends in the sea, he thinks of what Gotzun had said, "Viewing people on the beach from land is to see people entering the water; to view people from aboard ship is to see them emerge, born from the ocean."

He lies down, stretching his feet toward the water's curvy dance as the beach angles down to the shore, barely elevating his head. The receding tide has left the hot sand firm, and when he wiggles, it holds his shape. He shuts his eyes and the world turns bright red. He smells the salt and the birds, and hears the caressing rhythm of small waves. He feels the air rush into his chest and smiles, wondering what Revela might think if she could see him now.

Dante senses himself belonging to this primitive life, but is unsure he should feel this way. Revela can decipher feelings, and he craves her guidance. What might she say about his new friends and this magnificent adventure?

Satisfied with their catch, Atzi and Jayjo lead Dante back to the village, now animated with generations of dark skinned natives. Two tall men with insect huge eyes watch Dante. Clad in short aprons they are adorned with leather pouches around their necks, yellow feathers circling their ankles, and are armed with bows and arrows. An old woman, her shriveled body folded upon itself, sits in the dirt outside a hut and offers a toothless grin as Dante enters. Several children duck their heads into the hut to ogle him, but do not enter.

Five natives in the smoky room crowd with the three new friends, joining to eat the fresh roasted fish. Atzi encourages Dante to drink coconut juice from a half nut, and the semi-fermented liquid makes him dizzy. Dusk comes and cricket-like sounds announce the dark. In a moment of panic, Dante makes the half-hearted insistence, "I must go." But he stays, resolving instead to leave at dawn.

The room dims as the fire dwindles. An old man sitting across the fire, opposite Dante, begins an eerie chant, a muffled, dry murmur. Jayjo and Atzi gaze into the fire, arms wrapped around their knees, eyes narrowed to slits.

Dante makes no effort to understand the man. A story is being recited, the way Gotzun tells stories, and he thinks he understands the man though it makes no sense to him that he might. He looks to Jayjo who is rocking on his haunches, deep in concentration. Atzi catches Dante's eye and gestures, her hand waving behind her head, and Dante guesses at her meaning. Immersed in this primitive life Dante considers that the old man could be reading the clouds and the moon to explain why they live as they do.

The fire dies, the story teller is quiet, and the natives fade away. Jayjo swoops into his hammock. Dante cannot see in the darkened smoky room, but thinks the other sacks are also occupied. After two months at sea he is keenly aware of the jungle night sounds. He confuses the chatter of monkeys with birdsong and croaking frogs. Next to him, Atzi shudders to grunts and panting, discordant, sourceless sounds in the night. His thoughts accelerate. These people, the way they live, unimaginable to him as a farm boy, confuse him but at the same time render his own life more understandable. He thinks, 'What would my life on the farm be to them?'

Atzi places her hand on his shoulder as she did on the beach and looks into his eyes. His breath quickens. Trembling, he reaches for her. They kiss awkwardly at first, then embrace. Dante's hands rush over her body, touching and caressing. The nipple he admired is hard again, and in his mouth. He breathes heavily, fondling and groping Atzi's body in a furious ardor.

Pushing away, she slows him down, yet clings to him. "Wasto, Dante. Wasto." He curbs his passion, but only momentarily. She opens herself. The arrival of European man to the New World begins.

The girl remains in his arms as bird song and shrieking monkeys signal the morning. Dante, awash in visions, is uncertain he has slept or even closed his eyes. Atzi wakes, her cheeks flushed like a child, her black eyes alert. A new power has been launched in Dante's world. He has met the challenge and a sense of triumph coils within him.

Jayjo, Atzi and Dante slip out the hut and down the path that leads back to the beach where they met. At the water's edge, the three join hands and say farewell. Atzi and Dante hug, and Jayjo extends a closed hand motioning his friend to accept what he holds. Dante looks at the gift, the rock from Jayjo's talisman sac, the egg-shaped stone he held up to the sun.

Dante in turn, hands his knife to the astonished native, recalling for a moment, the last time he offered this knife, he'd taken a man's life.

Dante takes two backward steps, pivots, and begins to retrace yesterday's path along the beach. His lips tighten as if he might laugh or burst into tears. His walk is more erect, his head held higher, his eyes are lambent. He is fearless. Looking back after rounding the 'S' curve, he turns to see only the barren sea and the jungle, and curses for denying himself a last look of his friends.

That night, curled in his sleeping corner aboard the Santa Maria, his intuition senses he is in a place that joins here to there. He becomes a witness, testifying to his sister; "Revela, we went ashore and I met some natives. Atzi and Jayjo. They were my age and we went spear fishing. I stayed in their hut overnight. They sleep in hanging sacs. They were real! We swore a friendship, but I'll probably never see them again. I gave him my knife and he gave me his special stone. The captain and Harana were angry the way I disappeared. They thought I was aboard the Pinta and did not punish me. I showed the captain my stone. He liked it and is keeping it safe for me."

Chapter 31
Ygnacio & Lily

During the sail from Spain, confined below deck, Lily's fragile mind spun into a dislocated consciousness. But soothed by her week in the Canaries, where soft greens and yellows mute into each other, she begins to heal. Her sense of place returns, her psyche begins to reassemble. She wonders if perhaps this is somewhere she could survive her shattered self.

Following Ygnacio's orders, Berecillo de Arbolluvia arranged their passage to the island of Gomera. Lily learns she will be topside on the ship during the two-day sail from Las Palmas to the smaller, western island. The seas are following and the wind steady, the same weather system that sends the Voyage of Discovery across the Ocean Sea.

The pearl white sea dazzles Lily's eyes. She is euphoric, enjoying the gout of cool salt spray over the bow, the wind gusting through her hair, and the sharp ocean smells. Seagulls with their shrill quarreling fly to the ship, racing it almost within reach, then suddenly veer off at right angles. Lily lives with the orphaned feeling of being alone in the world and she senses a slim hope that this is may be her birth into a new life.

In the hacienda of the Governess, Elenora Bobadilla, Lily sits in a straight backed chair on the water stained floor. Hands flat on her thighs, her arms resemble the twin handles of the cracked urn beside her. Her pink mouth gapes like a child's, a weariness akin to age marks her face, not the full withering, but its early promise.

Lily's eyes flit around the room, as though her vision cannot keep up with her mind. She practices forgetfulness in the hope of creating a graveyard for Debrun's dungeon. The list of things she wants to forget is long. The place where her soul and spirit once flourished is hollow, still she is alive enough. 'I do not know what I was', she muses, 'but I've danced with death, and I am not afraid of what I might become. I'll never be afraid again.'

The farm girl's introduction to Elenora is brief, the Governess dismissing her with a quizzical expression and a slight, but welcoming smile. From the window the girl watches an exchange in the garden between Ygnacio and the Governess. The woman, dressed in simple peasant garb, wrings her long hands as though they are soiled.

Elenora instinctively takes the measure of Ygancio, evaluating his strengths and failings. She reads the soldier's expression as arrogant and cold. His face, once hinting of things to come with childhood faint lines, now defined with deep creases of cruelty. The Governess concludes he is a man not simply mistaken occasionally, but nearly always completely wrong.

Lily slides forward to the edge of her chair, straining to hear their conversation.

"Yes señor, this is a wonderful country. Majestic mountains surrounded by the great Ocean Sea." Then placing her finger to her chin, as if remembering, "Of course, the half-wit peasants are infested with lice and stupid. And their villages exude the stench of penury." She smiles at Ygnacio. "But no matter. The sky is immense and the fields are filled with food. Though primitive life does promote vulgarity, does it not?"

Ygnacio dips his head and raises his shoulders in a childish shrug, as if uncertain. "You are so correct, madam."

She tilts her head, flashing her profile, the sculpted beauty of a Greek goddess, "Tell me señor, what business might a knight of the *Cronistas de Armas* have with a boy?"

Ygnacio is not accustomed to answering questions, but does so with a creative confidence. Raising his chin slightly, his eyes beading like a monk at prayer and speaking as if he'd proven the roundness of the earth, he lies, "A message from his father. The man was like the same to me. God rest his golden soul. It is a matter of honor."

Elenora judges that the Ygnacio's face does not match his words. She knows Dante is safe, somewhere on the ocean, but probably safe. She picks a warm, ripe peach, examines it, then holds it to her cheek, the color of its skin identical to her own. Walking, her eyes widen again in the sham of remembering, not actually looking at Ygnacio but aware of him at the edge of her vision, and she says, "Yes, that young man. Dante, right? He sailed with my friend Cristóbal Colón the great Captain General. They seek the route across the Ocean Sea to India."

The governess leans forward jutting out her chin and fills her mouth with the soft fruit, thrusting her hand away from her body and shaking it to avoid a spurt of juice. Ygnacio reaches to his breast pocket, about to offer his handkerchief, the lace gift from Lily, but reconsiders. To camouflage the movement, he pats his chest.

Having questioned sailors at the harbor, Ygnacio already knows about Dante - and how he hates that news. Hearing it again causes a wicked tremor, a stinging pain in his side. He feigns surprise, but cannot conceal his contempt from the Governess. He also knows how her husband died at the hands of a mob. However, there remains a missing piece to the puzzle. With a level stare of his harsh eyes, he says, "And the girl?"

There it was. If there is one thing Elenora relies on, it is her assessment of men. The curl of his lips twist into an abyss of hatred, hatred so vile it demands another kind of blood to warm his body. Of course Elenora knows of Revela and her travel with the Jews to Tenerife. Repulsed, she watches Ygnacio lick his twitching lips. Ygnacio does not see the anger explode in her eyes. 'Yes', she agrees with herself. 'Shrewd and cunning, but lacking courage. He is not a *caballero*'.

The Governess, a woman quite able to keep things to herself, sets her chin into the wind. Her eyes drift to the horizon, as she recalls Cristóbal's attachment to Dante. 'His sister', she thinks. Her mouth betrays no tension as she says, "I never saw any girl." This is true.

Ygnacio and Lily leave the small fortress. Elenora Bobadilla sits on a red cushioned, high-back chair, her arms resting in her lap. She reflects on her position, her attributes. She has always been confident of her exceptional beauty and the power it affords her. How often has she said to that place deep inside, 'like the bird of paradise, beauty is my reason for living'. But so is her all consuming ambition. What does she want? She wants more - more wealth, more adoration, more power.

'This soldier, Ygnacio', she thinks, 'I hope to never see him again.' If she had looked directly into his eyes, she would have seen a cold, icy viciousness. The Governess of Gomera elongates her neck, holding her self-admired head high. She concentrates her gaze as if seeing a distant vision through a fog, a vision of herself, sitting exalted, a queen.

Ygnacio and Lily follow Revela's trail, sailing from Gomera to La Laguna, the deep-water port on Tenerife's north east coast. The soldier stands at the prow gripping the main-mast stay. Lily sits amidships, where motion is least felt.

Ygnacio juts his nose into the air, a habit since childhood. Although the scent of Elenora stays with him, he is not fascinated by those kohl-lined eyes and chiseled features. He is disappointed in the Governess. He found the lady lacking, not matching his expectations. He views her as he does most women of a certain age, wrinkly and unattractive. 'Clearly she has enjoyed too many years of life. Age does that', he thinks.

In truth, women have inevitably disappointed Ygnacio, starting with his mother who always sided with his sadistic father. As a boy he understood she did so under fear of a severe beating, and forgave her each time. But no matter, Ygnacio does not trust women. He often recalls his 'Ecclesiastics', "more bitter than death is woman..."

Dante can no longer be pursued, he was out of the game. Ygnacio shifts his consuming spite for the boy to Revela. He reasons that since the pair landed with the Jews, and Dante remained on board, then Revela stayed with the exiles.

In his childhood, he had trusted Revela, when she was a friend of his sister, Marta. But after the cat burning, and the thought flares his nostrils for the sweet stench of that screaming, furred devil, she had betrayed him. His lips curl. 'Elenora Bobadilla. Revela. Just another cunt', he mutters. Remembering the *romería*, he recalls what she said to him before turning her back. "Many in your family and mine are unhappy, but you are a beast. Evil and unhappy." 'The cunt.'

Arriving in Tenerife they learn that the five kingdoms of the island are divided like a pie, joined at the peak of Teide. The borders extend down from the volcano's lava dome to the sea, like spokes of a wheel. The ancient paths are major travel routes. It is easiest to cross from one kingdom to another where the borders meet, near the center of the pie, high on the mountain.

Barecillo de Arbolluvia had advised Ygnacio that Doramus brought the Jews to his father's kingdom of Adeje in the north of the island. Lily and Ygnacio depart La Laguna on horseback. Starting up the mountain, they plan to travel through the *bosque* to the rim of the lower crater, beneath the lava dome, then cross over to descend the trail on the northern slope into the realm of Bencomo.

Ygnacio has not told Lily of his dark mission. She rides a small black pony behind him. She sees in his face the stubborn set of a man with revenge on his mind, and overhears enough to know who he is looking for, but does not know why.

Travelling through the ancient forest, Lily's mind struggles to remain present. She floats in this liminal state, not fully a dream, but on the fringe of becoming one. Her thoughts are like being on the crest of a wave about to break, with a dark shield guarding her mind from brutal recollections, while another part of her mind tries to voice hidden memories. She hears Ygnacio speak the names Revela and Dante. They are familiar and should be part of a seamless chain from the past, before Debrun, but she cannot conjure a complete picture. Her history begins and ends with the suffocation of that barbarous terror and pain. After all, for Lily to survive means to forget.

Massive trees grow close together in the *bosque*, controlling the temperature and absorbing all sound. The stillness is remarkable, as if every audible aspect of life is sealed in place, awaiting a signal. The deep carpet of decay hushes the horses' shuffling hooves. Leaves fall as softly as snow. The flapping wings of a pair of blackbirds and their cawing break the quiet, each bird in turn flying from behind to just ahead of the travelers. Lily is startled, then shudders, sensing an ill omen as she watches them leapfrog above her. Ygnacio sees them and is thrilled.

Unable to focus, Lily sways in the saddle. Her mind blurs the birds and leaves. They merge together to all become a flurry of swirling leaves, then all a murder of blackbirds.

Reeling in a blaze of red light, as if staring at the sun with eyes shut tight, Lily drops the reins. Attempting to collect her senses, she presses her palms to her eyes, shakes her head, and feels a jolt, the feverish heat of blood rushing through her body. She is overcome by a sensation of sliding through a tunnel as her thoughts dissociate.

The girl's eyes goggle believing she sees the firmly rooted trees drawing nourishment from deep in the earth. She senses they somehow have an awareness of her, that they observe and know her feelings. In the utter silence, Lily imagines all their leaves drop in a single plunge, replaced by images of her childhood. Time reverses and Lily visualizes a flood of faces she recognizes but can't name.

Then, with no effort, it just happens, all barriers to her mind crumble and familiar images sweep through. She hears thoughts clearly as if she is speaking them. She recognizes the faces; Marta, Revela, Segundo, Dante. Lily trembles, her lips pout into a girlish smile and she feints, sliding from her horse onto a cushion of forest leaves.

Chapter 32
Cristóbal Colón & Dante

The sun has not fully risen across the wide ocean, but the day is already hellishly hot. On deck, Cristóbal Colón and Luís de Torres set the course for the next island. Dante overhears the captain say he wants "to chart each island for further exploration but having taken possession of one is like claiming them all."

The three ships sail in single file, leaving the depths of the Ocean Sea, searching with a sailor's eye for a passage to cross between treacherous reefs to calm, lagoon waters.

Standing near the helm behind the interpreter, Colón rests his forearm on the de Torres' shoulder and points to starboard. "There. You see that there, Luís? Where the water is smooth between the breakers? That's where we'll enter. There's enough room in this pond for all the ships of Christendom. If it's deep enough."

The boundless blue-green ocean is left to port as they sail into the coral protected pristine haff. Leaning over the rails the men watch the ship slide past pink and gold coral, aware that a mere brush against the razor sharp, stony growth could rip the hull open. Broad beaches border the palm covered island like a white sand necklace.

Peaceful Taino natives greet the sailors at each island, bringing fresh water and food to the landing party. Mystified by the huge ships, the billowing white sails, the appearance of the Spaniards - their clothes, their beards, their weapons - many Taino plunge into the sea and swim to the ships. Convinced he's reached the Indies, the Captain General calls the islanders 'Indians', and renames each island after Spanish Royalty or a Catholic Saint. The Europeans bring items successfully traded with African natives, red sailor caps, glass beads, and hawk's bells. The small bells fascinate the 'Indians' who covet them, trading their parrots, carvings, cotton, and necklaces of shells, teeth and bones.

The captain acknowledges the natives are not savage, and are "very friendly". He discounts the fear of cannibalism and admonishes the crew against doing them harm. He writes in the ship's log:

> *Their skin was emitted a golden glow as if the sun had taken residence in them. ..But they seemed on the whole to me, to be a very poor people. They all go completely naked, even the women, though I saw but one girl. All whom I saw were young, not above thirty years of age, well made, with fine shapes and faces; their hair short, and coarse like that of a horse's tail, combed toward the forehead, except a small portion which they suffer to hang down behind, and never cut. Some paint themselves with black, which makes them appear like those of the Canaries, neither black nor white, others with white, others with red, and others with such colors as they can find. Some paint the face, and some the whole body, others only the eyes, and others the nose. Weapons they have none, nor are acquainted with them, for I showed them swords which they grasped by the blades, and cut themselves through ignorance. ... I saw no beasts in the island, nor any sort of animals except parrots."*

Aware they are a small, poorly armed group, safe at sea but not on land, the crew avoids hostility with the natives. Harana, under Cristóbal Colón's orders, keeps a close watch on Dante.

"Careful now. Watch out for anything amiss. Any strange signal. Cause they'll gut ya like a fish."

The first day, when the 'Indians' grouped on the shore and swam out to the ship, the Captain General measured their worth. In his log:

> *Yes. They must all become subjects of Spain. Christians will do good business with these Indians.*

Not much later he wrote,

It appears to me, that the people are ingenious, and would be good servants and I am of opinion that they would very readily become Christians, as they appear to have no religion. They very quickly learn such words as are spoken to them. If it please our Lord, I intend at my return to carry home six of them.

Within a month of their arrival Dante hears the Captain General say to Harana,

With 50 armed men these people could be brought under control and made to do whatever one might wish.

When the marshal reports having been confronted by what he thought to be 'unfriendly looking' natives, their faces colored, long, wild, gleaming, black hair, and feathered headdresses, Colón concludes,

They will make good slaves.

Dante asks Luís if the 'Indians' would become slaves like the Canarians. At first, perhaps to avoid any thought of Spain, the interpreter resists his question. Then, he divulges to the boy, "Yes. Although the Queen is opposed to commerce in human beings, King Ferdinand need only hear they were captured in battle and will readily accept payment for them as slaves.

Dante reflects, 'How do you make a man a slave if not to capture him?'

Gotzun, well familiar with slavery and the logic of the Crown and Church, explains to Dante, "These natives are outside of Christ's law. The Spaniards call them 'heathens', like my people, not deserving to be treated as brothers. Or even human. At best they call us naked savages, wild beasts in human form, barking like dogs and eating uncooked food. Once captured and brought to Spain, they will be taught enough Spanish and the Catholic faith to be baptized. They'll pay for the blessing of their conversion with a lifetime of slavery."

Although Dante often heard Gotzun describe the brutality inflicted on his people, his own observation was that the Guanches seemed content to suffer their humiliation, as if feeling free to be enslaved. He had no idea of the killings. Wondering about the Guanches being oppressed, he asks Gotzun, "With your people at war, why didn't you stay and fight with them?"

An immense sadness rises in the Canarian. Eyes watery, he thinks, 'Here, this boy asks me to explain my life. Another omen that comes looking for me.' He says to Dante, "If I stayed it is certain I would die. And the story of the Guanches would die with me. I have pledged my soul to prevent that."

"But what if you never get back?"

Gotzun, gently pats the boy on the shoulder, and speaks in a pensive voice; "Little unfolds in life as we expect it to Dante. We each are on our own path. Our own destiny to face death. But wherever I am when I die, my spirit will be on the plains of Teide. My memories are fixed in that powerful place, it has marked me. It is there I will recount my last moments on earth."

Until now, it had not occurred to Dante that one's spirit might exist outside the body, transcending physical existence. He listens to Gotzun's thoughtful pledge and wonders, 'Where will my spirit be when I die?'

Tales of Marco Polo's travels in China and India describing an advanced civilization had resonated in Europe for over a hundred years. Predictably, the Voyage of Discovery crew's interest in shells and parrots was short lived. It was not long before they became disenchanted with the primitive living conditions. The nakedness became off-putting, the inability to communicate, frustrating, and the natives' fearful apprehension of the Spaniards, their total lack of understanding that other civilizations exist, was ultimately depressing.

Cristóbal Colón was searching for China with a view to contacting the Great Kahn and deliver the letter he held in trust from King Ferdinand and Queen Ysabela. Excursions inland were led by Luís de Torres as interpreter. If a village was not abandoned in fear before they arrived, the

Spaniards would be greeted formally by the natives, kissing their hands and feet, and even knelt before as if gods. But de Torres' language skills were of little worth, with communication made by hand gestures and sand drawings.

They sail on. There is no paucity of rainfall as in Spain and at the same hour every day, an entire isolated pearly curtain of water is visible in the distance as it showers over the green islands. At night, a silent avalanche of puffy clouds rolls off the mountains into the valleys. When the clouds clear, the sky opens to an ocean of spinning stars.

Cool katabolic winds sweep down the steep bluffs of larger islands, replacing the warm air rising off the water, pushing the ships along the coasts. Sometimes, especially at the mouth of a river, head winds slow their progress. With every new landfall, Cristóbal is hoping to arrive at Japan or China.

No sailor is more moved by the natural beauty of the islands than the Captain General. In the ship's log, directed to the King and Queen, he writes poetically of the majestic beauty of the islands:

> *This is so beautiful a place, as well as the neighboring regions, that I know not in which course to proceed first; my eyes are never tired with viewing such delightful verdure, and of a species so new and dissimilar to that of our country,*

> *This island is the most beautiful that I assure your Highnesses that these lands are the most fertile, temperate, level and beautiful countries in the world.*

> *This island even exceeds the others in beauty and fertility.*

> *Groves of lofty and flourishing trees are abundant, as also large lakes, surrounded and overhung by the foliage, in a most enchanting manner. Everything looked as green as in April in Andalusia. The melody of the birds was so exquisite that one was never willing to part from the spot, and the flocks of parrots obscured the heavens... A thousand different sorts of trees, with their fruit were to be met with, and of a wonderfully delicious odor...*

Finding land was paramount to Cristóbal Colón from the moment King Ferdinand acquiesced to the Voyage of Discovery, but matters changed. The primary goal, to reach the East, is forgotten. Taking center stage is what truly matters to King Ferdinand. When Colón sees gold pierced through the natives' noses, it is as if Gabriel's horn sounds. The Captain General, ever aware of the Capitulations, is determined to return with more than just a new chart. After all, the Capitulations grant him ten-percent of whatever fortune is discovered. All aboard are consumed with discovering a cache of the ore.

Where is the gold? Every native is questioned. What is the source? Where is the mine? Many 'Indians' say the metal is considered to be of little value and tell of islands where it is worn as decoration on arms and legs, places where it is so plentiful that pieces, actual stones of it, can be gathered from the ground.

Wasn't it logical? The source of the gold from the Maghreb, the 'River of Gold' from the west coast of the Nile, was thought to be directly inland from the Canaries, virtually on the same latitude of their current position. No less than Aristotle had advised that lands of the same latitude produce the same products.

Ended are the philosophical conversations enjoyed on the crossing between Luís and Cristóbal, the questions of religion, the existence of god and the soul, and the mystery of time. Gold becomes the single issue, and it breaks them.

Luís implores, "What's happened? Why are you doing this? When did we come for gold?

"Come now Luís, It has always been only about gold for most of these men, you know that. So why shouldn't they search for it?"

"They aren't just searching for it." He walks in a small circle in one direction, then the other, eyes on the ground, agitated, shaking his head. "They aren't miners. If that obsession comes on board, if you let that happen, all this will become a comedy of death."

The Captain General is aware there will be no reconciliation on this topic. His arms fold across his chest. "You forget the King, Luís. When we return with gold, make our report, Ferdinand will think that gold is easily secured. That natives actually keep it in their meager abodes." He extends his arm, opens his palm, then grips it into a fist, his eyes widening, "And since they do, how much is hoarded by the local regent and his hidalgos? And their church?"

Luís paces, exasperated, unable to look at Colón. "Whatever the reason, it all begins and ends in slaughter. This will become a land of blood. Just a few indiscriminate massacres, right? Do you want to risk that happening?"

Cristóbal shrugs, "Well, I can't control everything. Now can I?"

Luís reasons, "And so Ferdinand will be eager to send more ships and soldiers to secure his new domain. And you will be Viceroy of all the new land."

"Yes, that's right. That is the bargain. Part of it. But not just soldiers and gold seekers will come. Colonizers also. People seeking a new land and a new life."

The matter strikes a cord with Luís, and he feels Colón has taken advantage of his sympathies. "You know how I feel about that." He rakes his hand through his hair, his face taught, revealing the conflict in his mind. "There is nothing more that I could wish for. It would be the redeeming moment of my life. But that is not at issue here." His eyes rage, "You know what will come with men seeking gold. The same cruelty they practice in the Canaries. Slaves. Gotzun was right to pity these 'Indians'. Spain has put a lot of thought into how to murder. This will be child's play for them."

Cristóbal regrets the inference but finds refuge in reality. "Well Luís, we didn't sail here to hide from what we find."

"And the lives it will take to get that gold? The slaves? Are you not ashamed of your eagerness to exchange men's' souls for glittering stones? Wealth and honors for you. And what of wisdom? What of truth? The first battle is here. I've been to the Canaries. Let's not bring that here. Not now. Not you!"

The Captain General raises both arms as if in surrender to fate. "Well, surely you understand, Luís. I am the Admiral of this fleet. Would you have me serve some theological banquet for the crew? Tell them to 'calm down about the gold'? To pick plants? No, Luís. Those men we both dread are coming anyway. They are always coming. They will bring their sword and their cross. Nothing can be done to stop them." He grabs Luís' shoulders. "But we, you and I, are here now. And we are not them. There will be no blood spilt by us."

Sensing his defeat, the interpreter's head droops and slowly shakes, he sighs, "And what about exalting the glory of god's mystery? It certainly will be a mystery to these poor devils. Oh Gotzun, how right you are."

The ship shudders and rolls to its side with a great moan. What echoes in the Captain General's mind are Luís' words, "Who will you be when you return?"

A portion of the crew goes ashore at each landfall and the interpreter makes enquiries. Where might they find the Kahn? The sailors search for gold. Dante remains on the Santa Maria and is like a shadow to Colón. Despite their desire and persistence, the Voyage of Discovery does not find any significant amount of the ore. Colon notes in the log every mention of its existence on every island until finally writing as if in apology:

> to return in April and to circulate and find as much gold and spices as I can."... and "...I hope to God that when I come back here from Castile, which I intend on doing, that I will find a barrel of gold, for which these people I am leaving will have traded, and that they will have found the gold mine, and the spices, and in such quantities that within three years the Sovereigns will prepare for and undertake the conquest of the Holy Land...

A person could spend a lifetime learning about sailing, even without the actual experience. But a novice seaman couldn't dream of a more advantageous circumstance than to be at the elbow of the Great Navigator.

Dante begins to mimic Colón. Like the Captain General, he ties his hair to one side to read charts. He eats standing, alongside the Captain, bowl in hand. Each evening Colón pours a bucket of water over his head to wash off the salt, Dante uses what is left. When, like Colón, Dante goes barefoot on deck, his feet develop calluses and he thinks of his father's calloused hands.

The boy works with Colón to sound the depths of water, to note the winds and currents, and to chart the reefs and lagoons. He discounts Captain Pinzón's complaint that the Captain General is reckless, taking chances in shoals.

Colón calls Dante 'the boy', and keeps him by his side. He calls out, 'Boy!' And Dante wonders if he even remembers his name.

"Here, boy. Take a measure of this depth. Look. Those fish. Have you ever seen such colors?" Dante casts the sounding line forward and hauls in when the slack point is directly below. Noting the cloth knotted on the line, "She's four fathoms to bottom, Captain."

Colón is determined to teach Dante how to compute distances using the technique of triangulation, and is patient as a turtle with the boy. Choosing a landmark, he directs, "There. That rise, boy. Mark its compass-rose degree and gauge its height." Colón turns over the small ampuleta to measure time, and notes the speed and direction of the current. When the sand runs through, he marks the degree of a distant point and notes the information on a squiggly line, drawn as the shore. The calculation is a mystery to Dante, but the Captain General assures him he will understand it with experience. "The chart", he says, "is like a law. A sure, precise passageway into another world."

The boy is in earnest to remember the Captain General's teachings. On consecutive occasions Colón directs him to count the flock of birds, cruising the shoreline, feeding low to the water, first pelicans then gulls. Each time the count was nineteen. Colon laughed at the coincidence.

The lesson however, was that a distance behind each group was another bird, lagging behind their flock. "There is always a 'trailer' the Captain General instructed, and Dante said to himself, 'nineteen'.

Dante prided himself on noting an obscure comment of the Captain General. Before the landfall on August 6th, the Captain General said, almost to himself, but loud enough for the boy to hear, "The rhythm of the seas has changed." Then later, in conversation with Harana, he mentioned it again. "When the waves became jerky, marshal, it was like approaching the Canaries. The ocean floor has changed."

Perhaps Cristóbal Colón saw in Dante his own youth, how he once bore the fears and curiosities of first being at sea. He forgot the sorrow of his disappointments and wanderings and his heart returned to the day's when he was a boy. His mind's eye conjures a vision far in his past: a Portuguese sailor going up a mast, hauling the halyard that raises the wooden seat he straddles. His hand grips a flag with a red border around a white field and four blue shields; the sailor goes aloft to tie the banner from a yardarm; the flag blows in the breeze as he sways away from then back to the mast. For Cristóbal Colón that sailor floats forever in the air, and the Portuguese flag flaps forever in the wind. He doesn't need to imagine Dante's wonder.

The boy marvels at how all this has happened. How did he get here? How did his farm boy, concertina playing, family abused, short life bring him, like a trick, across the ocean to this strange land? Though close in time, his father and brothers, the farm, La Sirena Taberna, are distant thoughts. He looks at his life but does not recognize it. Only Revela remains fully present in Dante's mind. What has happened to her? What has he done to her life?

For Dante, the sail from the Canaries has taken on a dreamlike quality. It no longer feels real, as if each day was erased when it ended. What if he forgets something important? What if he forgets about touching the 'pope's hat'? What if he forgets about Testo the Greek? He wants to remember everything, especially Atzi, her dark eyes, her silhouette running in the jungle, the water shooting off her body, her laughter while buttoning his tunic, her touch. He worries that someday the past will be too vague.

Sailing between islands, the Santa Maria leaves a long wake, a frothy triangle in the gentle swells. In the prow, Dante's knees tightly hug the bowsprit, hands on his hips. He leads the ship forward, riding the waves, chest thrust out, his smiling face set into the wind and spray. He is a part of the air and sea as in a dream, without boundaries to his body. He feels like a king, he feels alive.

On Christmas Eve, 1492, a calm day under a blazing sun, the Santa Maria swings lazily at anchor not far from shore. The decks are clear of all but Cristóbal Colón and Dante as a faint breeze ripples the lagoon water. The Captain General is silent for an extended period, in a state of immanence. His white tunic is clinging wet from the oppressive heat. Careful to avoid touching the hot wood of the rail, he gazes past the island to the eggshell horizon.

Without turning to face the boy, his tone hushed, in an intimate, private voice, he says, "Dante. You will have much to tell your children. Tell them that their father crossed the Ocean Sea for a new land, leaving an old world full of superstition and hatred. Tell them that the sea that carried him taught that certain things are unchanging. That at sea a man must be steadfast in the face of danger. And tell them that honor and humility come before righteousness."

He becomes quiet again. A zephyr barely stirs the torrid air, the water is flat as a dish of mercury. Dante stands in Colón's shadow, raising his feet alternately off the burning deck, mulling over his words. Watching him, the way he tilts his head and narrows his eyes.

Then Cristóbal Colón turns to the boy. He has just remembered something important, and because he does, he believes it to be an omen. In a firm voice he says, "It takes great resolve, not just effort!"

Dante doesn't know what to think. Then, Colón raises a threatening finger to the sky, his moist eyes explosive. He bends to the boy and shouts, "Great conviction and courage! Everything of this world must rally to your side! The stars. The ocean. The mountains. The winds. God must lead you!"

The frightened Dante, wondering if the Captain General has gone mad, thinks, 'Well, how can one remain sane in this heat?

Chapter 33
Revela & Doramus & David

The Guanches are encamped near a *galería* where Teide's melted snow collects, a natural reservoir of cold water carved in the mountain. In a flurry of activity, the Jewish women fill water skins and pack food into carry sacs. The men speak with earnest, convincing gestures, their faces creased in worry, lamenting their circumstances, shaking their heads, rubbing their hands, keening. The children stay close in the care of each other. Despite what seems an overriding aura of anxiety, there is an undercurrent of excitement, a prospect of something new and wonderful.

Revela watches David combine their belongings into a single bundle to which he fashions leather straps.

He says, "Here, see how this works for you."

She hefts the pack, and swings it over her shoulder. "It's okay. But I don't understand. Why are we leaving, David?"

David retrieves the sack and says to himself, "Perhaps a bit more food will fit." and to Revela, "We don't have to leave. But we should."

Revela's face tightens and she pulls in her lips. She plants her feet wide as if to say, 'I'll make my own decisions', and says, "But why? And where to?"

David slows. Although he is in agreement with the elders, he understands the surrender Revela must make. She will think of her brother, and knows the decision will test her commitment.

Avoiding a condescending tone, but with mannered clarity, he says, "Well, this is still Spain. The Canary Islands. Tenerife belongs to King

Ferdinand & Queen Ysabela. The Inquisition is not long behind. If it hasn't arrived already. That's why. The elders have considered our situation and decided what's best for the community."

Revela's arms are crossed, her feet still planted, and in that sarcastic tone learned from her father, she says, "Oh. I see. And just where are we going?"

"Where? Well, to Jerusalem."

Revela's arms remain crossed. Her eyes squinch and a grimace invades her face. "Jerusalem? Where's that? What's there? Isn't that for Crusaders?"

"Right. It is for Crusaders. And it's far away. I wish I could tell you what it's like, but I really don't know. All I know is that it's been said to be our true home. For us Jews".

She extends her arms, palms up, and pleads, "But the Inquisition isn't here. Here in Tenerife. Do you think?"

"Not now. But what about a year from now? Two? What then?

No, we must keep moving. Get out of Spain."

Hands on her hips but dropping her confrontational tone, Revela tips her head to one side and asks, "But won't it be dangerous? Traveling there, I mean"

"Everything is dangerous."

"So why not wait a while? We just got here and it's, it's perfect."

David breaks eye contact and continues organizing provisions. "Well, besides the Inquisition, there's a war here. Well, a kind of war. Haven't you noticed? It seems Jews and Guanches are the Queen's favorite victims."

It was not hard to imagine war, in all its ferocity and carnage. But with life being so continuous and intense, it was hard to imagine death. David regrets the mocking question and drops the sack. He steps closer. Reaching out, he takes Revela's arms and pulls her to him. She tilts her head up, a soft smile beneath watery eyes.

"I love you Revela. I want us to have a life together." They embrace and David can feel Revela's body fold into his as she presses her head tight into his shoulder and consents to be a part of his life.

"I want to make a home for us."

To Revela 'home' now means something new and different, not simply where you were from, but where you were valued, were you were wanted, a home you can never lose.

David says, "But not everyone is going."

"What do you mean?"

"Arunas and Julia, Zelda, Evana, Milan. The old ones, they're staying." He pauses, and then, "My parents also. Only eleven of us will travel. And the children."

Revela is stunned, "But Merosa and the Rabbi? Why aren't they coming?"

"I think they should. But it's settled. They'll stay to care for the elders. I wish they were coming, but they're probably right. Elenora Bobadilla said we could stay on Gomera, under her protection. It's an option they may choose later. It was generous of the lady."

Revela's watery eyes roll up, and her chin trembles. How can this be happening? Dizzy at the thought of losing Merosa, her stomach churns with the empty feeling of abandonment. How can she be separated from the one woman she has ever known who validates her own beliefs? She grasps her mouth to hold back from crying out. Merosa, the mother she's longed for, an ally and teacher in whom she could confide, the mother she was cheated of by her dour, abusive father. 'It isn't fair", she thinks. 'David doesn't understand'.

Later in the day, as the sun approaches its ocean rest, the Jews gather near the cliff under the sacred drago tree. Below bellows the roar of the ocean. Merosa stands with the Rabbi, in itself an announcement that matters at hand concern family and are exempt from the religious ritual of gender separation. The Rabbi looks up and wonders if the impregnable canopy of this primeval tree will auger the protection they need.

Rabbi Moises' eyes drift over the congregation. Waiting for quiet, he whispers to himself each person's name and the names of their parents and siblings. Some are in exile but most are dead, many burned, and there are many. He knows this will be his last sight of these last faces. Hand over his heart, he thinks to himself,' I don't know where death takes people, but I know where they abide.'

Merosa's lips flutter silently, reciting the same names, a litany of grief. She twists a long, dry, drago leaf. She examines her hands but finds no comfort, for they are parched and her fingers bent like crooked branches.

The Rabbi's eyes drift up into an eternity of blue sky. A gust of wind lashes the exiles, but the drago stands firm. He begins;

"Brothers and sisters. Our hearts are exhausted on this mysterious journey. A riddle of the mind, but not a riddle of our spirit. We face the iniquity of circumstance but must stay alive for each other. It is the presence of God, not the absence of God, which rescues us from the demons that pursue us."

The Rabbi's sorrowful eyes are close to yielding to unrestrained tears. Merosa strokes his shoulder and he curbs his emotions.

"Just as every Jew before us, we are seeded into our lives. And every Jew in the future is our brethren. What was broken can never be the same. We can never go back to the way things were. But, you must not forget the places and loved ones of our homeland, that country of tears. We must teach our children what our people might forget.

"Yes, losing everything brings sadness, but we find hidden strengths. Remember what you have discovered in your hearts. Do not think of exile as a beginning, for there is no beginning, the beginning is only in your thoughts. We must remember our history the way our friends the Guanches remember theirs. Carrying it within ourselves, like a song you learn by singing it. Otherwise our story, our eternal inner lives, will be lost in time, like tears in the rain. Our tale is, in essence, a map of time. Exalted because of its simplicity.

"In this year of midnights, we have suffered an evil that leaves us hurtling toward death. Yet we are here, alive, and although no one can go back, everyone can go forward. Those who succumb to fear, who give in, are defeated. All others are triumphant.

"Our instincts tell us that great truths are awesome because of their simplicity. Remember Rabbi Hillel, the Prince of Rabbis, who taught that all our Torah is to say, 'What is hateful to you, do not do to your neighbor'.

"For centuries our forefathers searched for the ten lost tribes of Israel, hoping they might have ownership of land and provide a home for our exiled brothers and sisters. But in truth, we need not search. Ever since our exile over a thousand years ago, the call is for all tribes to return to the holy land and rebuild the temple in Jerusalem. Now the Lord asks us to heed that call. Though we part today, those that go take our spirit with them, and we who stay hold yours in our hearts."

The star-filled river of the Milky Way illuminates the sky. Revela sits alone in the moon shadow of the ancient drago tree, the constellation Pegasus seeming to rest on the tree's crown. Rubbing her arms for warmth in the October air, she thinks of the comfort and protection that home and family provided. What are her father and brothers doing? She smiles imagining Primero and Segundo harvesting grapes, loading them into the wooden tub, stained blood-red from years of use. Those were happy times, when all the children would wrap their arms on each other's shoulders as they 'danced the grapes'.

But unlike their neighbors their father failed to aerate the soil or control the aphids with garlic wash, and so the wine was usually sour. That was the way with her family, to just get by, to accept a misspent life.

The past spins through her mind, 'With Christmas coming, La Sirena will be packed with sailors from all over the world. If he were there, Dante would sing new shanties.... Yes, Dante. Who knows where he is now. Could he take care of himself? How will he ever find me if I go to Jerusalem? Perhaps I should stay in case he returns to the Canaries. He said he would, but what is the chance of that happening?

Why think about that dark pit of separation and blame? 'Better to think about the *romería*, the family extravagance, everyone singing and dancing, and parading the animals. Something different, something fun was always happening, like the time Alaldo rode that donkey into the river and nearly drowned. Or the time Lily and Dante saw Ygnacio by the mill. As a child Ygnacio had a sorrowful look, and I once thought the stories about him were exaggerations. But after the cat burning I knew. I said to him, "I know your sisters. They're not like you. You're not the only one unhappy in that house. But you are unhappy and evil too."

And then he said that strange thing to me, "Even though I'm a beast, don't I have the right to live?"

Even his sister, Marta, knew what he was. What a terrible blunder that awful night when Dante saw us by the well tree. There was nothing I could do to fix it. And really, what did I do wrong? I've thought it was all my fault. But maybe not. Dante didn't need to jump in like that.'

Her head lifts and her shoulders straighten as if this is a new path to think about, but later, not right now. 'David is everything I want in a man, kind, respectful, intelligent. Because of him I'm not alone. And Jerusalem, now that's exciting. It's wonderful here but the elders are right.

The Inquisition and the war against the Guanches, best to leave that far behind. I wish with all my heart that Merosa was coming. But I'm not surprised, she knows her duty.'

Revela hears voices and turns to see David and Doramus approaching. The Guanche's voice is low, confidential. "Gomera is in her grip, without hope. Her husband, Hernan Peraza, was killed in the revolt four years past. After that Elenora had no mercy. Most Gomerans have converted or are slaves in Spain. Or dead. And now Gomera is garrisoned by soldiers from Gran Canaria."

They join Revela under the drago. David touches her hand in greeting, and says, "Doramus is telling me of Elenora Bobadilla, the Governess of Gomera, where we first landed."

"Yes, I recall the name, Gotzun told me about the woman. He said she was beautiful but ruthless. Too bad we never met her."

Doramus nods, "It is best you didn't, Revela. Her hands are bloody and her heart is the shape of a scythe. I'm sure Gotzun warned you of her. He probably thought better of telling you what happened."

Doramus swells, his chest and neck stiffen. "All Gomerans were called to attend the funeral of Elenora's husband. Those that came were made prisoners and those that hid in the mountains were enticed to surrender. All were herded to the port where most were hanged, drowned, or drawn apart by horses. Hands and feet were cut off. The remaining men were banished to other islands but en route were thrown overboard. Their wives and children were sold as slaves."

David and Revela sit stunned. Spanish soldiers murdering men who had surrendered, enslaving women and children? Why not?

Doramus continues, "Yes, ruthless is a mild way to describe her. She has hanged many. Not only Guanches, but Spaniards as well. Anyone she deems a threat to her son's succeeding in title to the island."

Revela asks, "Is she a danger to you here, on Tenerife?"

"There is no doubt of it. Her consort, Alonso de Luga, a man known for cruelty, has conquered the island of Benahoare, which you call La Palma, just north-west of Gomera." Doramus' green eyes darken. He seems to sink into himself, his face a caul of shame. He runs a stick on the ground, stares at the senseless design, and continues, "It was treachery. The natives of La Palma, the Auaritas, betrayed their tribe. Years before on La Palma, an Auaritas woman, Francisca de Gazmira, became a Christian missionary. She possessed a great power over her people, claiming to be from another time and to have spoken with Jesus Christ. Many were baptized. When de Luga landed on the western shore, several Christian tribes joined him. They circled the island killing the little opposition they encountered. Led by the great *Mencey,* Tanausu, the Auaritas held their ground in fierce resistance in the caldera of the island's volcano, Taburiente.

Alonso de Luga proposed a parlay. Tanausu and other leaders met with him, but it was a trick. The Spaniards fell on them, nothing mattered except killing them all.

Sparing Revela and David the details of the ambush, Doramus continues, "Alfonso de Luga will next look to Tenerife. I'm certain of that. His victories will provoke interest from the Genoese, the money interests who know the worth of this land. They'll do the same as in the Cape Verde Islands. They'll create sugar plantations, bring in Spanish farmers and use us as slaves. I'm on my way to meet with Mencey Tegueste in Taganana, to seek an alliance."

The talk of Elenora in Gomera and the treachery in La Palma has created an atmosphere heavy with betrayal and death. Revela feels chaos in her stomach, learning how cruel people can be. Her face echoes a child in fear. She grips David's arm, her jaw firm. For the first time since Palos she feels the threat of real danger. She knows she has to be brave but has no practice or sense of how to do it. Stepping forward she asks Doramus, "Are you leaving soon?" and quickly to David, "when will we be ready?"

Taking Revela's lead, David says to Doramus, "We need some time. A day or two."

Doramus says, "Yes. That will work. We will leave the morning after this. Our paths will be the same for two days. At Guanchado, the balanced rock on the lower plane of Teide, I can double back a short distance for the trail to Taganana. You will head down to the port at La Laguna."

Revela asks, "How long to La Laguna?"

"From Guanchado, two or three days."

Revela, again, "And you'll take us there?"

Doramus, "Yes. It is a good place to rest. You can see the world from there."

Revela looks to David. She is more anxious than he, and David asks, "Where do we go then?

Doramus thinks the route through for a moment, "From Guanchado you will go down the Gezuk Trail to La Laguna. An easy path. You go through the bosque and enter the port from the west. In the Plaza del Puerto find a man named Nestor. He will help you secure passage on a ship to Las Palmas and tell you who to contact there for a ship to Africa.

"Can't you go with us to La Laguna?" Revela pleads.

"No. I must meet with Tegueste, a great mencey. I seek an alliance." To himself Doramus reviews Bencomo's plan, thinking, 'as if there was anything that could prepare you for these Spanish.' Being extremely difficult to reach, perched on the side of a great cliff, Taganana is protected and more easily defended. Doramus reveals to Revela what he has already told David. "If we are forced off the mountain it is where we will go. I will ask *Mencey* Tegueste to accept us."

The Guanche leaves the young Spaniards sitting in the light of a parchment moon, under tall alder trees. In the cathedral like silence, Revela leans into David and says, "Life isn't a dream is it? We are doing the right thing?"

David has been thinking ahead. La Laguna will be a test of how well organized they are. The trip to the port will be less strenuous than what the children have already endured. He says, "I'm certain we are. I must speak with Doctor Resi to plan."

Doramus leaves and they lay beside each other watching a waxing moonrise in the sky. Yoggi appears from the trail above and lowers himself in a heap next to them. Revela closes her eyes. A part of her still spins to the past. She wonders, if mistakes can destroy your life, can't they also create it, simply changing its shape like the dunes in the desert? She says, "Tell me again where we're going," as tears roll down her cheeks like leaking memories.

Chapter 34
The Return

Christmas Day 1492. The Santa Maria, flagship to the Voyage of Discovery, lay at anchor in the lagoon off the island Cristóbal Colón named Española. A young seaman, Marcelo, inexperienced in the art of ground tackle, is left at the helm for a short watch. When the tide rushes in it lifts the ship to a point above the great kedge, Esmeralda. Against the strength of the sea, the anchor breaks free. By the time Marcelo sounds the alarm it is too late. Settled on a reef high and dry, the Santa Maria is beyond saving.

With the help of a native chief, Guacanagari, whom Colón has befriended, the ship is dismantled. Its timbers and all else salvageable are used to build a small fort, appropriately named, La Navidad. Thirty-nine men of the Santa Maria will remain in the Bahia de la Navidad, commanded by Diego de Harana. Leaving them, Cristóbal gives orders to search for gold, but to avoid the natives, especially the women. No matter, they ignore the order and within two months they are all dead.

The Captain General believes this to be his final test. He has been true to his mission, never wavering from the goal, supplicating himself to lesser men and women, depriving himself of material wants, living as an aesthete, obeying the laws of the Church. Now he must return having lost his flagship.

The majestic islands no longer occupy Colón's thoughts. The King and Queen are on his mind. He will bring back a few Indians, some birds and plants, but only a small amount of gold. He will tell the Royals what they want to hear. They want to hear about gold, how much there is and that it can be taken. Will it be enough?

The Santa Maria's remaining crew board the Niña, a ship so small it deserves its name. Cristóbal can now consider the remarkable consequences that will flow to him from this voyage. His rewards are secured by the Capitulations, negotiated and agreed to by the Crown: Admiral of the Ocean Sea, inherited nobility for his family, the title of Viceroy of all lands discovered, ten percent of the treasure the new route will yield. With the fact now proven he can be a generous man.

Yet the titanic world impact this voyage will have is beyond anything he can comprehend. Now begins the conquest and slaughter of the indigenous peoples of the Western Hemisphere. The Catholic religion spreads its saving grace and its terror as European empires vie for dominance. The Voyage impacts matters of science and philosophy considered heretical, now they are conclusively proven to be true. The vast wealth accumulated from gold, silver and slaves is used to finance bloody wars and crusades to recover the holy land. But none of this can happen unless Cristóbal Colón returns.

It is mid-January, the month named for the Roman God with two faces, Janus. One face looks to the east and the other west, one to the past and one to the future. Janus, the symbol of Genoa, Cristóbal Colón's home, the god of the gates where time begins.

Cristóbal Colón and the Voyage of Discovery point East, to the rising sun and Europe. The first few days are a smooth sail as the Niña ploughs a northeastern course on the Ocean Sea. Again, as when leaving the Canaries, it is their good fortune to ride an ocean current and a favorable wind system, the prevailing westerlies. The air breezes up, the sails belly out, and the hearts of the shipmates set for home.

Soon the sail changes as the Niña's mainsail fills, her bow pitches up and then smashes down onto the sea, as if to hit back. This is not like the doldrums they had encountered on the crossing. That was a fearful experience, becalmed for days in a gloomy region of squalls. In that dead air, the sea was undecided on the run of its currents. The wind came from no place and went no place as the sails hung limp. Making no headway, every man was loathe to measure time and keenly aware of the slightest breeze, waiting, listening for a break in the weather. For ten days heavy rain clouds blocked the sun but no rain fell. At night there were no stars, no moon, as if the sky was lost to them. That had been one kind of a test.

Now came the sail the men first anticipated. The wind begins to blow hard as if in judgment and the intrepid ship strikes her way east with a bone in her mouth and spray awash her deck. Although the Niña is crowded, the crew tolerate the discomfort, for they dream of Spain.

Cristóbal Colón stands to port on the poop deck, near Lorenzo at the helm, and watches the sunlight dance on the ocean. This is a familiar isolation for him, apart from the crew and without the companionship of conversation other than the boy standing nearby. His feet firm on the pitching deck, he thumps the rail and thinks back to the day Luís de Torres told him he would not be returning. It was just after Martín Pinzón, the Pinta's captain, returned from his month-long, unauthorized excursion, seeking gold for his own glory. The Captain General grimaces at the distress the Paloan captain caused him, the mistrust, the challenge to his authority. He thinks, 'That man has been out for himself since we left Spain.'

The day they left 'Fort Navidad' and the garrison of thirty-nine men, Luís de Torres told Cristóbal he would not be returning. A hard blow for the Captain General, but more was said that truly shook him. The Captain General remembers:

"Is there nothing I can say to dissuade you, Luís?"

Luís de Torres gathers his belongings onto his sleeping pallet. "I'm afraid not. What is there for me to return to? It would simply provoke all the horror in my life. That's nothing I want."

Luís pivots but finds no space to turn where he is not confronted with Cristóbal.

A knot of confusion grows on the Captain General's forehead. His stomach aches, a feeling of abandonment, or perhaps betrayal. "But Luís. This is a wilderness, without the least necessity. You'll be lost, surrounded by heathens. Don't play the fool."

De Torres stuffs his paltry possessions into a small carry sack. "How can I be lost if I don't know where I'm going? No, I'd be lost in Aragon, my friend." He smiles to himself thinking about the tyranny he will not go back to, where a man lives in fear every day.

Stepping forward Cristóbal takes hold of de Torres' arm, "Look Luís, come on now. Stop that. Think this through. You needn't relive the past. Think to the future."

"I have no past. It fell into the sea." Luís has become resolute in his grief. Those he loved are not coming back. "No, they've taken my past. And I don't regret it being gone." He stops fumbling with his sack and turns to face Cristóbal. "And what is your future my friend? Can you say? Does it really exist or is it only a way of talking?"

Cristóbal Colón is certain of his future. Whatever Luís' choice, nothing can cheat Cristóbal's life of its meaning. "I know that. Hopefully those misfortunes will no longer weigh on your heart. Look Luís, either we fight to be miserable, or fight to be strong, the effort is the same. Yes. Step out of that fog of hatred. After all, life is all we have, isn't it?"

"That's right, Captain. But that doesn't change the reality of Spain. When you return, if you return, perhaps your life will be fulfilled. But still, there are no guarantees. It is a long way and those weasels will be there to greet you. You remember dealing with the impossible powerful? Don't you?"

Cristóbal Colón does indeed remember. Men with wolf-like faces, hidden by dark cowls, who measure their lives by the blood they spill. Monks who sleep in their coffins to be ready to meet God. He nods a reluctant concession. Still, he is certain nothing can stay his destiny.

Luís weaves his hand through the air snake-like, rubbing the tips of his fingers together. His eyes narrow, "How those bastards push and grind their way. Like teredo worms gnawing through a keel. Carving labyrinths of fear. Sitting on their fat asses as if on thrones."

Yes, Cristóbal does remember. But he has learned which bridges to cross and which to burn.

"Remember them, Captain? Those fat priests swarming like termites in church cellars, stuffing themselves on bread and mutton, guzzling red wine, torturing poor, starving peasants."

Luís pauses to take the measure of himself. He's no longer angry. His fists are not balled tight. His jaw does not ache from gritting his teeth. Yes, his heart remains filled with spite against the universe, but perhaps some hope remains. He thinks, 'a rather pleasant feeling' and continues in a cheerful tone.

"And then the fucking maniacs are in control, aren't they? Burning simple people. Rest assured Cristóbal, the future will judge us. There is no masking the injustice of obeying men who rule by torture and murder. Spain is an empire of the dead and someday it will be a country that cannot show its face."

The Captain General is astonished and elated by the change in Luís. Although his thoughts are as poisonous as ever, his words, normally caked in spittle and shouted, are spoken calmly, almost poetically. He says, "Luís. Think. This will be different. The whole idea was to return. Your place is with me."

"Captain, before we left Palos, I had an overwhelming feeling that I was moving closer and closer to catastrophe, suffocating in the stench of a hellish future." His voice stumbles and he unconsciously grabs his dry throat, a harsh taste at the back of his tongue. His eyes sting and he closes them. "...Something that would destroy everything about me and everyone near me. I didn't know what it was, but I knew I was on the brink of going mad. In fact, I did lose my mind."

Again he stops a moment to question what he is saying. Brightening, he grabs Cristóbal's shoulders. "I longed for someone's judgment. Anyone's contempt in place of my own disgusting self-hatred. This voyage seemed the only worthwhile thing to do with my life. I believe you've gathered that." He's looking directly into Cristóbal's eyes and sees a subtle flinch of agreement.

"Then you see, for the first time since I can remember, I awoke one morning feeling almost normal. I was astern. Simply resting against the rail. Watching the birds. And I awoke again. But not a waking up from sleep. This was an immediate and complete experience. And I understood that the sun and moon spread light in all directions. That the world is still living. You saved me Admiral! This absurd voyage. It's been like a bridge for me between lives. There's no doubt about it. Cristóbal, my friend, the world lies before me brighter than it was. How can I thank you?"

"Well, Luís, it is not my doing. I have found myself lost to myself many times." Cristóbal pats his friend's hands and removes them from his chest. He hesitates, his head tilts to the left to listen, then decides against mentioning the holiness of his mission and says instead, "Perhaps there's something about the sea, that it gave you a greater ability to forget. Perhaps its immensity put your life in an extended perspective. But until I return here, you will be alone, cut off from everything. From civilization."

Luís notices Cristóbal is leaning to the left, he thinks, listening? He finds the loop of rope he was looking for and begins to tie off the sheepskin sack. He says, "Alone? Really Captain. I was one with my family, in a community where everyone was connected to everyone else in what I thought to be a safe altogetherness. I believed if one was cut, we bled together, that we shared the cut. But we hemorrhage apart, Captain, we do not share anything at all. We live together but in all matters we are by ourselves. No, I have no fear of being alone, Captain."

"Oh come now, Luís. Return with me. You'll be by my side. You'll not be just an intellectual at court. You're an explorer. A man of action and courage." Smiling at his friend, "Besides, you'll be rich."

Luís says, "Everyone I loved or even admired, anyone whose trust I might seek, is either dead or in exile. It is beyond any logic. You understand that. It seems when taught the philosophies of enlightened minds, you tend to take the world personally. Captain, I have no future in Spain. I'll remain here. After all, there are others who are staying. Why them and not me?"

"Yes. Circumstances, Luís. Our full crew extra on the Niña?"

Colón accepts that his friend will remain. He knows that the return voyage will be very different without Luís and he smiles at the irony, of what might have been. Believing there is no risk too great for a chance at glory and immortality, he tries again, barely audible, "But you have a choice my friend. You can return."

Luís' eyes scan the possessions left scattered on his bedding: the colorful feathers, the stone and bone necklaces, the primitive carvings. He motions to the accumulation and says, "Take these back with you."

Something has opened in him, something beyond the horizon of his own imagination. He heaves a great sigh, and considers an unexpected inclination, that perhaps he is happy. He glances out the portal to the sea, and without looking at Cristóbal extends his palm to his friend and whispers,

"Captain, have you ever confused a dream with life?"

They face one another, each bewildered for their own reasons. Luís continues, "I've always thought that dreaming carried no risk. Only that perhaps it might be dangerous to try to translate one into reality. But I've had a dream for the past seven nights. The same dream each night. It is like looking through water. Along with the feeling of being lifted on a kind of wave."

The Captain's eyes widen.

"An awareness of being liberated. And a sensation of being nurtured. Each night. I'm lifted by that wave. Carrying me. Moving me with marvelous lightness."

The Captain General's eyes burn, the hair on his neck bristles.

Luís speaks into the air beyond Cristóbal, "Then I shoot through a tunnel. I have no peripheral vision and cannot distinguish any shapes or light. Only a ripple of amber glow. Somehow I know it's a secret passageway."

De Torres eyes shift, he sees that Colón is transfixed and wonders if he is hearing his voices. He hesitates, then pauses, biting his lip as if to say, 'the best is yet to come'.

"Then what you might call the 'real dream', begins. There's a tall man, directing a multitude of people emerging from a lacuna in the side of a hill. Everything is alive and in precise detail. Yet it's simple. There are families. And a winding blue road. The man is dressed in refined clothes and is wearing a black hat. There is a boy leading people. The boy has an expression of what seems to be.... well, something akin to wisdom. As if he knows something secret.

Behind the man a mountain is on fire. The people are singing. They are more than joyful, perhaps even holy. Then a swarm of large black birds dives on them. Pecking at their eyes. They beat off the birds. In a loud, piercing voice the man says, "Stay together."

A moment passes and Luís adds, "There is more, of course, but I can't remember it yet." He shakes his head of the vision and looks to the Captain General. "Each night the dream is more vivid. I melt backwards in time to what I know has already happened, as if I'm both awake and not awake, remembering something I have not yet experienced. For seven nights. Over and over. That's it."

Cristóbal Colón has barely moved an elbow to steady himself. Stunned, his pupils open as if in the dark. Thinking that Luís is unhinged to forego the glory and wealth that waits in Spain is no longer on his mind.

Pursing his lips, shrugging, Luís says, "I remember once thinking that it would be a highlight of life to have a dream come true. You know we Jews say a *chalom*, a dream, is never false. But ordinarily once you dream it, it doesn't exist anymore. I'm beginning to think that because the dream repeats itself, well", and he pinches a quizzical look, "it feels as if it is telling me what to do. Or if by watching, I am changing it. That it's using me. But I couldn't say for what."

Cristóbal Colón forgets to breathe. His throat closes and his blood rushes everywhere it shouldn't. The sensation is the same as on the crossing when he could not recall his brother's name. He wondered about his sanity then, and now he wonders if his dream has been stolen, that it's left him, that he will never dream it or see the boy again. He almost says, "You are dreaming my dream!"

This voyage has played out his life's inspiration. He looks right through Luís and speaks as if he is thinking of something else. "What do you think it means, Luís? Who is the boy?"

"I don't know. The Greeks say we are all shadows of a dream. Strange, isn't it, how in dreams you are certain, you just know, and yet, some-times in a dream you can't do the simplest thing? Personally, I have always believed that to follow your dream is to begin your intended life. And the boy? Well, the only boy I now know is Dante."

Cristóbal Colón blanches. He is shaking. He considers telling Luís his own dream. But the thought overwhelms him. How could he reverse a lifetime of guarding his most precious secret? Instead he says, "Perhaps it is someone else's dream, but it somehow found you?"

Luís shrugs off the suggestion. "Use a mystery to solve a mystery? I don't know."

Cristóbal asks, "Do you think one can share a dream?"

Luís shakes his head. "No. Dreams, like pain, belong to each of us alone."

Luís is touching things, his hands pushing into the odd alcoves in the ship's hull. As he searches, he is also saying good-bye to his home for the past six months, a sailor's home of bare necessities. Good-bye straight edge. Farewell charts. Good-bye hook. He finds what he is looking for and passes a book into Cristóbal's hand.

"Here. This is for you. I know how important you consider the writings of your countryman, Marco Polo. This tells of a Jew's travels to Asia and Africa one hundred years before that Genoan.

You know it?"

"Oh. Well. Thank you Luís." And he reads the title embossed on the green cloth spine, "The Travels of Benjamin of Tudela". Yes, he does know this Spaniard's story. "That is very kind. Look Luís, I'll no longer try to convince you to return. Of course, I'll leave you everything I can. I'm very concerned. I never considered you might want to stay. Is there anything else I can do?"

"Well, yes captain. There are two questions you might answer."

"Of course, Luís."

"First, let me say that I'm aware of the two distances you've written in the ship's log. The shorter version you've told the crew, and the true kilometers. A splendid idea."

"Who told you that?"

"The boy told me. And Harana knows also. Did you really think it would go unnoticed?"

The Captain General again hears "the boy". His face pales and falls into a confused frown. Is it his 'dream-boy? Or is it Luís' 'dream-boy'? He shrugs, "Oh, the kilometers. That doesn't much matter now."

"No, I suppose not. But it does relate to something else. I am curious about your initial calculations." Luís' hands are busy twisting his hair, crouching in a habit of knotting a ribbon in a mirror, he asks, "Did you purposefully underestimate the distance across the Ocean Sea? For the Talavera Commission and the Royals? A way to prove the voyage short enough to be worth the chance?"

Cristóbal Colón drops the book on the bed then turns to ask, as if a great confidence has been broken, "And who said that?"

De Torres sees the admission. He smiles and recalls an aphorism, 'lies are so infinite in number, and the truth so singular.' He says, "Santangel told me. Well, he suggested it might be so. It is true, isn't it?"

Colón waves his hand and laughs off the idea. "Oh, that. It's a small difference between Arabic and Roman kilometers. How do you think I got the chartists to, shall we say, condense the water?"

"You mean, mapped by your brother, Bartolomeo."

"Yes, that's right. Bartolomeo is an excellent cartographer. He did draft the charts."

His eyes fold and Luís thinks, 'The cleverness of the idea, the daring, and its spectacular success'.

"But you mentioned two questions, Luís. What else would you like to know?"

"A simple matter, Captain. One myself and others have wondered. Tell me, where did you learn your Spanish?"

The Captain General's eyes submit, as if the answer is the last secret he holds, but knowing it is not. "Why, 'en casita', Luís. At home of course."

The Niña lurches as a maverick wave disrupts the heading and the Captain General's attention is shaken from the memory of Luís and back to the ship. He has a last thought of his friend as he stands next to Lorenzo at the tiller. The Niña's sails belly out and the ship presses north-east in the confused ocean. Ahead in the darkness lies a monstrous sea. A tempest is forming high where the arctic polar wind and tropic heat clash like fighting dragons, a barbaric destructive force. It moves forward like an ice-capped mountain range, all teeth and fangs at the top and below black as night. The swelling combers absorb the ocean's power, malicious waves of uncontrollable force, terrifying and unpredictable, wolfing up the sea. The storm arrives without prelude other than an ominous silence. The water flattens, the birds disappear, and the wind ends. Then, like an erupting volcano, it hits. Alive with deepening waves that break at the top with a crackling roar, the ocean becomes one thunderous sound of hissing wind and sea. The ship is slick with sea and pelting rain. Ropes and timbers groan, the ship itself groans, the men groan. and land becomes an absolute inaccessible memory.

On the third day of the tempest a black mountain of a wave shoots the Niña into the sky, spirals the ship round and round, slams it down to the pit of its trough, then launches it again in a whirling arc. The Niña shakes from stem to stern, her planks moan, crackle and shiver. Everything not a permanent part of the structure flies overboard, claimed by the sea; spars, rope, cleats, hooks, toggles, blocks, pulleys, sails, hatches, anchors, barrels. The storm rages for six days and nights, sending the Niña far north.

What is a man in a storm like this? Two men, Lorenzo and Orkon, fight the sea to hold the helm, keeping the ship from going broadside to the waves and 'turning turtle'. All others are humbled to their core and huddle below, tying themselves to the Niña's ribs, clutching each other like terrified infants. Their bodies feel turned inside out, weightless, and they pray for salvation.

Cristóbal Colón cannot bear the thought of not returning to Spain, being denied the glory due him. All his life's minor sins, false starts, and small failures parade through his mind's eye. Despite his extensive nautical experience, this storm has given him a lesson of the sea's essence, its unfathomable magnitude.

Each day and night he seeks salvation in Jesus Christ. "Remember Lord, my ship is small and thy sea is so wide."

Dante stands beside the Captain General in his cabin. Every muscle hardens. His hands sweat and ache from his constant grip on the ship's under-mast, trying to avoid crashing into the hull like a loose coconut. He experiences a peculiar sensation inside his body of being both ice cold and burning hot. He smells himself, the foul odor of his body like a corrosive poison adding to the nausea rising in his throat.

When the storm is most ferocious, certain he is about to die, Dante renounces all: his life at sea, his feeling special to the Captain General, his encounter with Atzi and Jayo, his past on the farm, his concertina and shanties, everything. Still, he holds Revela in his thoughts. By doing so, he controls his fear and finds the power of courage in his mind, the kind of courage that requires no options, that acts as courage itself.

After a week of torment, the force-eight storm finally abates. The howling winds, the slap of the crushing waves, the terrified cries, wails, and screams of the crew all cease. An immense silence envelops the Niña. The ship makes landfall. Cristóbal Colón has calculated a course, and the storm has somehow delivered them to the Portuguese Azore Archipelago, fifteen-hundred kilometers off the coast of Portugal. Dante is once again awed by the Captain General's navigational skills. The men rush ashore to bow in the Church of Jesus Christ and comply with their promised prayers for salvation. After a week spent outfitting and provisioning the ship, they set out on the return sail to the Iberian Peninsula and home.

At noon on March 15, 1493, thirty-two weeks after its departure from Spain, the Niña enters the harbor of Palos de la Frontera, very near to the La Sirena Taberna.

Chapter 35
Cinchado

Wednesday, March 15, 1493, two hundred thirty-three days after leaving Spain, the Niña dropped anchor in Palos de la Frontera. News of their return was anticipated after the Pinta under the command of Martín Alonzo Pinzón was separated from the Niña during the great storm and landed far north on the coast of Galicia.

Dante sought out Juan Abreu, the gravedigger, hoping for news about his sister, perhaps a mention from a returning sailor. The Captain General, now Admiral, had been adamant Dante travel with him to Barcelona and be presented to the King and Queen.

With the news of Juan Abreu's murder, Dante was uncertain what to do. Despite the success, the exhilarating conquest, his prior selfishness haunted him. His face reddens thinking about that unconsidered decision to leave Revela. It was like Gotzun said, "Your story stays with you." Dante knew when they were on the beach and he said to her on parting, "it's all right", that in his mind he believed he would never see her again. He feels shame and is ashamed of that shame.

He asks Gotzun if he should stay with the Admiral. The tall Canarian places his hand on the boy's shoulder and says, "You're still young. What have you lost in this world? What is it you can never forget? Something you would always know isn't there? There are no known steps, Dante, no rule to follow. Your destiny is no better or worse than mine, or any man's."

Dante decides and rushes to find his sister. The barman at La Sirena, Miguel Conroso, reminds him of Juan Abreu's murder and the danger in the port, and then a stroke of luck, Dante learns the Scrimshaw is due to sail with the morning tide on her scheduled route to the Canary Islands.

The winter winds whip the caravel Scrimshaw from Palos past Gibralter and down the coast of Africa into the Canary Channel. Dante, wearing the red cap of a Spanish sailor, aboard as an able-bodied seaman, sprints from handhold to handhold with a barefoot swagger in his new weathered skin and downy beard.

For eight days the steady trade winds push the Scrimshaw toward the port in La Laguna. They enter the natural harbor, protected in the lee of the island by a low stonewall breakwater, green with slime. The air reeks of the fishy smell of decaying barnacles and the mineral odor of wet rock. Dante struts down a pier crammed with crates and barrels just off-loaded from a Portuguese caravel.

The young sailor finds the man known to Gotzun leaning against the gutting table of an open-walled fish house. Even taller than Gotzun with a long neck and triangular head, he says, "You are sent by Gotzun? Come with me. I will take you over the mountain."

The Guanche, Nestor, explains, "Two days through the bosque on the Gezuk Trail to the circle path at the base of Teide. At Cinchado we will rest, it is a place that joins here with there, a place of magic, where you can see the world. Then, another two days off the volcano and down through the north bosque into Bencomo's realm.

They hike in iron silence through the forest to the plain below Teide. Dante can see Cinchado in the distance, a gigantic inverted mass, like a triangular patch torn in the sky. He wonders what Revela's circumstances might be, the way her life has been turned upside down like that immense rock.

At the base of Cinchado they are dwarfed by the stone balanced on its vee bottom. Nestor leads Dante off the main trail to a well-worn path, a steep incline that winds up the mammoth, striated stone. They reach a flat shelf with enough room for two people to sit. Looking down Dante swoons at the dizzying height. Looking out is the rim of the world. Nestor drops to his haunches and the boy sits with his ankles crossed, knees high, like a grasshopper. They watch the last hour of light as the sun sinks into the Ocean Sea. A shaft of light, wide at the horizon, narrows and points to them. At the last moment there is a flash of green.

The Guanche says, "Tell me about Gotzun?"

"I sailed with him. Last year. Here to the Canaries. And then we sailed with the Captain General, the Admiral, across the Ocean Sea to India."

Nestor considers the concept, 'across the Ocean Sea', 'India'. He says, "And why did you decide to cast your fate to the wind? Why did you choose a life at sea?"

"Well, I didn't. It was what you might call, an unfortunate occurrence. I had to leave home. You see.... I killed a man. Two men. But I was defending myself. They attacked my sister."

"And did their family seek revenge?"

"No. They were soldiers. Important soldiers."

Dante thought about that fateful night. How he rushed to save Revela. He did defend himself against the first man, the short one, who came at him with his blade. He did fight the tall soldier. His mind reeled back and he remembered the instant before the strike, not the stab itself, but the moment before it happened. He could see the soldier's body receiving the blade - before it happened - his mind's eye saw the blade in slow motion pierce the skin, enter between the ribs, and distinctly disappear.

It thrilled him to think of it, but still, it was a great sin, a terrible sin. Then he spoke, a thought that had festered like an animal bite, something he was never able to admit. He sighed.

"I didn't have to kill the second soldier. He was unarmed. In fact, I had his weapon." He brought his arm up. His jaw tightened, his face twisted. "Although I held the knife in the air, it was as if it was someone else's hand. I knew the soldier would step into it. And he did."

'How strange,' he thought, 'to no longer want to recognize your life.' The fore-vision, not the act itself, was so odd, so otherworldly.

The Guanche says, "Cinchado has shown you a truth." Sitting on his haunches, the Canarian considers the tragedy and says, "Yes, sometimes the impossible happens. Sometimes a weapon has a mind of its own."

Dante wonders what that means.

Nestor gathers himself, and says, "King Per, was a great Mencey of the Kingdom Taora, where you are going. In the year of the dolphin his wisdom was tested. Two men from the neighboring kingdom of Icod had killed a troublesome man of Per's tribe. His name was Tuui. While in their realm Tuui had stolen an ara, a goat, and escaped back to Taora.

When the Icods confronted him he threatened them with his spear. There was a fight. Even several of Per's tribe joined the two Icods trying to subdue the thief. Tuui was stabbed with a tavona, a knife, and died. Tuui's family demanded punishment for the Icods. Both denied striking the fatal blow. King Per listened closely, giving each man his attention. Sitting beneath the sacred drago tree, the King took a drink of ahof chacerquea, sweet milk. The two men whose lives were in the balance stood before him with heads bowed. He poured the liquid at their feet. Then he declared the knife guilty and threw it into the sea."

Deep that night as the lambent moonlight fades, the sky turns black. Directly above, Dante recognizes the Canis Minor, the little dog, and on the horizon, Carina, keel of the greater constellation Argo Navis. The sailor knows the constellations. Feeling released, remarkably confident, as if he is certain he will be happy, he thinks 'I am now a sailor'. The memory of his life in Palos recedes like a wave drawn out to sea, but he is without a vision of his future. On his back staring above his raised knees, he watches the bright star Canopis. During the titanic tempest on the return, he discovered courage, and it moved him to honesty and confession.

He thinks, 'That trip. What was it Lorenzo said? "We all got back, 'cept them 'at stayed. None killed nr drown. No sailor will forget 'at storm. By the grace of Jesus, our captain was Cristóbal Colón."'

Dante inhales, the Atlantian air rushes into his chest. "Yes." he says." It is good to be alive, and I'm sorry for those two poor souls."

Lily's fall from her small black pony had been cushioned by the carpet of pine needles and leaves. After two-days rest, she is strong enough to resume travel. Her thoughts remain disorganized, she needs to forget one to get to another, but lacks the certainty of remembering to enjoy the comfort of forgetting. Nothing holds steady, her life broken quickly, like a stick.

Her fear of Ygnacio remains, that rodent gaze and curled lip. But Lily has never before seen him do what she can only call, a kindness. Through her days of delirium in the bosque, he stayed by her side. She could feel his hand on her forehead, drawing confusing thoughts from her mind. He nursed her back to strength feeding her herb broth and grains, calling her, 'my little bird'. It was as if he was of another species, keeping her warm and protecting her.

Gradually her sense of the world shifts away from the fog of hysteria. In Debrun's dungeon her life released its meaning. Now, as if floating up from the ocean bottom with waterlogged eyes, a lacuna of memory opens. Visions, like little waves, lick the edges of her mind, the long echo of memory, not recalled, but reborn.

Lily knows herself, her family, and her friends again. Their names are alive. And she knows Ygnacio.

What had been a labyrinth of secrets to Lily about where and why they were in the Canaries, is revealed. Ygnacio's intent is clear, his face a knot of anger and disapproval, his offhand malice focused on Revela. "I'll pay her back and then some," he says.

As Lily's mind repairs, something else cracks open inside her. A rage loosens, an anger more frightening than the fear she once lived. She wonders, 'who is this grown-up Ygnacio. When did he come into my life?' She takes her friend, Revela's side. "Why? For what? She didn't do anything. Why punish her for what her brother did?"

To himself, Ygnacio concedes she has a point. But so what? "She was there! If she hadn't been screaming! She helped him escape, didn't she?"

Lily stands her ground, her rage directed at Ygnacio. "She's his sister! Of course she helped him. Wouldn't Marta help you?"

Ygnacio can think of no answer, and that disturbs him. He asks himself, 'Why should Revela die? Actually, I like her.'

Then Lily steps in front of him, the hands of her skinny arms reaching up to take hold of Ygnacio's tunic. Looking straight into his dark eyes, she says, "If you harm her I'll never speak to you again."

She sweeps her auburn hair to one side and mounts the small black pony. They follow the old road through a grove of olive trees almost hidden among the pine and eucalyptus, down a pathway of crepuscular shadows, divided by branches of wild berries bending in lofty arcs. Streaks of pale clouds reflect the glow of a dark indigo sky. Lily is catching up with her life, remembering how she loved to play in the forest and the dangerous animals, men, and witches she was always wary of meeting. Wondering how she might escape from Ygnacio, she hums a childhood verse.

Look through the water to the bottom,
A fish swims like a fish.
Look up into the open sky,
A bird flies like a bird.
Look into your beating heart,

Your love awaits you.
See what is beautiful in life.

Riding on the Gezuk Trail, Lily runs her hands through the mane of her pony. In the fine morning mist her mind no longer wobbles, and memory returns. The droning cicadas and the 'qui-qui-qui' of finches blend with the soft rain; the forest in harmony, a sublime silence of grace and beauty.

Lily rewinds the spool of her life. Her childhood had been a happy period without any recollection of hardship. She was cheerful, pleasant to be with. But she sees her life through different eyes now. She remembers very clearly that somewhere just beneath the deepest layer of her memory, whether in the forest or playing on the porch, at church or during the romería, everywhere and always, there had been a peculiar constriction, a pressure-like pain in the pit of her stomach. A smell would precede the feeling— dank, like wet rock. Then an image of her father would flash in her mind, his face up close, more than she could see. A gnawing cramp would build, the pain doubling her over and clouding her reality. She had put it out of her mind and it formed a scar on her memory, but her body shakes recalling it. The smell is there now, the musty rot of a turned over log. She tucks her arm into the dull pressure in her side, believing it a loathsome curse, as if she trails a sticky liquid. 'It must be something mystical', she thinks. Magic is something she understands. Magic gives things life.

Lily is determined to protect Revela from Ygnacio. The overpowering frailty is gone from her eyes. She knows she is no longer a child, that she has broken with that view of the world.

She considers the brute and what she might say or do. She knows his secretive nature, that he is not one to let you know what he is thinking. And she knows Ygnacio controls his temper until he has the advantage, but then its release is a fierce onslaught of cruelty. If there is any hope for her to save Revela, to deflect his wrath, she will need to act before he explodes. She wonders, 'What does he want from me? What can I say?'

Under a deep green canopy of conifers, the wind does not blow, but still Ygnacio hears a howling. He wrestles a puzzling thought. 'I enjoy travelling with her. But who is she but a simple peasant? Why does it matter if she scorns me? And Revela? I've lived to taste her blood. She is her friend? What is that to me?' Ygnacio contemplates this idea of mercy, tasting it as the tongue tastes salt. Is there a place for it that can also accommodate the specialties he cherishes, to be shrewd and unforgiving? Probably not.

Moving above the tree line, Lily spurs her pony to ride abreast of Ygnacio. Not far in the distance they can see the flat top of Cinchado. As they near, their eyes bulge to take in the enormity of the rock. "How is that possible?" Lily asks. Ygnacio leans forward and turns his head to an upside-down look, but says nothing. They dismount and walk toward the rock.

On a small rise at the back of the Guanche camp, Rabbi Moises and Merosa, stand shoulder to shoulder with the elder, teary eyed exiles, whispering final good-byes to those leaving for Jerusalem. David leads the travelers past them on the trail to Cinchado. The seven children, paired and holding hands, surround Revela in the center. Yoggi, his triangular ears straight up, lopes from front to the rear as if herding his flock up the northern slope of the volcano.

Revela measures her companions, Arnaldo, Idit and the twins, Ernesto and Karyn, Esther, Ricardo, Inez, Elio, Chari, the Shifrin brothers. This was the same group she had seen together on the bluff when they first landed in Tenerife, when she watched, confused, as they threw bread on the water. David had explained its meaning; it was the beginning of their new year, 4277. "How could that be?" she asked.

"It just is. We've been around a long time." He said it was a day to think of all the regrets of the past year, all acts of unkindness and shameful thoughts — envy pride and guilt — and to cast them off into the water. He even quoted the Bible:

"The Lord will take us back in love; He will cover up our iniquities. You will cast all their sins into the depths of the sea."

Micah 7:19

Then, a few days later, everyone, David included, became sullen, withdrawn to a point that Revela became paranoid, worried that something had happened or was about to happen that was beyond her or anyone's control. A haunting lament, a strange chant, was on everyone's lips throughout the day. She heard it so often she remembered the beginning. It was like a list: 'ashamnu, bagadnu, gazalnu, dibarnu… David called it 'an alphabet of sins', recited as an act of atonement. He told her it meant, 'we have been guilty, we have betrayed, we have spoken falsely, we have caused others to sin...' Amid all this jewishness, uncertain of her place, Revela determines to live by her own decisions.

The exiles have taken control of their lives and feel a biblical connection to their forefathers. No longer running away, a contagious excitement ripples the camp. It is a parade of conquest, the joy of being in charge of their destiny. "Are we really going to Jerusalem? Can this be true?" They had remained steadfast, holding their ground, the last to leave their homeland; now, they might be first to fulfill an ancient, holy edict.

No longer slowed by the elderly, and the children now as trail worthy as their parents, Doramus sets a moderate pace. The exiles forge ahead through the sweet, misty scent of cedar and eucalyptus, and then into the higher altitudes of spiced fragrances from pine and conifer. Between, almost as a demarcation, is a grove of castañas, a carpet of black pods the children collect for roasting.

Above the tree line just below the lava dome, the flat terrain favors an unhampered wind blowing the thin, dry air. The breeze lifts a powder of fine volcanic sand from the mineral soil fields of alternating colors: a magnesium green cloud from the ash carpet of eruptions millennia past; then an avenue of copper red haze formed a thousand years ago; and a black mist over the tongue-like paths cascading down the volcano from the most recent eruption.

Puffs of yellow smoke pepper the area from faroles, holes belching magma heated sulfur, as if the huge caldron was cooking monsters. Again as in the ascent the acrid fumes burn their nostrils. Watery eyes pay little attention to the white and pink broom flowers. Even the bugloss plants with their red flowers in two-meter pyramids are ignored.

David leans in to Revela, "This paradise is a far cry from the misery of that boat ride." Revela nods, but the comment reminds her of Dante and she enjoys a worried smile. Although she never had a desire for elsewhere, she reflects on her own great adventure.

The mention of the Santa Maria prods an obscure memory and she muses that perhaps Dante was destined to be at sea. When he was a toddler, almost three, they were at the beach near the harbor collecting the blue-black crabs that made the rocky shore home. The waves were strong and the ebb dragged the weathered stones that blanketed the beach back into the sea with a hollow, deafening hiss. Revela was stooping, trying to catch the scurrying creatures, when, in the tail of her eye, she saw what she thought was a log, or perhaps a mass of sea weed, rolling in the surf among the tumbling stones being dragged into the sea. She shielded her eyes from the sun's glare and then realized it was her small bother caught in the rolling surf. Overpowered in the water, Dante's tiny arms stretched over his head, his spinning body accelerating down the beachhead incline and disappearing into the white foam.

Revela could not hear her own terrifying scream over the crashing ocean. Then a tall man she had not noticed before raced into the water. Reaching below the waves he grabbed Dante by the scruff of his neck as if he was a mewing kitten, raised him to eye level, and with an outstretched arm, brought him to her and asked, "Is this yours?" She laughed out loud remembering that absurd question. At home when she rinsed the dried salt off her brother, he was clutching in his tiny fist a small reddish beach-rock, pierced by a hole. Revela strung the stone and her brother wore the necklace as a talisman for many years.

Unattentive, Revela stumbles on a rock. She rights herself as her face puckers to a distant sadness, then a deep breath and the anxiety of that seaside event becomes a distant memory again.

The exiles cross the tree line onto the plain of Teide. The beauty of the island enchants Revela, but the change in terrain moves her to consider the travel to Jerusalem, and she wonders, "When did all this begin? She thinks of what Rabbi Moises said, "There is no beginning, only a thought in your mind."

She will miss the comfort of Merosa's friendship and counsel. Although she does not fully comprehend her own feelings, it puzzles her that David's mother and her mother have thoughts not that different. Merosa had laughed saying that, "They were together in a conspiracy of women", and her mother, conspiring against her father, had admonished her, "Make no mistake, we are in it together." More apparent were matters with an ocean of difference; her mother discouraging a trip to Moguer, "Away from home, the soul can slip away." and Merosa, "You don't ever leave home. You take your home with you."

Encamped that night, the stars like sprinkled salt, Revela stares at the constellations she cannot name. She does not sleep well, dreaming of Palos and her brothers. Up at dawn she scouts a short distance further on the trail, almost to the balancing rock where Doramus will leave them and they will travel on their own en route to La Laguna and a passage to North Africa.

Walking alone just beneath the overhang of Cinchado, Revela drops her eyes to avoid a rut and looking up sees people ahead. Startled, she looks again. Something confuses her and she blinks as if waking from a mid-afternoon nap. Walking closer, eyes straining, a flash of recognition jolts her when she hears,

"Where's your little brother, sweetheart?"

Revela's heart jumps. Her arm shoots across her chest, then to her mouth and she thinks, 'How can it be? You're, dead.' Then she connects the sibilant voice with the curled lip and is certain. 'Yes! It's him! It's Ygnacio!' Her mind is in turmoil. 'He's alive! What can this mean?' Her breath first too much and then too little, Revela gasps, becoming dizzy, unburdened by a titanic release of guilt.

Even though Ygnacio stands before her, there is no correcting the past. Where she is, where Dante is, this reincarnation only serves to remind her of the mistakes made, the lives changed. She doesn't attempt to unravel the multiple consequences of this colossal turn. She knows something is going to change. Her life is once again both gone and begun again.

An impulse to embrace Ygnacio ends as she gathers herself and says, "I'm so glad to see you." Though difficult to avert her eyes from him, she senses something else. Another familiar face? 'Is that Lily?' She rubs her eyes. 'Are these ghosts? How can this be happening? It's as if we are children in Palos.'

Lily also gasps, as startled as Revela. 'It's her! Already! What should I do?' She gags in a moment of fear.

Ygnacio is warmed by the luck of this meeting, but squirms. Lily's warning plays in his head and he thinks, "I must decide'.

Then Lily lurches at Ygnacio. Grabbing his arm and leaning into his ear, in a harsh, resolute voice she does not recognize, "Don't forget what I said. Do not harm her."

Ygnacio draws a deep breath, his lip curls and he jerks his arm away. Lily's gaze is no longer shy, but steady, her iridescent eyes piercing. She holds his gaze and says, "There is something depraved in you Ygnacio. Something sadistic, and foul in your heart. I don't know what you want of me? What you want of Revela? I'm warning you— do not harm her!"

Revela and Ygnacio look at each other through a long, dangerous silence. As if the thought was an old friend, Ygnacio decides, 'Her punishment is due, it's time to pay for her crimes.' His hand grips the hilt of his basilard, when they hear a familiar voice.

"Revela!" At the peak of Tiede the rising sun reflects off a patch of snow, so dazzling it seems to be on fire, and Revela squints in the glare. Then, not looking at the soldier, though she has not even turned her head, but peering beyond Ygnacio just over his shoulder, out of the blue-sky space between Cinchado and Tiede, Revela sees a figure rushing down the path.

Again the call, "Revela!"

She does not know, but thinks, as if it inevitable, 'Of course he's here also!'

Ygnacio immediately knows who it is, and becomes enraged. His checked fury awaits only some small detail, as if his next breath will trigger an explosion.

Lily's eyes dart from Ygnacio and Revela to Dante rushing down the path. An avalanche of silence is broken by her screams, "No! Dante! No!"

Her cry sends a shock through Ygnacio. 'Yes!' His eyes goggle and a single thought explodes in his mind like a ruptured blood vessel. Ygnacio turns to his left as Revela circles to his right. The girl steps forward with her arms raised to receive her rushing brother. But Dante's reunion with his sister is interrupted as the force of his rushing embrace meets the point of Ygnacio's familiar blade. With no chance to avoid that knife, it slips into his abdomen releasing a spray of blood.

A heavy numbing sensation radiates through his body as fear strikes him like an anchor plunging in the sea. His knees shake and his legs buckle. Dante is deliriously excited to see Revela and at the same time realizes this is his ruin. Sinking to the ground, his fall is broken by his sister's arms. He attempts to say something but a bubble of blood rises in his mouth. As he lay there bleeding he thinks, 'Is there supposed to be something else? Am I supposed to have something more?' He looks at Revela but sees his mother. He hears his mother calling him home, or was it the sea? He misses her. An immense dark wave comes over him. He feels it first, then hears it, and finally sees it coming for him.

He has lived his future, it is behind him, and he is slipping out of existence. He remembers Gotzun saying, 'It is everyone's experience, there are no survivors.' On her knees Revela cradles her brother. Searching for a noise to express her grief, she makes a repeated low, choking sound.

Just then Yoggi streaks around the base of Cinchado, his eyes on fire. The dog lunges for the soft fleshy part of Ygancio's neck. But the soldier catches the snarling mouth with his forearm, and Yoggi tears into the offering. His teeth sink deep and the rancid taste of Ygnacio's blood makes him gag, but he holds on, shaking his jaws deeper, tearing to the bone, his saliva mixing with Ygnacio's flesh and blood. The soldier hammers the dog's snout with his fist and the pommel of his knife, but Yoggi's grip matches Ygnacio's fierceness. They battle savagely; Ygnacio spinning and trying to crush the dog's face, Yoggi clenching tighter and tighter. The soldier violently swings the dog from side to side, twisting its neck and foreleg, until finally Yoggi must let go. Ygnacio throws the dog aside and cradles his mutilated arm. His skin is ripped open and he sees bone as his blood gushes. He drops the knife. His strength sapped, he stumbles backwards, regaining his balance on top a small boulder.

But Ygnacio, although disorientated, is nothing if not focused on killing. Now disarmed, he remembers his loving weapon of choice. Seldom in actual combat, his preference being a stab in the dark from behind, he remembers the blade for close-in killing, the golden charm. It will be perfect for finishing off Dante and, yes, Revela. His lips curl into his special sneer of superiority and unbridled cruelty. He thinks, 'Oh, it is time for an accounting'.

His undamaged hand fumbles inside his vest pocket and fingers the handkerchief Lily had tatted that cushions his treasure. He never thought until this moment it a gift of love. He looks to Lily, bending over the body of Dante, and as if his eyes have become unbuttoned for the first time, he does not see her as a prisoner but as a companion, someone he wants to be with, someone who he wants to want to be with him. He feels the wrapped amulet and pulls, but the white lace foams out his pocket like a crashing wave, and his murderous partner bursts free. As the handkerchief flutters in air, the amulet soars in an arc. He twists his body, grasps at it, and like magnets, the goat-head weapon finds his hand and he senses the heat of its power.

Yoggi lies on his side in pain, his neck throbbing from the wicked whipped twisting, his right foreleg hideously bent, his snout crushed on one side. But this dog is not finished with this devil. His eyes are frenzied like a wolf. He can see de Silva teetering as if skipping a jig, and, as any animal might, he eyes the deadly golden totem in the man's hand. The dog has no fear. Rising, he lunges and with all his strength strikes Ygnacio in the gut with his snout, like a porpoise slamming into a shark. But the dog's strength has ebbed and Ygnacio absorbs the full force of the blow. Still Yoggi's charge further unbalances the soldier and he continues his clownish contorted dance, one foot on the boulder and one foot in the sweet, thin mountain air, until wobbly, near feint from exhaustion and the loss of blood, he falls on his backside into a bed of pink broom flowers.

With foes in sight amid crimson pools, Ygnacio senses no danger. Clutching his golden partner-in-death he once again feels invincible. Sprawled in the wildflowers, he looks up into the island sky. He inhales the smell of fresh warm blood and savors the wonderful cold taste of revenge. He has dispatched his victims with ease and his lips curl to one side to produce a crooked smile on his face. Then he recalls the childhood memory of his cousin, Leo, laughing at him as he lay in the wildflowers, the wooden sword fight, how he felt humiliated and how he had bounced up to strike that murderous blow. But he's not playing any child's game now and he laughs, a wild convulsed howl.

But this time there is no cousin Leo, and there is no bouncing up after the fall. He takes a giant step forward from the wild flowers to finish Yoggi but his foot never reaches the ground. He stumbles and bounces, not up, but down. Down the mountain. He grabs at a jagged volcanic rock that slices his hand open. He says, "Oh". He falls down an incline of razor red ash, surfing on the skin-ripping, ancient lava. He bounces farther and his eyes goggle watching himself unable to stop, tumbling from ledge to ledge down the mountain, and he wonders, 'What did I do to deserve this?' As he falls he screams a hollow noise, the cry of a tyrannical child. The plunge seems unnaturally long, as if the forest below wants no part of him and is rushing away as quickly as he falls. His hip crushes against a boulder. Picking up speed careening down the cliff face, he is spiked by a spear shaped obsidian rock, a quick, in-out his stomach. A parade of his victims races through his mind — the quarterings and severed limbs, the unearthly screams. Then a long drop, speed-bouncing, the left side of his face ripped off; twirling head over heels like a pinwheel, cracking his skull open — the hairy crushed skulls, the torture drownings. His neck fully twists his head to face backwards — the stretched innards, the smell of burning children, the pink guts. His body folds in half as he slaps the ground, hitting with such force that his spine snaps and his intestines explode out his anus. As he plummets down the mountain the images come faster and faster, and then slower, and then yet faster, and then slower, and slower still, and then they stop, and the pinpoint of light in his mind's eye goes out. Then Ygnacio is dead.

At dawn five days later, the Scrimshaw slips out of La Laguna harbor en route to Agadir on the northwest coast of Africa. The exiles are aboard as passengers. Their journey to Jerusalem has been mapped out using The Travels of Benjamin of Tudela as guide, but reversing a portion of his journey. Across the Canary Channel to Agadir, then skirting the African coast north past Gibralter into the Medditeranian Sea to Syracuse on the Island of Sicily. Cross to the port of Granada and finally a short leg on land to Alexandria where a Jewish community will welcome them. Caravan to Darnietta, Qulzum, and Fararna. Then across the Sahara by camel through Ascalan and then the final fifty kilometers into the holy city of Jerusalem.

Lily and Revela stand close, leaning on each other at the prow of the ship. Each has sketched to the other the basic details of their desperate journey. Father Barragio, Debrun, Ygnacio – the depths of their cruelty astounds Revela. Recalling Lily to have always been demure, almost timid, Revela refrains from questioning her. She can see the pain in Lily's eyes and the skeletal body of the once robust farm girl.

The lanteen rigged ship tacks against the trade winds. The rolling waves carry them toward the dark continent as they luxuriate in the warm Sahara wind.

"I wonder if there ever was a way out for Dante?" Revela asks.

"What do you mean?"

"Well, that night at La Sirena. He had no business attacking two soldiers. He probably should have died then. Did Death forgo claiming him? Was there a reason? Was he needed to serve some purpose?"

Lily is not familiar with the concept of serving a purpose. For her, survival of Ygnacio is a completion, as if a circle of life has closed. She knows she is changed in a profound way and no longer a submissive, fearful child.

Revela ties her hair. She finds no comfort in sadness and accepts Dante's death as real, as death without hope. "Well, it's as if his life was a piece of parchment, folded to bring the two ends together. You see what I mean?"

Lily prefers not to think about Dante or Ygnacio or anything and everything that has happened to her since being brought to the St. George's Church. Wanting to close the subject, she says, "Yes, I suppose so."

Lily had seen Ygnacio disappear over the ledge of the mountain. During the fight with Yoggi, she had a sense of fear for the soldier, a moment of empathy, a moment of care and concern, but only a moment. She knew she would recall that small instant for the rest of her life and would be ashamed of it.

Revela puts her arm around Lily, pulling her tight, slicked up beneath her arm, the way she used to hold Dante, and says, "I suppose all we have is one another in this heartless world."

END

READINGS

The Canary Islands after the Conquest by Felipe Fernandez-Armento

The Canary Islands Cultural History by Peter Stone

The Canary Islands Through History by Salvador Lopez Herrera

Christopher Columbus The DNA of his Writings by Estelle Irizarry

Columbus by Bjorn Landstrom

The European Discovery of America The Southern Voyages by Samuel Elliot Morison

The Fortunate Isles: Or, The Archipelago of the Canaries by Eugene Pegot-Orier, Frances Locock

The Guanches of Tenerife by Sir Clements Markham, K.C.B.

The Guanches Survivors and their Descendants by José Luís Concepcion

The History of the Discovery and Conquest of the Canary Islands by Juan de Abreu Galindo

The History of the Jews by Paul Johnson

Salt-Water Poems and Ballads by John Masefield

Sailing Alone Around the World by Joshua Slocum

Tenerife Guide and Memories Distributed by Garcia Y Correa

A Voyage Long and Strange by Tony Horwitz